In Short Supply
Jobs and Skills in the 1980s

ECONOMIC COUNCIL OF CANADA

In Short Supply

Jobs and Skills in the 1980s

161 415791

1982

Available in Canada through

Authorized Bookstore Agents
and other bookstores

or by mail from

Canadian Government Publishing Centre
Supply and Services Canada
Ottawa, Canada,   K1A 0S9

Catalogue No. EC 22-108/1982 E   Canada: $7.95
ISBN 0-660-11134-9   Other countries: $9.55

Price subject to change without notice

Contents

This report reflects a consensus of the Economic Council of Canada.

Members of the Economic Council of Canada

DAVID W. SLATER, Chairman
PETER M. CORNELL, Director
PATRICK ROBERT, Director

PHILIP C. BARTER
Partner,
Price Waterhouse and Co.,
Vancouver

PIERRE BRIEN
Vice-President,
Canada Lands Co. (Mirabel) Ltd.,
Ste-Scholastique

ROBERT B. BRYCE
Retired public servant,
Ottawa

MILDRED S. DOBRIN
Vice-President and General Manager,
Miracle Mart,
Montreal

G. CAMPBELL EATON
Managing Director,
Newfoundland Tractor and Equipment Co. Ltd.,
St. John's

EILEEN FORBOM
General Manager,
United Broadcasting Limited,
Sudbury

DONALD F. FORSTER
President,
University of Guelph,
Guelph

SHIRLEY B. GOLDENBERG*
Professor, Faculty of Management,
McGill University,
Montreal

T. EARLE HICKEY
Former Minister of Finance of P.E.I.,
Charlottetown

KALMEN KAPLANSKY*
Senior Fellow,
Human Rights Centre,
University of Ottawa,
Ottawa

PIERRE LORTIE*
President,
Montreal Stock Exchange,
Montreal

DONALD H. MCDOUGALL
Partner,
Stewart MacKeen & Covert,
Halifax

PAUL L. PARÉ*
Chairman and Chief Executive Officer,
Imasco Limited,
Montreal

ALASTAIR H. ROSS
President,
Allaro Resources Ltd.,
Calgary

PATRICK SHIMBASHI
Farmer,
Taber, Alberta

RALPH G. M. SULTAN
Vice President,
Starlaw Holdings Ltd.,
Toronto

ROY VOGT*
Professor, St. Paul's College,
University of Manitoba,
Winnipeg

*Member of the Council's Advisory Committee on the Labour Market study.

READER'S NOTE

The reader should note that various conventional symbols similar to those used by Statistics Canada have been used in the tables:

- – amount too small to be expressed
- .. figures not available
- ... figures not appropriate or not applicable
- – nil or zero
- e estimated figures.

Details may not add up to totals because of rounding.

Figures for Canada from the Labour Force Survey and gross flow data provided by Statistics Canada exclude the Yukon and Northwest Territories.

1 Focus and Rationale

Canada's job creation record since the Second World War has been one of the best in the industrialized world, and by far the majority of its labour force enjoys challenging and rewarding work. Nevertheless, the Canadian labour market today is characterized by imbalances, with jobs and skilled workers both in short supply. The stresses and strains engendered by this situation, if they do not receive careful attention, could become deep-rooted problems.

The average number of jobless persons in recent months has exceeded 1 million, and about three times that number may experience some unemployment during the course of a year. Yet in some regions, some industries, and some occupations, there are shortages of people to fill the jobs that are available, especially in the skilled category. Clearly, these imbalances are costly in terms of overall output loss and in terms of financial and psychic hardship for individuals. And, since the skill shortages in some areas push salaries up while workers elsewhere are jobless, the dilemma of high inflation coupled with record levels of unemployment is exacerbated.

Imbalances and Change

Such imbalances are the central focus of this report. Developments in the demand and the supply of people and jobs in the past and their possible course in the future are examined. And, through an analysis of the process by which the demand and the supply of labour adjust to one another, we consider the potential role of policy measures in assisting that process.

The present combination of severe unemployment and high inflation – a problem that has been with us for nearly a decade – makes a study of the Canadian labour market appropriate at this time. More generally, however, it is apparent that the market faces considerable challenges that will test severely its capacity to adjust to the changes in the economy. Thus, while evolution rather than revolution is, more often than not, the hallmark of change, it can be argued that the labour market of the 1980s will contrast markedly with the experience of the recent past.

The most basic and thoroughgoing set of changes derives from the demographics of the Canadian labour market. One of its major characteristics in the last two decades has been the rate of growth of the labour force, which is virtually unsurpassed in the developed world. Despite Canada's enviable record of job creation, this rapid growth has engendered persistently high unemployment levels. It is here that we see the first dramatic change for the future: while the labour force grew, on average, at a rate close to 3 per cent per year during the 1960s and 1970s, it is expected to rise by close to 2 per cent annually over the 1980s.

Moreover, the structure of change is important. For example, while the increase in the participation of women is expected to continue and their share of the labour force is projected to rise from 40 per cent to more than 44 per cent over the decade, other developments show much less conformity with the past. The proportion of young workers, for instance, will drop substantially during the 1980s, with correspondingly fewer new entrants into the market, lower unemployment rates relative to the national figure, and lower mobility of the work force. Most of the young people who entered the labour market in the 1960s and 1970s, at a time of growing youth unemployment, are now swelling the "prime working age" group, in which women will be almost as numerous as men by 1990. The increased numbers of women in the prime age group, combined with a changing mix of job opportunities in the service sector, suggest the need for innovative policies to ease the entry of women into nontraditional jobs. Finally, a substantial addition to labour force growth in the 1980s is expected to derive from the native population of working age, which will grow at an average rate of nearly 2.9 per cent annually, compared with 1.1 per cent for Canada's total working-age population. All of these changes suggest that flexibility and adaptability will be at a premium in the work force of the future.

Next, it is apparent that Canada is one of many countries in which technological change can be expected to bring about far-reaching alterations in the labour market. For example, while the present debate about the possible employment effects of the advent of microelectronics is characterized by more heat than light, we must at least acknowledge the prospect of pervasive redeployment, even if we do not accept the gloomy prophecy of unprecedented labour displacement. In addition, the changing patterns of international trade — reflecting, in particular, the growing influence of Third World countries — are also expected to affect the structure of output and labour utilization in Canadian industry. If, finally, we superimpose upon this the effects, already in train, of internal shifts in Canada's economic centre of gravity, it is apparent that the 1980s will test our capacity for effective industrial, occupational, and regional allocation of manpower.

The uncertain global economic environment is regarded with increasing apprehension because of the stringent constraints under which macroeconomic policies operate in many countries. The impact of severe external shocks in recent years, combined with the exigencies of the inflation/unemployment trade-off, have cast doubt on the ability of traditional policy instruments to deal with economic stabilization problems. It is fitting, therefore, to focus on the labour market as a principal component of the economic adjustment mechanism and as the target for policy action. There are misgivings, for example, about the impact of labour market policies in the past, and there is concern that these policies might well be quite unsuited to the changing circumstances of the future. Mixed with these reservations, however, is a measure of optimism suggesting that the labour market affords opportunities for the implementation of targeted policies that could relieve the stranglehold of the trade-off and could thus provide more room for manoeuvre to conventional macroeconomic policies.

Particular Concerns

Our preliminary investigations indicated that skill shortages were both widespread and acute in the midst of generally high unemployment and in the context of job scarcity in many areas, sectors, and occupations. Thus an even-handed treatment required us to investigate imbalances rather than just the skill shortages that had recently been attracting attention.

In addressing this issue we soon became aware of the difficulties involved in the seemingly simple task of identifying imbalances. The well-known shortcomings of any macroeconomic forecasting exercise tend to

be exacerbated in the labour sector; and the information about particular sectors, occupations, and areas, though plentiful, is marked by gaps, overlaps, and inconsistencies that impede one's view of the overall picture. We therefore carried out our research at both levels of investigation. First, we undertook an exercise in occupational projection, for both demand and supply, at the national level. Second, we obtained skill shortage information directly from individual establishments in various industries and geographical areas across the country.

Since skill shortages are only one manifestation of labour market imbalance, we also decided to devote particular attention to the problem of unemployment. Recent theoretical and methodological advances in the United States suggest the need for a new approach to this problem, and we applied such an approach in our study of the situation in Canada. This work on the dynamics of unemployment breaks new ground in the diagnosis of labour market infirmity in this country.

From the analytical portion of our research there emerges a view of the labour market that has oriented our evaluation of adjustment processes and existing policies and shaped the measures that we recommend. Some elements of that view are as follows. First, it is apparent that many problems derive from what economists call the "structural" evolution of the market, caused by shifts in product demands, technical change, demographic developments, institutional and attitudinal change, and the like. Second, there is a category of problems associated with fluctuations in economic activity that may react with structural problems in a mutually reinforcing way. Furthermore, it is apparent that, regardless of whether our difficulties arise from the nature of the economy's structure or from its variable level of activity, the consequences are unevenly shared by those who participate in the labour market. Segmentation, in other words, is a principal characteristic of the Canadian labour market. It is reflected in regional disparities, in the relative prospects of various industries and occupations, and in the experience of different age and sex groups.

Such considerations constitute the backdrop for the ultimate aim of this report — namely, to formulate policy recommendations that might contribute to a better functioning of the labour market. Thus we draw upon the lessons of our projection exercises, our detailed examination of the nature of unemployment, and our investigation of various adjustment mechanisms to suggest various policy measures about training, job creation, and labour market information and analysis.

The Policy Context

Observers have long been aware of the possibility that labour markets might not always work properly. In the 1930s it was recognized that governments might have to intervene in order to maintain demand. More recently, particularly in the 1960s and the 1970s, with greater focus on the problems of growth, increasing emphasis has been placed on measures to improve the supply and quality of labour and on the provision of the information and services required for labour markets to allocate people to jobs rapidly and efficiently.

In fact, of course, the labour market is so central to the workings of the economy that, in the broadest sense, practically all policies affect it in some way. Fiscal and monetary policies alter the growth and structure of labour demand, for example, while such programs as unemployment insurance, pensions, and immigration, in addition to training and education, affect labour supply. Within the labour sector itself, there is an enormous array of policies and programs concerned with wages and hours, safety and health, grievances and job security, and they, in turn, have effects beyond the labour market. Measures affecting the deployment of labour, for example, have far-reaching implications for the efficacy of policies aimed at improving growth, price stability, and income distribution, among others. To further complicate the picture, the policies that interact in this complex manner may well have been instituted with different objectives in view, so that they may be complementary in some cases but conflicting in others. And in virtually all cases there are both short- and long-run consequences to consider.

The policies on which we focus in this report are rather narrowly defined, however, as a result of our concentration upon the question of imbalances and the process of adjustment in the labour market. The existing array of programs directed at facilitating such adjustment in Canada is impressive. At the federal level, for example, there is a variety of demand-side programs (such as the Canada Employment Program) that cost about $380 million a year and affect 90,000 persons. On the supply side, manpower training figures most prominently among a variety of measures costing over a billion dollars and servicing more than 400,000 clients. Among the programs designed to reconcile supply with demand, the operations of the Canada Employment Centres (which serve over 1 million people a year) account for a major portion of the annual expenditures of $185 million.

In this document we discuss many of these programs, though our major emphasis is on manpower training. This program is one of the largest and, primarily because of the conflicting goals it was given in the past, one of the most contentious. We examine the existing training system, in order to determine its appropriateness for the adjustment tasks that lie ahead. One of the major attractions of manpower policy, and of training in particular, is the possibility that by reducing bottlenecks it may contribute not only to the growth of employment, output, and productivity, but to the reduction of inflation as well. Thus, much of our concern is with the efficiency aspects of the labour market's allocation mechanism and, in particular, with its potential to alleviate the twin evils of inflation and unemployment. An important message of our policy conclusions is that the Canadian manpower training system can – indeed, must – be reoriented in the interest of greater efficiency.

We are convinced, however, that labour market policy can achieve even broader aims. Our analysis suggests that there exist considerable differences in the extent to which different segments of the population share in the general prosperity – differences not wholly explained by variations in productive potential and diligence. Thus the objective of equity continues to be a major concern. And it is in this context that the powerful role of labour market processes and policies can be seen. Not only could they lend to traditional policies more room for manoeuvre by simultaneously addressing objectives in a complementary (as opposed to conflicting) way; they could, in addition, address social and economic inequities through their characteristic ability to be targeted. More specifically, job creation programs could play an important role if they were targeted at those persons with special disadvantages in finding and keeping jobs.

But our focus on job creation stems from more than consideration of labour market inequities. It also involves the distinction between cyclical and structural economic problems and between short- and longer-run, more strategic, issues. Quite apart from the short-run, cyclical downturns in economic activity that may signal the need for direct job creation, such programs may have important long-run potential. Our analysis of unemployment shows that much of it is of the long-run variety, thus suggesting that job availability (quite apart from mismatching problems) should be a major concern. Without programs to take up this slack, a portion of the work force may be condemned to repeated and continuous bouts of unemployment, interspersed with occasional and ephemeral job holding.

Finally we are concerned with the crucial role that information plays in labour market adjustment. It is clear that accurate labour market data are necessary in order to anticipate, and respond to, future problems. We indicate the types of data that are required for such purposes. Better information permits better planning by both workers and employers, and it promotes better decisions by policy makers. We also emphasize the role of analysis, since faulty diagnosis can give rise to inappropriate treatment. We believe that our investigation of long-term unemployment is a good case in point, since it specifically contests traditional views of joblessness. This leads, naturally, to different policy suggestions.

Distinguishing Features

In concluding this introduction to our report, it might be useful to offer a few comments on how it relates to some other recent investigations of the Canadian labour market. The Special Parliamentary Committee on Employment Opportunities in the 80s, which published its report in 1981, focused on issues very similar to those addressed in this report. The approaches are very different, of course, reflecting the terms of reference of the respective investigating bodies. While we have attempted to obtain advice from businessmen, labour representatives, government officials, and others, as to relevant issues and approaches, and while we have obtained labour market information directly by questionnaire in some of our projects, we have been unable to amass the enormous amount of practical advice that is contained in the testimony presented to the Committee. As a result, a larger part of our research is based upon detailed economic and statistical analysis of labour market data.

The Task Force on Unemployment Insurance established by Employment and Immigration Canada addresses issues of wide concern and consequence, but its focus is obviously narrower than ours. On the other hand, the scope of the study undertaken by that same department's Task Force on Labour Market Development in the 1980s is perhaps a little broader than ours, addressing in greater depth such issues as job creation programs in the context of community development, adjustment assistance to declining industries, and the special employment needs of the native population and of women, for example. In general, however, there are a number of shared concerns.

Nevertheless, while there are numerous overlaps in emphasis and aims, some aspects of the Council's work can reasonably be claimed as unique. In addition to extending existing work on projections of occupational demand and supply, we are able to draw upon original material from our Human Resources Survey. Second, in an area singled out as deficient in analysis by the Task Force on Labour Market Development, we offer some fresh approaches: not only does our work on unemployment deal with its cyclical and noncyclical components, but it also examines the dynamics of joblessness in a way that should help to alter radically the perception of Canadian unemployment. New empirical data on wage differentials and on job creation are presented in the chapter on labour market adjustment, and the section on the process of job search is based on a comprehensive study that is the first of its kind in Canada. Finally, our approach to training policy leads us not only to consider benefit/cost relations but also to seek the personal assessments of a variety of federal, provincial, and local training practitioners, and to examine empirical evidence on the conduct of both public and private training.

2 Recent Developments

In many respects, Canada's labour market has shown considerable vigour over the last two decades. Employment has expanded at a remarkable rate, placing Canada among the top industrialized countries in this respect. This success, however, has been clouded somewhat by the even more rapid growth rate of the labour force, which averaged 3.2 per cent a year over the same period. Partly as a result, the national unemployment rate rose to generally higher figures in the 1970s, compared with the previous decade,[1] and now ranks among the highest of the advanced industrial countries. In addition, this country has suffered increasing structural unemployment, as shown by the presence of widespread skill shortages in the midst of high unemployment levels. The salient aspects of these developments, and in particular those factors often cited as having contributed to them, deserve careful scrutiny.

The Unemployment Experience

Except from 1960 to 1962, Canada's unemployment rate did not exceed 5.5 per cent during the

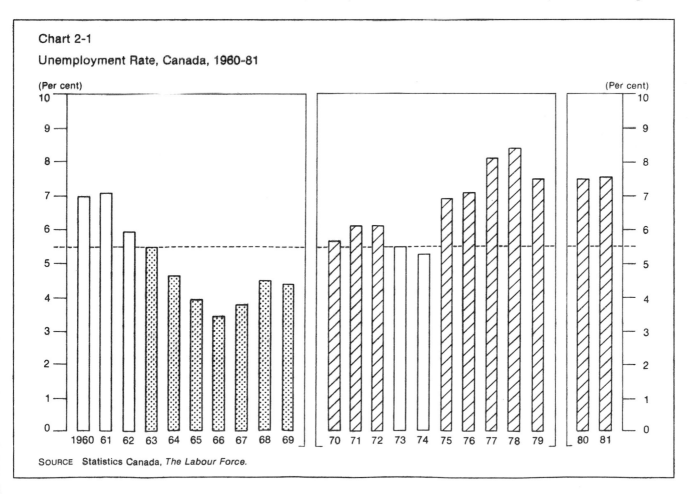

Chart 2-1

Unemployment Rate, Canada, 1960-81

SOURCE Statistics Canada, *The Labour Force.*

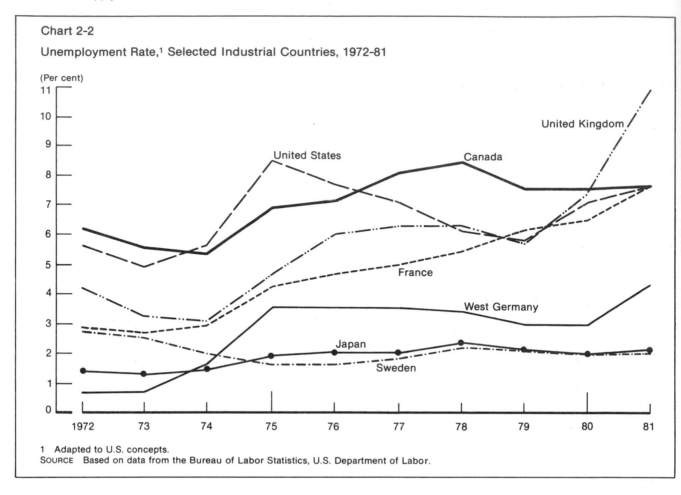

Chart 2-2

Unemployment Rate,[1] Selected Industrial Countries, 1972-81

1   Adapted to U.S. concepts.
SOURCE   Based on data from the Bureau of Labor Statistics, U.S. Department of Labor.

decade of the 1960s; after that, it never fell below that figure, except in 1974 (Chart 2-1). This upward drift has made Canada's unemployment record one of the worst in the industrialized world, with the United States, the United Kingdom, and France also experiencing high rates of joblessness (Chart 2-2).

Regional disparities are a well-known dimension of the Canadian economy, and unemployment is an important element of these differences: the national unemployment rate of 7.6 per cent in 1981 masked rates of 11.6 per cent in the Atlantic provinces, 10.4 per cent in Quebec, 6.6 per cent in Ontario, 4.5 per cent in the Prairie provinces, and 6.7 per cent in British Columbia. The regional rates tend to move up or down together, although not at the same pace: in the last decade, for example, unemployment has grown faster in Quebec and the Maritimes than in the Prairies or British Columbia. Unemployment dispari- ties are also present among occupations (highest for loggers and lowest for managers) and among age- sex groups (much higher than average for teenagers and lower for older workers of both sexes).

The various emphases revealed by different interpretations of the malaise – most cite demo- graphic and institutional changes as significant factors – are in turn reflected both in the official responses of governments and in the foci of research- ers.

The impact of the changing composition of the labour force is most readily apparent in the increasing proportions of women and of young people. In 1966, persons aged 15 to 24 accounted for 24.2 per cent of the labour force; men over 25, for 55 per cent; and women over 25, for 31.3 per cent (Chart 2-3). In 1981, the corresponding figures were 26.2 per cent, 45.2 per cent, and 40.7 per cent, respectively. The arguments concerning the impact of demographic changes on the nature and evolution of the labour market are simple and familiar. First, it is contended that by dint of sheer numbers the attitudes, charac- teristics, and behaviour of the majority of labour force participants in recent years no longer coincide with those of the "prime-working-age male bread- winners," who formerly made up the bulk of the work force. Second, the demographic groups whose labour force share has increased are precisely those whose unemployment rates are higher than average.

As far as institutional changes are concerned, the 1971 revision of the Unemployment Insurance Act is thought to have been particularly important. This amendment amounted to considerable liberalization of the law in the form of extended coverage, reduced eligibility requirements, an increased benefit rate, and

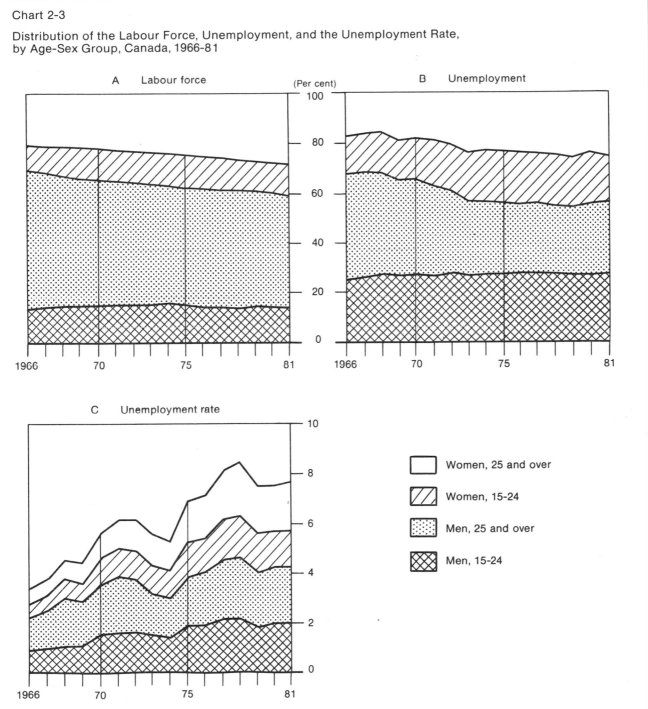

Chart 2-3

Distribution of the Labour Force, Unemployment, and the Unemployment Rate, by Age-Sex Group, Canada, 1966-81

A   Labour force   (Per cent)   B   Unemployment

C   Unemployment rate

Women, 25 and over

Women, 15-24

Men, 25 and over

Men, 15-24

NOTE   In panels A and B the graphs add up vertically to 100 per cent. In panel C the graphed lines add up to the aggregate unemployment rate.

SOURCE   Based on data from Statistics Canada.

an extended duration of the benefit period. These developments are regarded by some as having caused an increase in the duration of unemployment and in labour force participation, but the empirical evidence is rather mixed. Among the studies indicating a significant effect, the addition to the official unemployment rate ranges from 1 percentage point (e.g., from 6.5 per cent to 7.5 per cent) in a number of early works to as high as 2 percentage points in more recent studies.[2] It should be pointed out, however, that amendments to the unemployment insurance legislation in 1975, 1977, and 1979 rendered the overall provisions less generous, so that the unemployment insurance system is likely to have had a reduced impact on unemployment in recent years.

A second institutional arrangement often cited as having significantly altered the nature of the labour market is the minimum wage. The argument proceeds from the hypothesis that the imposition of a fixed minimum will cause disemployment for those persons for whom the market wage, in the absence of such intervention, would have been established at a lower level.[3] It suggests, moreover, that this effect may be strongest for precisely those groups whose labour force share has been growing, thus strengthening the impact of the demographic and unemployment insurance factors described above. Minimum wages exist not only in the federal jurisdiction but also in each of the provinces; thus their potential for good or ill is frequently, and hotly, debated. There is as yet no overwhelming body of empirical evidence supporting either side of the argument, although several recent studies claim disemployment effects. Suffice it to say for the moment that substantial upward adjustments in minimum wages took place in all jurisdictions in 1974, 1975, and 1976. For example, no less than six provinces raised their minimum wage by over 20 per cent in 1974, and the average adjustment that year was 20.3 per cent. However, the ratio of minimum wages to average wage rates in manufacturing, which had increased up to the mid-1970s, has tailed off again in recent years.

Other government programs may also have contributed to a change in the characteristics of the national labour market and of its participants. For example, since the late 1960s the Canada Manpower Training Program has served about 300,000 clients per year, and this country has disbursed more training funds per labour force member than any other developed nation save Sweden. It seems likely that if to this enormous federal presence in the labour market is added the manpower programs of the provinces, a sizeable proportion of the work force has experienced labour market episodes that are quite different from the traditional concepts of work and joblessness.[4]

For such reasons, many observers contend that Canada's labour market differs markedly today from what it was two decades ago and that its traditional performance measures — particularly the aggregate unemployment rate — do not adequately capture the changed circumstances. This perception has led many to stress that the labour market is actually characterized by a good deal more tightness than meets the eye. In other words, the inflationary potential associated with any given unemployment rate is greater than formerly. Back in 1976, this Council emphasized the need for judicious interpretation and supplementation of traditional labour market indicators, and it reiterated this concern in its Fifteenth Annual Review two years later.[5] In this regard, there has been a significant development on the statistical front, with the appearance of a published series for the employment/population ratio (see Appendix Table A-1) highlighting Canada's impressive job creation record.

The demographic and institutional factors described above have combined to yield unemployment rates that are high by historical standards. Yet, because inflation rates have also been high in recent years, the degree of tightness or inflationary potential signaled by a given unemployment rate is considerably greater than would have been implied in earlier periods. Thus the message of the unemployment rate must be extracted with caution. In any event, there is little doubt that, as far as the labour market is concerned, the legacy of the 1970s is a more stringent trade-off between inflation and unemployment, severely constraining the options of policy makers.

The Anatomy of Unemployment

The worsening trade-off has been summed up by some observers as an increase in the "natural" or (in the terms of the Council's Sixteenth Annual Review) "equilibrium" rate of unemployment.[6] Recent estimates of this figure, generally defined as the rate below which inflationary pressures can be expected to increase, are in the order of 6.5 to 7.0 per cent. The factors causing this unemployment are often labelled as either "frictional," "structural," or "cyclical" in nature. If, for example, lack of job market information causes people to search more extensively for suitable work, this can be expected to extend the duration of the "frictional" unemployment usually associated with the quest for a job. On the other hand, to the extent that particular age-sex groups tend to have different human-capital characteristics and to be concentrated in particular occupations, demographic changes may lead to a "structural" mismatching of workers and jobs. By contrast, the labour market slack associated with the economy's failure to operate at its productive potential is generally referred to as "cyclical" unemployment. These names are important inasmuch as the treatment designed to alleviate each type of unemployment will vary substantially.

Thus, if unemployment were judged to be primarily cyclical in nature, the policy response would consist of measures to move the economy closer to its potential path of output growth. If it were primarily of a frictional nature, unemployment might be addressed by providing prospective employees and employers with fuller and faster information about each other's opportunities and requirements. Structural unemployment would require policy makers to tackle the more deep-seated mismatches based on the mutual unsuitability of vacant jobs and jobless workers. A reconciliation might then be needed as to their respective locations, wage requirements, skill, or education; this could, in principle, be promoted by measures affecting either the demand or the supply side of the mismatch.

Now, while there is a good deal of agreement that frictional and structural factors have played the major role in recent unemployment increases, there is much less accord about their relative contributions. A popular extension of the findings concerning the additional unemployment induced by unemployment insurance (UI), for example, has been the notion that the bulk of joblessness is of the "voluntary" or "turnover" variety. This benign view, which maintains that most people experience short spells of unemployment and obtain UI benefits anyway, might engender a rather complacent attitude on the part of policy makers or even a call for tighter UI regulations[7] and more streamlined job information services. Recent research suggests, however, that a substantial proportion of measured unemployment emanates from long-term joblessness. We consider this an important development, in that it will affect the diagnosis and treatment of unemployment.

Another research project carried out by the Council recently attempted to break unemployment down into "cyclical" and "noncyclical" components and to address directly the question of whether structural and frictional factors (lumped together under the "noncyclical" heading) have indeed figured more prominently in recent years. This approach posed the basic question: "How many of the idle person-hours could have been employed, in any year in our period

Table 2-1

Cyclical, Noncyclical, and "Hidden" Unemployment,[1] Canada, 1961-79

	Unemployment rate			Distribution of unemployment			Hidden unemployment rate[2]	Labour hoarding rate
	Cyclical	Noncyclical	Aggregate (official)	Cyclical	Non-cyclical			
	(Per cent)							
1961	4.4	2.8	7.2	61.1	38.9		..	4.3
1962	3.7	2.2	5.9	62.7	37.3		..	2.6
1963	3.4	2.1	5.5	61.8	38.2		..	2.1
1964	2.3	2.4	4.7	48.9	51.1	Average	..	3.1
1965	1.3	2.6	3.9	33.3	66.7	1960s:	..	3.1
1966	–	3.6	3.6	–	100.0	55.2	..	2.8
1967	2.1	2.0	4.1	51.2	48.8		..	6.1
1968	2.3	2.5	4.8	47.9	52.1		..	4.0
1969	1.7	3.0	4.7	36.2	63.8		..	3.7
1970	4.4	1.5	5.9	74.6	25.4		..	4.7
1971	3.5	2.9	6.4	54.7	45.3		0.8	3.0
1972	2.6	3.7	6.3	41.3	58.7		1.5	3.3
1973	0.1	5.5	5.6	1.8	98.2	Average	1.3	3.7
1974	0.2	5.2	5.4	3.7	96.3	1970s:	0.4	5.2
1975	3.2	3.8	7.0	45.7	54.3	64.3	0.1	6.1
1976	2.1	5.1	7.2	29.2	70.8		1.8	4.1
1977	2.8	5.4	8.2	34.1	65.9		2.0	3.5
1978	3.0	5.5	8.5	35.3	64.7		2.2	3.6
1979	2.8	4.8	7.6	36.8	63.2		2.1	3.4

1 Based on old (pre-1976) Labour Force Survey concepts.
2 Basically, the proportion of discouraged job seekers who, in slack periods, withdraw from the labour force. Estimates for 1961 to 1970 were found to be insignificant.
SOURCE Estimates by the Economic Council of Canada; for technical details on hidden unemployment and labour hoarding, T. Siedule and K. Newton, "Discouraged and Additional Workers Revisited," and "Tentative Measure of Labour Hoarding," Economic Council of Canada Discussion Papers 141 and 128, Ottawa, December and March 1979, respectively.

of study, if the economy had been operating at full capacity?'' The procedure was to calculate the real output gap – i.e., the difference between full-capacity and actual output in any year – and the corresponding idle person-hours.[8] The results bear out the suggestion that the rates of noncyclical (i.e., structural and frictional) unemployment were higher in the 1970s than in the 1960s, at least when the official national unemployment rates are used as a basis (Table 2-1).

There are, however, two other important forms of "hidden unemployment," both associated with cyclical fluctuations in economic activity, that should be taken into account by a more balanced and comprehensive interpretation of unemployment. The first is associated with what is often called the "discouraged worker" effect. In times of cyclical recession and slack labour markets, some unemployed workers, frustrated by their inability to find suitable jobs, may give up the search and withdraw from the labour market. Such persons are not included in the official unemployment count despite the fact that they are, in fact, "jobless." Our estimates suggest that discouraged workers form a rather substantial group. For example, if they had been included among the jobless in 1978, the effect would have been to raise the official unemployment rate from 8.5 per cent to 10.7 per cent. The other factor is an estimate of "labour hoarding" – the practice by which employers faced with a cyclical decline in the demand for their output choose not to lay off workers because they judge it to be cheaper to keep them on the payroll than to search, screen, hire, and train new ones at the time of the subsequent upswing. While such workers do not feature in the official unemployment statistics, it is safe to assume that they may be considerably underutilized. The approach used to measure this effect involved the estimation of the difference between the *actual* number of person-hours employed to produce the output observed in any year and, on the basis of historical relationships, the number of person-hours *required* to produce that same output efficiently. As can be seen in Table 2-1, the overall magnitude of this form of hidden unemployment is considerable when compared with the official measure – almost equal to it in some years.

These points lend weight to the contention that, when interpreting the familiar national unemployment statistics, there is much more than meets the eye. The U.S. Bureau of Labor Statistics recently took the lead in this field by publishing a variety of unemployment measures based on different definitions, including the "discouraged worker" phenomenon. The corresponding estimates calculated by Statistics

Canada clearly show the relative importance of these phenomena in the overall unemployment picture in this country (Table 2-2).

Table 2-2

Estimates of Alternative Unemployment Measures,[1] Canada, 1976-80

	U_1	U_2	U_3	U_4	U_5	U_6	U_7
	(Per cent)						
1976	2.4	3.7	4.6	6.1	7.1	6.9	7.2
1977	2.8	4.4	5.3	7.2	8.1	8.1	8.5
1978	3.1	4.6	5.7	7.5	8.4	8.6	9.0
1979	2.6	4.1	5.0	6.6	7.5	7.8	8.2
1980	2.6	4.2	5.2	6.6	7.5	7.9	8.3

1   The U_1 figures represent those who have been unemployed 15 weeks or longer; U_2, those who have lost their jobs; U_3, the number of unemployed heads of households; U_4, unemployed persons seeking full-time jobs; U_5, the official aggregate rate; U_6, a weighted measure that includes U_4 plus unemployed persons looking for part-time work, as well as part-time workers seeking full-time jobs; and U_7 adds to U_6 an estimate of the number of discouraged workers who have left the labour force.

SOURCE   Estimates based on unpublished data from Statistics Canada's Labour Force Survey.

In sum, the unemployment history of the last two decades must be examined carefully in the light of the institutional and demographic changes that have altered the character of the labour market and in the light of factors, such as labour hoarding and discouraged workers, which, though quantitatively important, are not covered in the published statistics. The message of the unemployment figures – what they tell us about how tight the labour market is, about the kind of hardship that joblessness entails, and so on – clearly has changed. Moreover, we have recently come to appreciate more fully that our "snapshots" of the state of the labour market at a point in time are merely clips from an action-packed moving picture of the dynamic, complex, and continuous interplay of people and jobs. One further set of recent developments must now be briefly described since it, too, helps to place our unemployment experience in perspective and is a central focus of subsequent chapters.

Skill Shortages

The current problem of occupational shortages is not a new one, nor was it unexpected. In the early 1960s this Council, in its First and Second Annual Reviews, expressed concern about the adequacy of the supply of the specialized technical and scientific personnel that were deemed essential for continued economic growth. Job vacancy data for the early

1970s suggest that significant shortages appeared again at that time. Moreover, while current imbalances have only recently received considerable attention, the prospect of general shortages has been raised several times since the mid 1970s. In any event it is apparent that the Canadian labour market, at the outset of the 1980s, is suffering from severe and widespread skill shortages in some areas. The Council's nationwide Human Resources Survey showed that about half of the participating establishments had experienced such shortages in the 1977-79 period and that well over 40 per cent anticipated further difficulties in the next few years, particularly with respect to high-level, blue-collar skills.

The causes of this problem are discussed in detail in Chapter 5. Suffice it to say here that the number of skilled immigrants destined for the labour force declined substantially in the 1970s, compared with the 1960s; that the skilled labour force is rather aged; and that Canada's vocational training system has not produced the requisite skills in sufficient quantities. Furthermore, there are strong indications that the imbalance problems may be exacerbated by technological change, by shifts in the pace of economic activity among sectors and regions, and by the labour market adjustments associated with Canada's adaptation to the changing patterns of international trade and competitiveness.

The Problems of Particular Groups

One aspect of labour market performance on which we are not able to report new research results does, in our view, deserve special emphasis nevertheless. It has to do with those workers or would-be workers who, for whatever reason, are unable to enjoy the rewards that normally flow from the mainstream of labour market activity. Various words are used to try to capture the essence of their predicament: the "working poor"; the "chronically unemployed"; the "marginal worker"; the "handicapped" or "disadvantaged" with respect to physical or mental characteristics, education, experience, or other human circumstances. While none of these epithets fully describe the concept, together they nevertheless convey some indication of the object of our concern. Because we believe that the economy should be able to assure to all Canadians equality of access to the labour market, careful identification of those factors and circumstances which at present deny people such means of access is required.

Among the unemployed, we find that women, young people, and those lacking formal education or with problems of insufficient or inappropriate training,

illiteracy, and skill obsolescence are overrepresented. Labour market problems are experienced not only by the unemployed but also by the employed and by people who for various reasons do not participate in the market at all. Data from Statistics Canada's Survey of Consumer Finance, for example, show that roughly 1.5 million households in Canada have income that is below the poverty line. Of these low-income units, about 600,000 (40 per cent) have heads in the labour force and thus derive the bulk of their income from employment-related activities in the form of wages, salaries, and unemployment insurance. While the proportion of low-income family heads experiencing unemployment in 1979 was nearly twice as high as that for all family heads, it appears that many who are steadily employed are nevertheless poor. But by far the majority of low-income family heads who worked in 1979 did so on a part-time basis, and their representation in low-wage service occupations was twice the national figure. Thus, while the plight of the unemployed is fairly well documented, the problems of the working poor in low-skilled, unattractive, short-term, and part-time jobs, facing confiscatory marginal tax rates, are less well known.

Next, we must call attention to those for whom the primary problem has been simply that of access to the labour market. Native Canadians, in particular, figure prominently in this group. A recent study estimates that the unemployment rate of the native population of Winnipeg and environs is about 30 per cent — more than five times that for the city's overall population.[9] In other parts of the country, it is likely that the joblessness rate is even higher. For example, estimates by native groups in Saskatchewan and several communities in Alberta place the unemployment rate among Indians at 80 per cent or more.[10] And such figures are by no means exceptional. Employment is heavily concentrated in a few low-skill, low-wage occupations, particularly in construction, manufacturing and processing, and services. But, as suggested above, the participation figures are also shocking: in the Winnipeg study cited above, native labour force participation rates among men and women are 25 and 40 per cent lower, respectively, than those for the general population. The National Indian Brotherhood firmly opposes the view that the native people themselves are responsible for this situation:

We reject totally the myth to which some government officials still subscribe: that our people do not want to be involved in the economic life of this country, or to share in the benefits of modern technology, because such participation is incompatible with our traditions and cultures. Their line of argument explains nothing. Its effect is to place the burden of blame on Indians, and to acquit government for their role in creating and reinforcing Indian poverty.[11]

The outcome of this deplorable labour market experience is that — to cite Canadian Indians as an example — the ratio of dependent to employed persons is about 10:1, compared with 2:1 in the larger community. This abnormally high dependency ratio is manifested in disproportionately high rates of social assistance: in some Indian communities, over 95 per cent of all households receive some form of public aid.

Finally, the underutilization of the resources of persons with physical or mental disability is a continuing cause for concern. Their numbers are sizeable — about 1.3 million working-age Canadians, more than half of whom are potential labour force participants. For those who do participate, however, the unemployment rate is probably well in excess of 50 per cent.

We raise these points in order to underline the fact that in assessing the recent performance of the Canadian labour market, one must take careful account of a wide variety of severe problems that are frequently masked by the conventional data pertaining to earnings, employment, and productivity. Indeed, large numbers of the native people of this country are not even covered by the Labour Force Survey, on which the principal official statistics of labour market activity are based.

Conclusion

The lessons of the recent past are many and varied. First, it is apparent that demographic change can substantially alter the characteristics and behaviour of the labour market and force us to modify our perception of it. This lesson must be borne in mind for the coming years, since the well-publicized baby boom is now swelling a new stratum of the age structure and since women will continue to increase their rate of participation. Second, the possibly unintended and undesired consequences of measures aimed primarily at even the worthiest of goals will be monitored closely in the future, as a result of the experience gained with unemployment insurance legislation in several countries. This has been one of the most controversial and intensely studied issues in recent labour market research. Third, imbalances in the form of skill shortages and joblessness are costly in terms of output lost to the economy as a whole and in terms of financial and psychic hardship to individuals. The need to identify as accurately as possible the locations and dimensions of such imbalances in the future is therefore both obvious and of paramount importance. Such concerns are the focus of the next four chapters. Fourth, it is clear that underlying the familiar official statistics concerning labour market performance are a host of less well-known facts about the hardship of particular groups. For many Canadians, mere access to the labour market is a major practical problem. For others — even though, nominally at least, they have a job — the nature of the work and the earnings associated with it are far below the standards enjoyed by other Canadians. Finally, it is apparent that policy makers, caught on the horns of the inflation/unemployment dilemma, must focus more than ever before on the labour market as the locus of a variety of measures that, taken together, could facilitate the functioning of the economy as a whole.

3 Occupational Demand

We noted earlier the crucial contribution of the labour market to economic development and the potential role of labour market adjustment processes and policies in the attainment of macroeconomic objectives. In order to frame labour market measures that are efficacious and just, the policy maker requires a causal explanation of past performance and as accurate a view as possible of future developments.

The consequences of information inadequacy may be painful on occasion, as all who have witnessed severe shortages and subsequent gluts in various professions are well aware. Since four or more years are required to "produce" the entrants into many occupations, their supply depends crucially on estimates of needs made some time before. This, in turn, puts a premium on accurate projections of work force requirements.[1]

It is therefore of paramount importance to monitor the nature and direction of the progress of the economy and to anticipate the resource requirements that this progress implies. In the labour market this means, among other things, anticipating the manpower requirements that stem from the changing growth patterns of different industries and areas. In this way, growth-inhibiting bottlenecks may be avoided and the employment opportunities of the labour force enhanced.

Information and Methodology Shortcomings

Information on labour demand by occupation is essential to the human resource managers of public and private organizations, to educational planners, and to economic policy makers. For a variety of reasons, however, such information has generally been rather limited in scope, quality, and availability. During the 1970s a number of nationwide models were developed to describe and forecast various aspects of the Canadian economy.[2] While these efforts no doubt contributed much to general economic research and policy making, none of the models explicitly incorporated the occupational-demand dimension. Indeed, outside of a handful of individual efforts, very little has been accomplished in this area of investigation over the last 15 years.[3]

The problem stems largely from the paucity and the inadequacy of detailed data at the occupational level. The three main sources of such data in Canada are the Occupational Employment Survey (OES), the Job Vacancy Survey (JVS), and the Census. The OES was intended to be a continuing survey, but after the recent revelations of quality deficiencies it was halted, and only the 1975 figures were made public. The JVS provided detailed quarterly vacancy data from 1971 through 1978, but this survey was also discontinued.[4] The Census provides information on occupational employment but nothing on vacancies; moreover, because it is decennial, it fails to provide a picture of the changing patterns of labour demand across occupations and industries from year to year. In addition, definitional changes pose problems of compatibility from one Census to the next.

Along with such data problems, the methodology in general use for occupational employment projections poses problems also. The technique used by Employment and Immigration Canada, as well as by the OECD and the U.S. Bureau of Labor Statistics, is based on the assumption of fixed occupational shares of employment within industry sectors. In other words, the employment shares of, say, mechanical engineers, maintenance personnel, and secretaries in a particular industry are taken as constant over time. These shares are then simply applied to projections of employment for the various industries in order to estimate occupational projections. The difficulty with this approach stems from the absence of frequent, regular, and continuing observations, thus precluding the availability of a time series of data that would show, from year to year, the shifts in the patterns of occupational employment reflecting changes in technology, for example. As a result, we must generally assume that the occupational employment shares within each industry at the time of the 1971 Census hold true today and will hold true in the future.

It should be pointed out, however, that even if these difficulties were surmounted, we would still face severe theoretical and methodological problems. First, even a regular time series of occupational employment could still limit us to a "fixed shares" approach, albeit with more constant updating. Second, a comprehensive model with which to determine occupational demand should, ideally, take account of the allocative function of such crucial factors as the relative wages in various occupations. In practice, no one has yet succeeded in rendering operational the inclusion in a comprehensive model of the hundreds of equations needed to provide sufficiently detailed occupational projections.

Given one of the central tasks of this study — namely, the identification of labour market imbalances — and given the data constraints described above, we have attempted to project occupational demand by taking a number of new approaches. First, we have taken explicit account of the fact that occupational demand should include not only employment but vacancies also. Second, we have used a "fixed shares" model for occupational employment projection but have modified the traditional COFOR (Canadian Occupational Forecasting Model) approach by reorganizing the industrial groupings in order to link up directly with the industry employment figures from our own CANDIDE 2.0 model. Third, because the "fixed shares" approach yields implausible results for some occupations, we have developed an alternative model in which the industry employment shares of various occupations are related to industry output shares and capital intensity.

The Projected General Economic Climate

Our present projection of labour demand by occupation is based on the general economic projections developed with the Council's CANDIDE 2.0 model in the third quarter of 1981. The assumptions behind those projections included estimates of average annual real growth in the United States of 3.1 and 2.9 per cent for the periods 1981-85 and 1986-90, respectively, and a slight decline in that country's unemployment rate throughout the 1981-90 period. For Canada, these projections suggested growth prospects for the present decade that were slightly lower than in the late 1960s and early 1970s, but an improvement on the late 1970s. They called also for relatively high employment and a decline in unemployment rates during the first half of the decade, but with inflation in the double-digit range during 1981-84, and just below that range during the second half of the decade.

Quite clearly, however, there have been some pronounced changes in the economic climate since the original basic projections were made. Some corrections and revisions have already been made to the Council's base case but further revisions were in the process of incorporation at the time the present document went into print. These will involve a somewhat lower growth rate in GNE, particularly in the period up to 1985, and lower employment growth and higher unemployment than had earlier been anticipated. On the other hand, price increases seem likely to be lower, on average.

Should the projected general economic climate change, all of the figures for labour demand by occupation would likely be altered. The degree of sensitivity would not be large, however, because the changes generated by the shift in the general economic scenario would have to be distributed among a large number of occupations. Nevertheless, changes would occur, particularly if the sectoral or industrial pattern of growth were altered in any substantial way. Although we anticipate that no more than a modest scaling-down of the occupational demand figures would occur as a result of this, the impact of changing circumstances will be monitored as the Council's base case is revised.

Labour Market Tightness and Job Vacancies

Within the context of the economic environment described above, how tight will the labour market be? Traditionally, economists have used the unemployment rate as a quantitative indicator of this elusive concept. This approach has generally been rejected in recent years, however, on the grounds that the nature of the unemployment rate has changed: the economic implications that a 5 per cent rate had in the 1960s differ from those of the same rate now. Indeed, in our last major study of the Canadian labour market, we discussed the message of the unemployment rate, concluding that basic changes in the nature of the market had also altered the message and that supplementary information was needed for a balanced interpretation of labour market performance.[5]

As far as the tightness of the labour market is concerned, we specifically suggested examining job vacancies in conjunction with unemployment, and we drew attention to the relationship between these measures over time. Generally speaking, the vacancy rate and the unemployment rate move in opposite directions over the course of economic cycles: when economic conditions improve, vacancies tend to increase, unemployment decreases, and the labour market "tightens"; when recessionary conditions appear, vacancies diminish, unemployment grows, and the market "slackens" (Chart 3-1). In the relatively tight labour market conditions of 1974 (second quarter), a high vacancy rate was paired with a low unemployment rate; the reverse was true in the slack conditions of 1978 (third quarter). These cyclical movements tend to produce curves that generally run between the upper left and the lower right of the chart.[6]

Apart from such cyclical movements, however, the relationship is also affected by factors that determine how quickly vacant jobs and unemployed workers are matched. If this matching process is improved, for example, we may observe fewer vacant jobs and fewer unemployed people at the same time; compare, for example, 1972 (fourth quarter) with 1973 (first quarter).[7]

We have made use of this long-standing economic relationship in conjunction with basic projected information from CANDIDE 2.0 to develop our vacancy projections. They must, of necessity, be regarded as possibilities – estimates of what could happen should

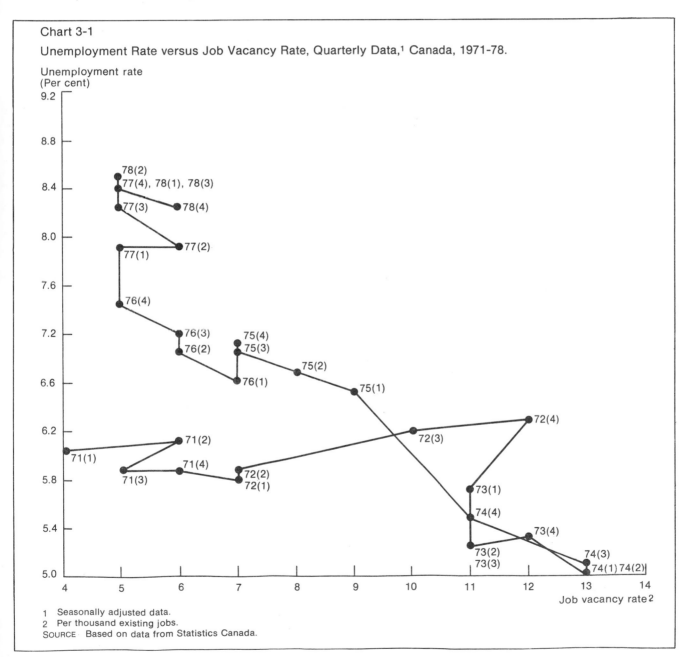

Chart 3-1

Unemployment Rate versus Job Vacancy Rate, Quarterly Data,[1] Canada, 1971-78.

Unemployment rate
(Per cent)

1   Seasonally adjusted data.
2   Per thousand existing jobs.
SOURCE Based on data from Statistics Canada.

Table 3-1

Observed (1971-78) and Projected (1979-90) Average
Annual Job Vacancy Rates, Canada

	Job vacancy rate[1]
1971	5.5
1972	9.0
1973	11.3
1974	12.8
1975	7.8
1976	6.0
1977	5.3
1978	4.8
1979	6.2
1980	5.0
1981	5.6
1982	6.5
1983	7.8
1984	8.2
1985	8.1
1986	7.8
1987	7.9
1988	7.2
1989	6.9
1990	6.8

1   The job vacancy rate is defined as the number of vacancies per
    thousand existing jobs in all industries, except agriculture, fishing
    and trapping, domestic services, and the noncivilian component of
    public administration and defence.
SOURCE   Based on data from Statistics Canada and estimates by the
    Economic Council of Canada.

previous relationships between vacancy rates and
unemployment rates hold true in the future.

The observed (1971-78) and projected (1979-90)
total job vacancy rates are shown in Table 3-1. On
the basis of these vacancy figures it appears that the
labour market in the 1982-90 period may not be as
tight as that of, say, the 1973-74 period. It is
expected to be more comparable to that of 1975 but
tighter than that of the years 1977 to 1980.

Where Will the Bottlenecks Be?

One of the most troublesome problems of recent
years has been that of shortages. Despite widespread
claims of such shortages, however, we know of no
analysis using detailed job vacancy data, nor have we
seen any interpretation of future skill shortages in
terms of job vacancies by occupation.

We have addressed this shortcoming by projecting
occupational vacancies on the basis of the shares
observed in the 1971-78 period and of the estimated
course of aggregate vacancies; the summary results
are presented at the two- and three-digit CCDO
(Canadian Classification and Dictionary of Occupa-

tions) level[8] in Table 3-2. The code itself is explained
in Appendix B. For convenience, we describe occupations with an average annual vacancy growth rate
exceeding the national average (12.6 per cent) as
having "high vacancy growth" during the 1981-85
period.

A few words of caution about the interpretation of
vacancy figures seems appropriate at this point. First,
the existence of vacancies does not necessarily
indicate a shortage: for some high-turnover occupations the posting of vacancies is a regular event.
Second, the growth of vacancies does not necessarily
indicate a worsening shortage either, since the labour
market itself grows in size over time. Similarly, of
course, the results of employer surveys such as our
own Human Resources Survey, with which some of
the present findings may be compared, must be
treated cautiously, since the needs of individual
employers may not always be accurately measured
by the sheer stridency of their pleas.

With these caveats in mind, it is interesting to note
that many of the "high vacancy growth" categories
identified in Table 3-2 are also expected to experience skill shortages, according to our Human
Resources Survey.[9] Examples of this include architects and engineers (CCDO 214), other occupations in
architecture and engineering (216), metal machinery
occupations (831), other metal shaping and forming
occupations (833), and a number of occupations
concerned with fabricating, assembling, and repairing
metal, electrical and electronic, wood, and rubber
and plastic products (851, 853, 854, 857, 858, and
859). In the same survey, systems analysts, computer
programmers, and related occupations (218) are also
predicted to experience shortages in the future. Even
though this category is not, according to our criterion,
classified among the "high vacancy growth" occupations, information on the projected level of vacancies
and vacancy shares for 1981-85 indicates that
graduates in these disciplines should nevertheless
also be in an advantageous position when seeking
desirable employment in the future.

Thus far, we have not touched upon the vacancy
share statistics shown in Table 3-2. These figures are
informative, especially when the vacancy time series
in question is relatively erratic, thereby creating
artificial growth rates.[10] Under close scrutiny, however, the vacancy shares tend to reinforce most of
what has been said above, as can be seen by the
consistency between the observed and projected
figures. Also, it should be noted that high vacancy
growth may or may not be an indication of serious
bottlenecks for the total economy. For instance,
wood machining occupations (835) have a growth

Table 3-2

Summary of Observed (1971-78) and Projected (1981-85) Job Vacancies in Selected Occupations,
Annual Averages, Canada

	Number		Share in total vacancies[1]		Vacancy growth	
	1971-78	1981-85	1971-78	1981-85	1971-78	1981-85
			(Per cent)		(Per cent)	
Occupation code (CCDO)[2]						
113	704.1	1,108.5	1.2	1.4	11.4	8.9
117	1,364.1	2,827.5	2.3	3.6	18.0	10.2
211	292.8	597.3	0.5	0.8	16.9	10.0
214	1,226.9	2,517.3	2.0	3.2	13.3	12.7
216	1,438.2	2,940.0	2.3	3.7	17.9	14.1
218	449.6	1,110.2	0.8	1.4	21.4	10.5
231	192.1	323.4	0.3	0.4	6.5	12.8
233	402.6	583.2	0.7	0.7	4.5	5.9
234	64.5	132.0	0.1	0.2	16.7	11.9
235	127.4	182.3	0.2	0.2	3.9	8.4
239	58.8	132.4	0.1	0.2	13.8	9.2
25	22.4	42.9	--	0.1	13.2	4.8
271	176.9	275.8	0.3	0.4	6.0	1.7
273	232.2	293.6	0.4	0.4	3.3	8.7
279	279.0	487.6	0.5	0.6	10.4	7.6
311	106.3	89.5	0.2	0.1	-3.5	7.7
313	2,565.8	3,049.1	4.1	3.8	-2.3	12.5
315	551.3	514.6	1.0	0.7	-2.9	4.0
331	226.2	383.4	0.4	0.5	4.1	8.1
333	59.3	102.3	0.1	0.1	8.8	9.5
335	125.5	259.4	0.2	0.3	14.0	7.0
337	91.8	189.9	0.2	0.2	7.4	9.3
411	3,398.5	4,593.0	5.7	5.8	2.4	9.5
413	1,959.6	3,080.7	3.3	3.9	6.7	10.6
414	519.3	869.2	0.8	1.1	5.1	13.2
415	836.0	1,092.4	1.4	1.4	3.9	13.4
416	234.9	351.9	0.4	0.4	2.6	8.8
417	931.1	1,372.3	1.5	1.7	7.3	9.8
419	1,965.3	2,719.0	3.2	3.4	4.0	11.4
513	4,085.6	3,536.1	6.8	4.5	-3.7	7.4
517	1,490.4	605.0	2.6	0.8	-2.8	-6.9
519	241.0	103.3	0.4	0.1	-10.0	13.6
611	1,203.0	1,344.0	1.9	1.7	1.2	16.1
612	3,598.4	5,633.9	5.6	7.1	3.4	15.1
613	307.1	544.0	0.5	0.7	11.8	13.4
614	1,062.6	889.7	1.7	1.1	-6.7	11.6
616	242.1	250.6	0.4	0.3	-9.2	6.9
619	1,061.3	1,560.7	1.7	2.0	4.9	14.6
71	272.3	124.2	0.5	0.2	-9.3	--
73	41.3	58.9	0.1	0.1	5.4	4.8
75	1,295.2	714.2	1.9	0.9	-10.1	11.2
77	836.9	1,224.0	1.4	1.5	3.7	12.4
811	73.3	78.9	0.1	0.1	-10.7	9.6
813	585.5	1,117.2	0.8	1.4	8.1	26.3
815	115.4	153.6	0.2	0.2	-2.4	14.9
816	277.5	384.2	0.5	0.5	5.4	10.7
821	1,109.6	384.1	1.7	0.5	1.1	-1.0
823	149.8	120.5	0.2	0.2	-4.2	12.8
825	60.5	95.5	0.1	0.1	11.5	10.1
826	314.3	331.9	0.5	0.4	-7.6	17.5
829	49.1	7.9	0.1	--	-10.2	-31.6
831	1,307.7	2,440.5	2.1	3.1	18.7	16.0
833	1,766.7	2,800.7	2.6	3.5	6.4	20.0
835	138.5	150.7	0.2	0.2	-1.6	22.8
837	71.3	68.2	0.1	0.1	-3.7	14.6
839	196.2	293.4	0.3	0.4	9.7	13.6

Table 3-2 (Concl'd)

Occupation code (CCDO)[2]	Number		Share in total vacancies[1]		Vacancy growth	
	1971-78	1981-85	1971-78	1981-85	1971-78	1981-85
			(Per cent)		(Per cent)	
851	682.0	1,376.8	1.1	1.7	18.3	14.8
853	1,135.8	1,166.5	1.8	1.5	2.4	15.6
854	476.3	493.2	0.7	0.6	−1.1	16.9
855	2,732.3	1,593.5	4.4	2.0	−6.2	10.2
857	378.0	586.9	0.6	0.7	3.0	21.2
858	3,453.0	4,791.3	5.5	6.0	5.4	13.5
859	514.1	662.0	0.8	0.8	−0.1	17.3
871	405.6	584.5	0.7	0.7	0.5	10.6
873	588.4	670.7	1.0	0.8	−3.7	10.9
878	2,887.3	3,653.2	4.6	4.6	−2.8	13.6
911	87.0	48.8	0.2	0.1	−16.3	6.4
913	44.1	124.3	0.1	0.2	21.6	9.1
915	63.8	132.0	0.1	0.2	12.2	14.4
917	1,764.2	1,936.4	2.8	2.4	−1.7	14.2
919	39.8	113.2	0.1	0.1	28.0	8.4
93	1,743.8	1,221.6	2.7	1.5	−6.7	18.5
951	350.2	575.1	0.6	0.7	5.5	12.9
953	298.2	530.6	0.5	0.7	4.7	12.5
955	35.3	68.8	0.1	0.1	6.0	8.8
959	39.1	87.4	0.1	0.1	11.7	13.2
Total[3]	61,816.0	79,334.0	100.0	100.0	2.5	12.6

1   Vacancies in a two- or three-digit CCDO occupation ÷ total vacancies × 100.
2   See Appendix B for occupation descriptions.
3   Includes a few occupations not listed above.
SOURCE   Data from Statistics Canada and estimates by the Economic Council of Canada.

rate of 22.8 per cent between 1981 and 1985, but the number of vacant jobs involved is too small to have much impact overall.

Many vacancy problems — for example, those involving architects and engineers (214) — can, in principle, be eradicated by government policy measures. Medium-term postsecondary education policy could be redesigned to increase the supply of these workers or, as is sometimes suggested in the media, foreign students graduating from these courses could be encouraged to stay in Canada. Vacancies in the highly skilled trade occupations might be less easy to fill, because the supply of skilled tradesmen has in the past come largely from a formidable task in providing the requisite numbers of such workers.

While occupational vacancies have been projected to 1990, only the 1981-85 results are presented here to indicate the medium-term implications. Over the longer term (1986-90), there will be more vacant jobs in most of the occupations, but the vacancy growth rates will be substantially lower than those of the 1981-85 period.

Where Will People Be Employed?

Some information on the future configuration of employment by industry is available from the CANDIDE 2.0 projection. While agriculture, fishing, and trapping will continue to decline gradually, the manufacturing sector will experience some moderate employment growth. Relatively speaking, however, its employment share (i.e., manufacturing employment as a proportion of total employment) is expected to drop slightly. The service sector will continue to grow in both absolute and relative terms.

As far as the occupational dimension is concerned, the vacancy figures must be supplemented with some estimates of occupational employment (Table 3-3). The average annual employment growth rate for the total economy is estimated at 2.7 per cent for 1981-85 and at 1.6 per cent for 1986-90. As before, we call those groups with average annual growth rates exceeding the national average for the 1981-85 period the "high employment growth" occupations. While the 1986-90 information is included as a reference for long-term development, we shall concentrate on the medium-term scenario (1981-85).

Table 3-3

Summary of Occupational Employment Projections,
Annual Averages, Canada, 1981-90

Occupation code (CCDO)[2]	Employment growth		Employment share[1]	
	1981-85	1986-90	1981-85	1986-90
	(Per cent)			
113	2.3	0.8	2.3	2.2
117	2.8	1.1	2.3	2.3
211	3.2	1.2	0.4	0.4
213	2.8	1.4	0.2	0.2
214	3.3	1.3	1.0	1.0
216	3.1	1.2	0.9	0.9
218	2.9	1.1	0.3	0.3
231	2.6	1.2	0.1	0.1
233	2.6	1.2	0.3	0.3
234	2.6	1.3	0.3	0.3
235	2.6	1.2	0.1	0.1
239	3.2	1.5	0.1	0.1
25	4.2	2.6	0.3	0.3
271	--	-1.3	0.3	0.2
273	-0.8	1.4	2.0	1.8
279	-0.1	-0.5	0.6	0.5
311	2.6	1.3	0.5	0.5
313	3.1	1.7	3.5	3.5
315	2.6	1.2	0.7	0.7
331	1.8	0.6	0.3	0.3
333	2.4	1.1	0.2	0.2
335	3.0	1.1	0.2	0.2
337	2.7	1.3	0.2	0.2
411	2.6	1.1	4.0	4.0
413	2.8	1.0	4.5	4.5
414	2.6	1.0	0.6	0.6
415	2.2	0.7	1.7	1.7
416	2.6	1.1	0.4	0.4
417	2.0	0.8	1.7	1.7
419	3.6	1.5	3.6	3.7
513	2.6	1.1	8.2	8.1
517	3.6	1.1	1.3	1.3
519	2.6	1.8	0.2	0.2
611	2.6	1.5	1.4	1.4
612	2.6	1.3	3.1	3.1
613	2.9	1.5	0.5	0.5
614	2.6	1.3	1.8	1.8
616	1.9	0.9	0.4	0.4
619	2.6	1.2	2.8	2.7
71	-0.5	-0.8	4.4	3.8
73	-0.6	-0.8	0.2	0.2
75	-1.5	-1.1	0.5	0.4
77	6.0	2.9	0.7	0.8
811	5.0	3.2	0.1	0.1
813	2.4	-0.2	0.7	0.6
815	2.3	1.2	0.2	0.2
816	0.9	0.9	0.5	0.5
821	0.5	0.2	1.4	1.3
823	3.4	1.4	0.5	0.5
825	1.1	2.2	0.4	0.4
826	0.5	-0.8	0.4	0.3
829	1.1	-0.2	0.1	0.1
831	1.5	0.3	0.8	0.8
833	2.0	0.8	1.6	1.5
835	2.9	0.9	0.1	0.1
837	3.0	1.6	0.1	0.1
839	2.1	0.4	0.2	0.2
851	0.9	0.1	0.8	0.7

Table 3-3 (Concl'd)

Occupation code (CCDO)[2]	Employment growth		Employment share[1]	
	1981-85	1986-90	1981-85	1986-90
	(Per cent)			
853	2.2	0.8	1.1	1.0
854	2.8	0.8	0.3	0.3
855	0.6	--	1.7	1.6
857	1.0	1.9	0.5	0.4
858	2.4	0.9	3.0	2.9
859	1.9	1.6	0.8	0.7
873	2.2	0.9	1.3	1.3
878	2.7	1.0	4.3	4.3
911	0.9	0.4	0.2	0.1
913	0.4	-0.1	0.3	0.3
915	1.0	0.6	0.2	0.2
917	2.5	1.0	3.0	2.9
919	3.4	2.0	0.1	0.1
93	2.2	1.0	2.4	2.4
951	2.0	1.6	0.7	0.6
953	3.4	1.5	0.6	0.6
955	1.5	0.8	0.1	0.1
959	2.6	1.1	0.1	0.1

1 Employment in two- or three-digit occupations ÷ total employment.
2 See Appendix B for occupation descriptions.
SOURCE Estimates by the Economic Council of Canada.

Note, also, that the employment growth figures alone do not tell the whole story of an occupation's impact on the total economy. For instance, clay, glass and stone, and related material machining occupations (837) are projected to have an employment growth rate higher than the national average. However, this occupation involves only a few workers (its employment for the 1981-85 period accounts for less than 0.1 per cent of total employment), so that its significance for the total economy is accordingly small. To obtain a proper perspective of the employment picture, the growth rates must therefore be read in conjunction with the employment-share figures and the strategic role that an occupation plays in the economy.

The highlights of Table 3-3 are as follows:

• Managers, administrators, and related occupations (113) – a category that includes management-related occupations in public administration, education and health services, and other service industries but excludes officials and administrators unique to government (e.g., postmasters) – are expected to grow at a rate slightly lower than the national average for 1981-85.

• Accountants, personnel and related officers, and other occupations related to management and administration (117) will grow at a pace only slightly faster than average.

• The other highly trained professionals – occupations in physical and life sciences (211, 213); architects and engineers, and other occupations in architecture and engineering (214, 216); and occupations in mathematics, statistics, systems analysis, and related fields (218) – are expected to enjoy a healthy growth. While all of these groups are projected to have relatively small employment shares, this does not minimize their significance to the total economy. Because of their strategic importance, a lack of trained personnel in these occupations could constitute a potential bottleneck to growth.

• Employment for social scientists and social workers (231, 233) will grow at a rate slightly lower than average over the next few years, as will employment in law and jurisprudence (234) and in such fields as physicians, dentists, veterinarians, and other diagnosing and treating occupations (311).

• The employment levels of teaching and related occupations (271, 273, 279) will likely experience a decline during the 1981-85 period. This bleak outlook for the teaching profession is due to the expected decrease in the school-age population over the medium-term future.

• Nursing, therapy, and related assisting occupations (313) are expected to have an employment growth rate significantly above the national average.

• Bookkeeping, account recording, and related occupations (413), other clerical and related occupations (419), and sales occupations in the services (517) are all projected to enjoy employment growth well above the national average. These are not only large groups; they are also the type of occupations that are not age- or sex-specific. Since the labour force groups other than prime-age men are expected to grow relatively quickly, the projected figures for these occupations carry some elements of hope for the future labour market because of their absorptive potential. There is some fear that technological change in such occupational groups may replace workers with machines. Thus far, there is no conclusive evidence that this is necessarily the case, though the nature of many jobs will undoubtedly be changed. For instance, a bookkeeper may have to learn how to use a microcomputer for bookkeeping purposes. But, since the level of output for the service sector is projected to grow relatively faster than other sectors, the overall employment growth for such service-oriented occupations can be expected to be above the national average.

• Employment normally found in agriculture, fishing, trapping, and forestry (71, 73, 75) is not expected to experience growth in the upcoming years.

• Mining and quarrying, including oil and gas field occupations (77), and mineral ore treating occupations (811) are two relatively small groups that are projected to have average annual employment

growth rates of 6 and 5 per cent, respectively. These rapid rates are, of course, the result of the expected expansion in the energy sector.

• Although there are shortages in a few cases, occupations found in manufacturing are not expected to grow dramatically in the medium-term future. Among the occupations found mainly in this sector, only those in wood processing, except pulp and papermaking (823), machining in wood, clay, glass, and stone and other materials (835, 837), and wood fabricating, assembling, and repairing (854) are projected to have employment growth rates higher than the national average. Many of the occupational groups in the manufacturing sector that are expected to experience some kind of shortage are not among the fastest-growing employment groups identified here. This is not surprising, because *ex ante* demand cannot always be met. Unsatisfied demand would show up as job vacancies, rather than as an increase in employment.

• Jobs in the service sector, in the broadest sense of the term, will have average growth rates better than, or close to, the national average.

It should be re-emphasized that total labour demand must include vacancies as well as employment. Only in this way can the "unsatisfied" and "satisfied" components of demand be considered. Estimates of employment growth and shares suggest the importance of potential job availability, but they do not necessarily indicate shortage problems. Employment growth in a particular field may be extremely rapid, but as long as adequate supplies of qualified personnel are forthcoming, bottlenecks can be avoided. Conversely, an occupation showing little employment growth may nevertheless have substantial unsatisfied labour demand. As a result, its growth of realized employment may be slight, while its accumulation of vacancies may be large. Employment projections, then, represent merely a part of the labour demand story, so taking them as an indicator of shortages could prove misleading. To identify imbalances more accurately, vacancy estimates must also be incorporated.

Conclusion

In Chapter 2, we discussed the deterioration of the Canadian labour market performance in terms of rising unemployment rates, and some of the factors associated with greater degrees of structural mismatching of labour demand and supply were considered. Our analysis of the unemployment/vacancy relationship in the present chapter generally corroborates the finding of a greater mismatching in the 1971-75 period. Our work also suggests, however, that the strong growth of the service sector in the

1970s helped to absorb the large influx of women and young people and averted a potentially intensified maladjustment problem. Inasmuch as current macroeconomic models project a continual growth of service sector employment, we can hope for similarly beneficial effects on the absorption of women and young people in the current decade. Our optimism in this respect must nevertheless be tempered by the observation that it is precisely the jobs that have traditionally afforded opportunities for female and youth employment — clerical, stenographic and other office occupations, as well as jobs in retailing, for example — that are jeopardized by the rapid technological changes based on the microprocessor. This does not necessarily mean that there will be large-scale displacement (though there will undoubtedly be some), but rather that the nature of the tasks will likely change substantially. And while one might argue that it is precisely those who have invested less in human capital who are best able to adapt, one must nevertheless feel concerned about the nature and quality of the new employment opportunities. Whether or not the microprocessor will reduce most of the work to an uninteresting button-pressing chore, and what influence it will have on the wages and salaries of the workers, are moot questions.

In the absence of any comprehensive forward-looking information, decision makers — including potential members of the labour force, educators, human resource managers in private enterprise, and government policy makers — are likely to react to the current market conditions. But it takes a minimum lead time of five years for a bright high school graduate to become a licensed engineer, and about seven years to become a registered architect. Because the time required to develop many occupational skills is considerable, in the absence of accurate and detailed projections overshooting and undershooting of supply could therefore occur. This is too important an aspect of the Canadian economy to be left as is. We believe that the government can improve the present situation by providing the general public with regular, comprehensive, projected information on occupational demand. This can be accomplished only by improving the Canadian occupational data base, by intensive and continuous efforts at improving occupational-demand modeling and projection techniques, and by efficient means of disseminating this information.

In the short run, however, the urgent requirement is for the establishment of a capacity to analyse and project the limited data currently available. To be useful, such an exercise must be carried out regularly and continuously, with continual updating and with widespread dissemination and publicity.

4 Labour Supply

The supply side of the labour market – the working-age population in the labour force – underwent substantial, and in many ways fundamental, change during the 1970s. Those born in the postwar baby boom reached the working age; the declining labour force participation rates of young people first arrested and then reversed; and the participation of women continued to increase. The extensive demographic changes in the working-age population combined with the participation rate changes to produce a labour force that grew at an accelerating pace during most of the decade.

While the labour force of the 1980s will continue to grow, the demographic trends described below will induce deceleration in the rate of growth throughout the decade. The generalized oversupply of labour that characterized much of the 1970s will ease, making the task of new job creation more manageable. Although no generalized shortage of labour is expected to emerge, difficulties have already been experienced with respect to certain critical skills. Without corrective measures, they may endure or worsen when the economy expands.

To obtain an understanding of future trends, we have developed a labour supply projection to the mid-1980s. This has enabled us to see where increases and declines are expected to occur, as well as to assess some of the factors causing these changes. For our purposes, we have defined "labour supply" as comprising both employed persons and the officially unemployed, but not the hidden unemployed – a concept corresponding to the definition of "labour force" by Statistics Canada in its Labour Force Survey.

The 1970s

The changes that have occurred in the household sector provide a useful starting point for an examination of labour supply, as this perspective makes it possible to discern the shifts in the relative importance and changing behaviour of heterogeneous subgroups within the labour force. At present, the only way to accomplish this in Canada, other than through the census, is by recourse to the Survey of Consumer Finances.

An examination of the distribution of "census family" types,[1] based on the surveys for 1971 and 1979, reveals an increase in the older age groups, especially among single women, reflecting in part the general aging of our society (Table 4-1). The rise in the incidence of marriage breakdown is reflected in the greater number both of unattached persons and

Table 4-1

Distribution of Census Families,[1] by Type, Canada, 1971 and 1979

	1971	1979
	(Per cent)	
Unattached persons,[2] 65 and over		
Men	3.5	2.7
Women	6.5	8.0
Subtotal	10.0	10.7
Families of 2 or more persons, where the head is 65 or over	8.1	8.0
Unattached persons[2] under 65		
Men	11.4	12.6
Women	10.6	12.1
Subtotal	22.0	24.7
Single-parent families of 2 or more persons, where the head is under 65		
Female head	4.1	5.2
Male head	0.6	0.9
Subtotal	4.7	6.1
Husband-wife census families of 2 or more persons, with the head aged under 65 and with no children under 16	19.0	20.1
Husband-wife census families of 2 or more persons, with the head aged under 65 and with children under 16	36.2	30.4
Total	100.0	100.0

1 A census family consists of the husband, wife, and any unmarried children resident with them, or one parent and any unmarried children.
2 The expression "unattached persons" used here corresponds to Statistics Canada's "persons not in families."
SOURCE Statistics Canada, Survey of Consumer Finances, special tabulations.

of single-parent families, predominantly headed by women. The rise in the greater number of unattached persons also reflects to some extent the increase in the number of informal relationships not bonded by marriage. The most dramatic change, however — and the one with the greatest implication for labour supply — is the decline in the number of families with two parents and children under 16 years of age, caused in large part by the drop in the fertility rate. Since married women with children at home tend to have a higher propensity to remain out of the labour force than working-age women in other situations, this compositional shift alone explains part of the increase in the aggregate female participation rate over the past decade.

Unattached Persons

Looking beyond these simple compositional shifts, new patterns in work effort have emerged in most groups as the result of changes in demographic trends and in the behaviour of individuals. Consider, first, the case of unattached persons aged less than

65 years (Table 4-2). A visible change has occurred in the age structure, with the proportion of persons aged 25 to 44 increasing substantially between 1971 and 1979. In itself, this demographic shift is quite sufficient to raise aggregate participation rates, since they are higher in that age group for both unattached men and women than in the younger age group, where continuation of schooling is a factor. In addition, there has been an increase in the propensity to work within each age-sex group, except for men and women aged 45 to 64, who tend to seek opportunities for early retirement.

Single-Parent Families

A group that is often singled out for special attention is that of single-parent families headed by women. This is especially so not only when consideration is given to social assistance and services but also, increasingly, when labour market access and supporting services are being considered. During the 1970s, the number of such families rose by about 59 per cent — resulting in no small measure from the liberalization of divorce laws in Canada. The importance of this factor is indicated by the 82 per cent

Table 4-2

Distribution of Unattached Persons[1] under 65, by Age and by Sex and Labour Force Status, Canada, 1971 and 1979

	1971	1979
	(Per cent)	
Age		
24 and under	33.1	31.1
25-44	30.6	38.2
45-64	36.3	30.7
Total	100.0	100.0
Sex and labour force status[2]		
Men		
Worked full-time	39.6	42.3
Worked part-time	4.2	3.3
Did not work	8.1	5.5
Subtotal	51.9	51.1
Women		
Worked full-time	32.4	34.7
Worked part-time	3.6	4.2
Did not work	12.1	10.0
Subtotal	48.1	48.9
Both sexes		
Worked full-time	72.0	77.0
Worked part-time	7.8	7.5
Did not work	20.2	15.5
Total	100.0	100.0

1 The expression "unattached persons" used here corresponds to Statistics Canada's "persons not in families."
2 Full-time or part-time status is determined by whether the weeks worked were mostly full-time or mostly part-time. For 1979, full-time employment meant 30 or more hours of work per week.
SOURCE Statistics Canada, Survey of Consumer Finances, special tabulations.

Table 4-3

Distribution of Single-Parent Census Families[1] Headed by Women under 65, by Selected Characteristics, Canada, 1971 and 1979

	1971	1979
	(Per cent)	
Age of head		
24 and under	8.3	12.3
25-44	47.4	50.6
45-64	44.3	37.1
Total	100.0	100.0
Labour force status of head[2]		
Worked full-time	36.2	47.7
Worked part-time	8.9	13.5
Did not work	54.9	38.8
Total	100.0	100.0
Age of children in the family		
No children under 16	27.4	29.9
Children under 6 only	14.9	19.7
Children under 6 and aged 6 to 15	14.6	7.6
Children aged 6 to 15 only	43.1	42.8
Total	100.0	100.0

1 A census family consists of the husband, wife, and any unmarried children resident with them, or one parent and any unmarried children.
2 Full-time or part-time status is determined by whether the weeks worked were mostly full-time or mostly part-time. For 1979, full-time employment meant 30 or more hours of work per week.
SOURCE Statistics Canada, Survey of Consumer Finances, special tabulations.

increase in the number of divorced women between the 1971 and 1976 censuses.

There was quite a striking change in the age structure of these families between 1971 and 1979, with the proportion of young women increasing substantially (Table 4-3). Concomitantly, the proportion of single-parent families with children under 6 years of age increased, and the proportion of children under 6 years of age as a percentage of all children under 16 in these families also rose (Table 4-4).

Work effort, as indicated by the labour force status, has increased substantially for the group as a whole, reflecting the higher propensity to work (full-time or part-time) within all age groups. The declining family size has contributed to this trend, since it is generally much easier for mothers with few children to make child care arrangements and to work. The proportion of single-parent, female-headed families with children aged both under 6 years and 6 to 15

years in the same family — families that have the highest average number of children — nearly halved between 1971 and 1979. More importantly, however, the average number of children per family declined irrespective of family size. Despite this, the increase in labour market participation by heads of single-parent families has meant a rise of about 149,000 children under 16 who had working mothers. While not all of these children required care, those who did had to compete for scarce resources with children from the growing number of families with both parents working. Thus, while many factors indicate an increasing participation in the labour force by single mothers, a major barrier for many — and an issue for social policy — is the lack of affordable day care.

The number of single-parent families headed by men under 65 increased over the decade, but this group continues to represent a very small proportion of all families. The proportion of such families with children under 16 did not change significantly.

Table 4-4

Distribution of Children under 16 in Single-Parent Census Families[1] Headed by Women under 65, by Selected Characteristics of Families, Canada, 1971 and 1979

	Age of children					
	1971			1979		
	Under 6	6-15	Total under 16	Under 6	6-15	Total under 16
	(Per cent)					
Age of head						
24 and under	25.3	1.1	7.5	43.6	1.5	14.2
25-44	69.5	69.4	69.4	55.1	76.7	70.2
45-64	5.2	29.5	23.1	1.3	21.8	15.6
Total	100.0	100.0	100.0	100.0	100.0	100.0
Labour force status of head[2]						
Worked full-time	19.3	30.4	27.5	39.7	47.7	45.3
Worked part-time	8.0	10.6	9.9	12.6	15.9	14.9
Did not work	72.7	59.0	62.6	47.7	36.4	39.8
Total	100.0	100.0	100.0	100.0	100.0	100.0
Age of children in families with children under 16						
Under 6 only	52.4	–	13.9	73.6	–	22.1
Under 6 and from 6 to 15	47.6	27.8	33.0	26.4	14.5	18.1
From 6 to 15 only	–	72.2	53.1	–	85.5	59.8
Total	100.0	100.0	100.0	100.0	100.0	100.0
All children	26.4	73.6	100.0	30.1	69.9	100.0

1 A census family consists of the husband, wife, and any unmarried children resident with them, or one parent and any unmarried children.
2 Full-time or part-time status is determined by whether the weeks worked were mostly full-time or mostly part-time. For 1979, full-time employment meant 30 or more hours of work per week.
SOURCE Statistics Canada, Survey of Consumer Finances, special tabulations.

Husband-and-Wife Families without Young Children

The number of husband-and-wife census families with no children under 16 increased slightly in relative terms over the decade (Table 4-1). This result might be expected, given the increase in the absolute number of couples in the 45-64 age group, whose children tend to be older as well. This is not the predominant feature, however: the share of older couples among families without young children declined because of the increase in the 25-44 age group (Table 4-5). The change in the latter group reflects both the aging of the baby-boom generation and the decision of married couples not to have children, or at least to postpone having them.

The most distinct change, however, was within the under-25 group. As a proportion of all husband-and-wife families with no children, this group declined only slightly despite the massive movement of the baby-boom generation into the 25-and-over category. What this reflects is a very definite change in the attitude of young married couples towards having children. In 1971, of all husband-and-wife families aged 24 and under, just under one-half had no children; by 1979, nearly two-thirds fell into that category. Thus, while the number of young families declined from 1971 to 1979, the number of those without children actually increased. There is little doubt that these shifts are very strongly related to the changing labour market activity of women.

Within these families without children, the labour force status of husbands changed very little from 1971 to 1979. There was a slight decline in the incidence of full-time work and an increase in the proportion of husbands who did not work at all during the survey year. This was entirely accounted for by husbands in the 45-64 age group, as the two younger groups moved in the opposite direction. These results are consistent with the overall decline in the labour force participation rate of older men. The incidence of full-time work among wives in these families increased substantially from 1971 to 1979, as did the incidence of part-time work. While, in 1971, 45.3 per cent of wives did not work at all during the year, by 1979 only 35.3 per cent reported that they had not worked.

Husband-and-Wife Families with Young Children

A substantial decline in the proportion of two-parent families with children under 16 was recorded between 1971 and 1979 (Table 4-1). Again, a large shift in the age structure of this category has been noted (Table 4-6). The 25-44 age group was the only one that increased in absolute numbers during the 1970s. The under-25 and the 45-64 age groups declined in both relative and absolute terms. As noted before, this is a result of both the aging of the baby-boom generation and the decision of married couples to postpone having children.

Within this family type, the labour force status of husbands changed only slightly during the decade. In 1971, 94.9 per cent of husbands were full-time workers; by 1979 this proportion had risen to 96.0 per cent. The proportion of husbands engaged in part-time work diminished, while that of husbands who did not work at all during the year remained at about 2.3 per cent. As in the case of husband-and-wife families without young children, there was an

Table 4-5

Distribution of Husband-Wife Census Families[1] with Husband under 65 and No Children under 16, by Selected Characteristics, Canada, 1971 and 1979

	Labour force status of wife[2]							
	1971				1979			
	Worked full-time	Worked part-time	Did not work	Total	Worked full-time	Worked part-time	Did not work	Total
	(Per cent)							
Age of husband								
24 and under	8.1	1.0	1.7	10.8	7.8	1.3	1.0	10.1
25-44	18.7	2.2	6.1	27.0	22.2	2.6	3.7	28.5
45-64	17.3	7.4	37.5	62.2	21.6	9.2	30.6	61.4
Total	44.1	10.6	45.3	100.0	51.6	13.1	35.3	100.0

1 A census family consists of the husband, wife, and any unmarried children resident with them, or one parent and any unmarried children.
2 Full-time or part-time status is determined by whether the weeks worked were mostly full-time or mostly part-time. For 1979, full-time employment meant 30 or more hours of work per week.
SOURCE Statistics Canada, Survey of Consumer Finances, special tabulations.

Table 4-6

Distribution of Husband-Wife Census Families[1] with Husband under 65 and with Children under 16, by Selected Characteristics, Canada, 1971 and 1979

| | Labour force status of wife[2] | | | | | | | |
| | 1971 | | | | 1979 | | | |
	Worked full-time	Worked part-time	Did not work	Total	Worked full-time	Worked part-time	Did not work	Total
	(Per cent)							
Age of husband								
24 and under	1.9	0.7	3.2	5.8	1.5	0.8	1.3	3.6
25-44	16.0	10.0	41.6	67.6	28.6	15.1	30.4	74.1
45-64	5.2	3.9	17.5	26.6	7.4	4.6	10.3	22.3
Total	23.1	14.6	62.3	100.0	37.5	20.5	42.0	100.0
Age of children								
Under 6 only	7.6	3.2	15.7	26.5	12.0	5.7	11.5	29.2
Under 6 and from 6 to 15	3.6	3.4	19.4	26.4	5.8	3.5	11.4	20.7
From 6 to 15 only	11.9	8.0	27.2	47.1	19.7	11.3	19.1	50.1
Total	23.1	14.6	62.3	100.0	37.5	20.5	42.0	100.0

1 A census family consists of the husband, wife, and any unmarried children resident with them, or one parent and any unmarried children.
2 Full-time or part-time status is determined by whether the weeks worked were mostly full-time or mostly part-time. For 1979, full-time employment meant 30 or more hours of work per week.
SOURCE Statistics Canada, Survey of Consumer Finances, special tabulations.

increase in the proportion of men aged 45 to 64 who did not work at all during the year.

The labour force status of wives in families with children under 16 indicates substantial increases in the incidence of full-time and of part-time employment, both for this category as a whole and for all age groups. The incidence was highest in the youngest group and declined as age increased. The incidence of part-time work among the youngest wives moved from the lowest of the three age groups in 1971 to the highest in 1979, with the result that the proportion of women in the youngest group who did not work dropped from nearly 55 per cent to just above 35 per cent over the decade. These trends reflect two basic changes: there are fewer children in families; and the inhibiting effect of children on the working decisions of mothers is declining.

With respect to the first of these factors, the average number of children in two-parent families with young children dropped from 2.3 in 1971 to 1.9 in 1979. While the incidence of full-time employment by wives increased during that period, regardless of the age of their children, the incidence was lowest among wives with children in both the under-6 and the 6-15 age groups. These were the families with the highest average number of children: 3.4 in 1971 and 2.7 in 1979.

The influence of the second factor was most visible in the under-25 group with children aged less than 6

years only. The incidence of full-time work by the wives in this group increased by about 10 percentage points while the average number of children declined only marginally; the increase in the incidence of part-time work was of similar magnitude but was accompanied by a slight increase in the average number of children. This would clearly have implications for labour force growth even if the fertility rate were to stop declining.

In summary, what have the household surveys revealed? The main message is that the observed changes in participation rates have been due to large demographic shifts and to changing labour market behaviour, particularly among women. Within the male population, the main changes have been the advancement of the baby-boom generation to prime working age and the decline in the participation of older men mainly because of earlier retirement. While the participation rates of women have been affected by the same demographic evolution, their advance has resulted from participation increases in virtually all types of family units. It is still true that the incidence of full-time or part-time participation among mothers decreases with increasing family size. Not only is family size decreasing, however, but the participation rate of mothers is less affected by the number of children in the family. These changes have direct implications for the future direction of the labour force and for broader social issues.

The Source Population, Participation Rates, and the Labour Force

The projection of labour force trends to the mid-1980s is not an exploration of virgin territory. A paper written at the Department of Finance in 1980 examined participation rates and labour force growth to the year 2000.[2] In the same year, this Council published, as part of its research program on pensions, a study containing population and labour force projections to the year 2051.[3] Last year, the Institute for Policy Analysis published a report in which population and labour force growth in Canada and the provinces during this decade was examined.[4] As well, a task force of Employment and Immigration Canada studied the labour supply developments that are expected in the 1980s and also made some projections of the occupational composition of employment growth.[5] Our own projections in this report have a more modest time horizon, in large measure because our use of a broader occupational dimension imposed data limitations on us.[6] In many respects, the projections to mid-decade for most labour supply studies are similar; yet they do differ in detail — importantly at times.

Labour force growth is generally decomposed into its two elements: changes in the source population and changes in the participation rates of different groups within that population. We are not concerned here with the total population but with the labour force source population: the civilian, noninstitutional population aged 15 years or more. The domestic portion of this population for the entire decade of the 1980s is already with us.

The decline of the birth rate in the last 20 years was partly offset by the maturing of the baby-boom generation during the 1970s; thus the lower number of births per woman was partially counterbalanced by the increase in the number of women of child-bearing age. While most analysts predict a reduction in the number of new entrants to the labour force source population, this trend will be less severe than indicated by the lowering birth rate.

The source population of domestic origin will be decreased by deaths. While age-specific death rates may remain constant, an aging population will have an increasing overall death rate because of compositional shifts. Finally, the size and composition of the overall source population will be affected by net immigration. In the set of projections presented here, we have assumed that net immigration will remain at 50,000 persons a year, which is in line with recent experience. Under this assumption, most labour requirements will have to be met primarily from the domestic population and not from abroad.

We have examined figures for the recent past and medium-term projections of the labour force source population by age-sex groups (Tables 4-7 and 4-8, and Appendix Table C-1).[7] The progressive slowing down of the overall growth rate of the source population from 2.3 to 1.0 per cent over the 1975-85 period is in line with the decline in the birth rate that commenced in the 1960s. The total source population is projected to increase by almost 3 million persons over the period. It will undergo a striking compositional change, with the youth portion actually declining from 1980 onwards and representing only

Table 4-7

Distribution of the Source Population,[1] by Age-Sex Group, Canada, 1975-81 (Actual) and 1982-85 (Projected)

	15-24		25-44		45-64		65 and over		Total		
	Men	Women	Men	Women	Men	Women	Men	Women	Men	Women	Both sexes
					(Per cent)						
1975	13.2	13.1	18.2	18.2	12.8	13.4	4.9	6.1	49.2	50.8	100.0
1976	13.2	13.1	18.3	18.3	12.7	13.3	5.0	6.2	49.1	50.9	100.0
1977	13.2	13.0	18.4	18.4	12.6	13.2	5.0	6.3	49.1	50.9	100.0
1978	13.1	12.9	18.4	18.5	12.5	13.1	5.1	6.4	49.1	50.9	100.0
1979	13.0	12.8	18.6	18.7	12.3	13.0	5.1	6.6	49.0	51.0	100.0
1980	12.9	12.6	18.8	18.9	12.2	12.8	5.2	6.7	49.0	51.0	100.0
1981	12.6	12.3	19.0	19.2	12.1	12.7	5.2	6.8	49.0	51.0	100.0
1982	12.2	11.9	19.5	19.5	12.0	12.6	5.3	7.0	49.0	51.0	100.0
1983	11.8	11.5	19.9	19.8	12.0	12.5	5.4	7.1	49.0	51.0	100.0
1984	11.4	11.2	20.2	20.1	12.0	12.4	5.5	7.3	49.0	51.0	100.0
1985	11.0	10.8	20.5	20.4	11.9	12.4	5.5	7.4	49.0	51.0	100.0

1   The source population, as defined by the Labour Force Survey, includes the population aged 15 and over, except residents of the Yukon and Northwest Territories, persons living on Indian reserves, inmates of institutions, and full-time members of the armed forces.
SOURCE   Data from Statistics Canada; and calculations from Economic Council of Canada, "base case" solution of the CANDIDE 2.0 model, September 1981.

Table 4-8

Source Population[1] Growth Rates, by Age-Sex Group, Canada, 1975-76 to 1980-81 (Actual) and 1981-82 to 1984-85 (Projected)

| | 15-24 | | 25-44 | | 45-64 | | 65 and over | | Total | | |
	Men	Women	Men	Women	Men	Women	Men	Women	Men	Women	Both sexes
					(Per cent)						
1975-76	2.3	2.2	2.8	2.8	1.5	1.6	2.6	3.3	2.3	2.4	2.3
1976-77	1.9	1.6	2.5	2.7	1.2	1.3	3.0	3.9	2.1	2.2	2.1
1977-78	1.6	1.1	2.3	2.5	1.0	1.2	2.9	3.9	1.8	2.0	1.9
1978-79	1.0	0.7	2.5	2.7	0.6	0.8	3.1	4.0	1.7	1.9	1.8
1979-80	0.5	--	3.0	3.0	0.7	0.8	3.1	3.9	1.7	1.8	1.8
1980-81	-0.3	-0.7	3.1	3.1	0.9	0.9	2.4	3.4	1.6	1.6	1.6
1981-82	-2.2	-2.0	3.3	3.0	0.4	-0.1	3.1	3.5	1.1	1.1	1.1
1982-83	-1.9	-1.8	3.4	3.0	0.9	0.6	2.7	3.3	1.4	1.3	1.3
1983-84	-2.2	-2.0	3.1	2.7	1.1	0.9	2.6	3.2	1.3	1.3	1.3
1984-85	-2.1	-2.1	2.4	2.6	0.5	0.8	2.5	3.1	0.9	1.2	1.0

1 The source population, as defined by the Labour Force Survey, includes the population aged 15 and over, residing in Canada, with the exception of: residents of the Yukon and Northwest Territories, persons living on Indian reserves, inmates of institutions, and full-time members of the armed forces.
SOURCE Data from Statistics Canada; and calculations from Economic Council of Canada, "base case" solution of the CANDIDE 2.0 model, September 1981.

approximately one-fifth of the total in 1985, compared with more than one-fourth in 1975. The 25-44 age group shows strong gains throughout the period, as the baby-boom generation moves into prime working age. These compositional shifts, which are large by any standard, are a major determinant of the labour supply changes noted in our study.

The projection of participation rates, notably those of women, prove to be the trickiest element of any analysis of future labour supply. Generally, past attempts have resulted in substantial underestimation of the female rates.[8] The participation rates used in this report were derived from the "base case"

solution of the CANDIDE 2.0 model (Table 4-9).[9] The equations used to derive the estimates are fairly standard in form, and they incorporate most of the variables generally found in such models but in a manner consistent with the overall operation of the economy.

The relationship between the participation rates of married women and the earnings of their husbands is a particularly troublesome element of all female participation rate projections, and one on which findings are mixed. The evidence from the household surveys is that a relationship does exist. Within

Table 4-9

Labour Force Participation Rates,[1] by Age-Sex Group, Canada, 1975-81 (Actual) and 1982-85 (Projected)

| | 15-24 | | 25-44 | | 45-64 | | 65 and over | | Total | | |
	Men	Women	Men	Women	Men	Women	Men	Women	Men	Women	Both sexes
					(Per cent)						
1975	68.8	56.8	95.6	52.3	87.0	39.4	18.5	4.9	78.4	44.4	61.1
1976	67.9	56.8	95.7	53.6	85.7	41.1	16.0	4.2	77.6	45.2	61.1
1977	68.8	57.5	95.5	55.4	85.4	41.5	15.6	4.4	77.6	46.0	61.5
1978	69.7	58.9	95.8	58.7	85.7	42.6	15.2	4.5	77.9	47.8	62.6
1979	71.4	61.0	96.0	60.0	85.5	43.7	15.3	4.2	78.4	48.9	63.3
1980	72.0	62.6	95.6	62.2	85.2	44.5	14.7	4.3	78.3	50.3	64.0
1981	72.5	63.2	95.6	65.1	84.8	45.2	14.0	4.4	78.3	51.6	64.7
1982	74.3	64.5	95.5	65.1	85.0	47.1	14.2	4.3	78.8	52.2	65.3
1983	75.1	64.7	95.5	66.9	84.9	48.2	13.9	4.3	79.0	53.1	65.8
1984	75.9	65.5	95.4	69.0	84.7	49.2	13.6	4.3	79.2	54.2	66.4
1985	76.6	66.1	95.3	71.1	84.8	50.2	13.3	4.3	79.3	55.3	67.0

1 The participation rate for a particular age-sex group is the labour force in that group as a proportion of the source population for that group.
SOURCE Data from Statistics Canada; and calculations from Economic Council of Canada, "base case" solution of the CANDIDE 2.0 model, September 1981.

families, there is greater reliance on working wives, not only to keep families out of poverty but also to enable them to meet their standard-of-living expectations. This factor is particularly relevant in times of declining real wages and spiraling housing and energy costs. Clearly, the poor results of female participation rate projections to date show that much more work in this area needs to be done, particularly with respect to family effects.

Not only do the differing family structures impose differing costs and constraints on the ability of individual persons to participate in the labour market, but – in conjunction with social transfer programs and the income tax system – they also cause returns from such participation to vary widely. A study done at the Council as part of an international project on income maintenance contains the results of detailed simulations for a number of family types that show some of this variability.[10] The families were assumed to be living in Metropolitan Toronto and thus came under federal and Ontario jurisdiction; the year chosen as the basis for the simulations was 1979. The first case considered was a single-parent family in which a mother did not participate in the labour market but remained at home to care for two children aged 2 and 7. In such circumstances, the mother would receive social assistance under the Ontario Family Benefits Act. In addition, she would receive financial assistance from such programs as Family Allowances, the refundable Dependent Child Tax Credit, and the Ontario Tax Credit. Despite these various contributions, her total income for 1979 would have amounted to only $6,131. In comparison, the Statistics Canada "low income cut-off" for a family in these circumstances in 1979 was $9,775. Any alimony or other payments under a separation agreement would close the gap somewhat, but this would also cause a reduction in social assistance equal to 75 per cent of the payment received.

Would this mother not be better off to place the children in someone else's care and participate in the labour market? As we have seen, the incidence of full-time work among mothers in this situation increased more rapidly than their numbers. Since the answer to our question depends upon many variables, it could only be: "Possibly."

Consider an identical family except that the mother worked full-time (that is, 30 hours a week) but averaged no more than 120 hours a month – a necessary condition in 1979 to prevent disqualification from social assistance under the Ontario Family Benefits Act. Assume that her annual income from employment amounted to half the 1979 average "industrial composite wage," or $7,494. In such

circumstances, her social assistance payments would be reduced by over $4,500, leaving her with just over $30 a month from that source. The other allowances and tax credits would remain the same, but the working mother would have to make contributions to the Unemployment Insurance and Canada Pension plans. Assuming that she could have placed her youngest child in a Metropolitan Toronto day care centre, she would have been faced with a minimum charge of $189. When all the calculations are done, she would have ended the year with $8,679. That is, a full year of work would have netted her an additional $2,548 on gross earnings of $7,494, resulting in an effective tax rate of 66 per cent on employment income. To put it another way, her effective wage rate would have been about $1.77 per hour, and she would therefore have joined the ranks of the working poor. Note, also, that if she had little control over the number of hours of work, she could quite easily have been disqualified from receiving any social assistance and, possibly, from having access to a range of social and medical services provided with social assistance. Moreover, if space were not available in the public day care system, she would likely have had to pay much more for child care. These, and many other problems, could have occurred, leading to an even bleaker financial situation.

Even as it stands, the results show extremely high effective tax rates up to an earnings level of around $8,000, where social assistance payments cease, not because of any bureaucratic callousness but as a result of the need to target programs to those who need them most. For those who could not command half the industrial composite wage, the picture would be even more grim. While the long-term benefits of labour market participation may be touted, the problem for women in this situation, with little labour market experience and poor wage prospects, is one of cash flow. Like a potentially profitable company that cannot capitalize on prospects because of bankruptcy, these women cannot always benefit from labour market participation because of near-term cash flow problems. One of the few acceptable solutions to the problem of the poverty trap faced by too many in this situation is to increase the immediate returns to participation. In this vein, consideration could be given to an "employment expenses tax credit," similar in operation to the Child Tax Credit,[11] but intended to assist with the costs of working.

The foregoing notwithstanding, one of the major conclusions reached in the Kahn-Kamerman study, based on the results for eight western industrialized countries, was that from the point of view of a family's annual financial situation, labour market participation is much better than nonparticipation, and participation by two family members is superior to participation by one.

The results for Canada were in line with the overall results of the study and reflected important features of the tax and transfer systems faced by Canadians. First, the personal income tax, both federal and provincial, is based upon the individual as the unit of account. This means that the incremental family income provided by an additional earner rather than by the incremental earnings of a single earner is taxed at lower marginal rates. In families where total earnings are identical, a two-earner family has a sizeable tax advantage over a single-earner family. For families bearing substantial child care expenses in order to earn this income, the tax gain provides a significant offset, while the gain is relatively clear for families without additional child care expenses.

Second, because unemployment insurance benefits are also based upon the individual earner, subject to an earnings ceiling, the risk of a severe cash flow decline in a multiple-earner family is reduced, even though the risk of partial earnings loss may increase. When one also considers social attitudes and the longer-run returns to labour market participation for the individual, the rapid advance of the labour market participation of married women is not surprising.

The participation rates of the under-25 group are projected to continue to rise, so that by 1985 they will be higher than in 1975 by 7.8 percentage points for young men and by 9.3 points for young women. The participation rate for men aged 25 to 44 — the highest rate of all groups — is expected to remain virtually constant. Women in that age group are expected to show the largest increase — 18.8 percentage points over the 10-year period, with the increase from 1980 to 1985 being only slightly below that for 1975-80. While men in the 45-64 age group will continue to show slight declines in participation largely because of early retirements, women of that generation will show fairly strong increases. The abolition of mandatory retirement laws, already enacted in some jurisdictions and expected to be universal before long, will have an effect on the labour supplied by older workers. Although the impact will be minimal during the period covered by our projections, the aging of the Canadian population, along with the decision of older workers to postpone retirement, could be a source of experienced labour in the future. The aggregate participation rate is predicted to increase by 5.9 percentage points, with the aggregate rate of men increasing by just under 1 point and that of women by just under 11 points.

The resulting composition and growth of the labour force between 1975 and 1985 are shown in Tables 4-10 and 4-11, and in Appendix Table C-2. Despite the rising participation rates of young people, the decline in the growth of the source population is sharp enough that their share of the labour force is also reduced. The largest labour force increase is expected to be for women in the 25-44 group, with compound annual rates averaging 5.6 per cent between 1980 and 1985. Given the stability of the participation rates for men aged 25 to 44, their labour force growth rates are simply a reflection of the increase in their source population. In aggregate, labour force growth will continue to slow down, following a trend that started in 1978. Increases in participation rates will keep labour force growth rates

Table 4-10

Distribution of the Labour Force,[1] by Age-Sex Group, Canada, 1975-81 (Actual) and 1982-85 (Projected)

	15-24		25-44		45-64		65 and over		Total		
	Men	Women	Men	Women	Men	Women	Men	Women	Men	Women	Both sexes
	(Per cent)										
1975	14.9	12.2	28.5	15.6	18.2	8.6	1.5	0.5	63.1	36.9	100.0
1976	14.7	12.2	28.6	16.0	17.8	8.9	1.3	0.4	62.4	37.6	100.0
1977	14.7	12.2	28.5	16.5	17.5	8.9	1.3	0.4	62.0	38.0	100.0
1978	14.6	12.2	28.2	17.3	17.1	8.9	1.2	0.5	61.1	38.9	100.0
1979	14.7	12.3	28.1	17.7	16.6	8.9	1.2	0.4	60.7	39.3	100.0
1980	14.5	12.3	28.1	18.4	16.3	8.9	1.2	0.5	60.0	40.0	100.0
1981	14.1	12.0	28.2	19.3	15.9	8.9	1.1	0.5	59.3	40.7	100.0
1982	13.9	11.8	28.5	19.5	15.7	9.1	1.2	0.5	59.2	40.8	100.0
1983	13.5	11.3	28.8	20.2	15.5	9.2	1.1	0.5	58.9	41.1	100.0
1984	13.0	11.0	29.0	20.9	15.3	9.2	1.1	0.5	58.4	41.6	100.0
1985	12.6	10.7	29.1	21.7	15.1	9.3	1.1	0.5	57.9	42.1	100.0

1 The labour force is composed of that portion of the civilian, noninstitutional population aged 15 and over who are employed or unemployed.
SOURCE Data from Statistics Canada; and calculations from Economic Council of Canada, "base case" solution of the CANDIDE 2.0 model, September 1981.

Table 4-11

Labour Force Growth Rates,[1] by Age-Sex Group, Canada, 1975-76 to 1980-81 (Actual)
and 1981-82 to 1984-85 (Projected)

	15-24		25-44		45-64		65 and over		Total		
	Men	Women	Men	Women	Men	Women	Men	Women	Men	Women	Both sexes
	(Per cent)										
1975-76	0.9	2.2	2.8	5.5	-0.1	5.9	-10.7	-12.0	1.2	4.3	2.3
1976-77	3.3	2.7	2.4	6.0	1.0	2.4	–	6.8	2.1	4.1	2.9
1977-78	2.8	3.7	2.6	8.7	1.3	3.9	–	8.5	2.2	6.0	3.7
1978-79	3.5	4.2	2.7	4.9	0.4	3.1	3.8	-3.9	2.2	4.2	3.0
1979-80	1.3	2.7	2.6	6.9	0.4	2.7	-0.7	6.1	1.6	4.7	2.8
1980-81	0.4	0.4	3.1	7.8	0.4	2.5	-2.2	5.8	1.6	4.3	2.7
1981-82	0.3	-0.1	3.2	3.0	0.7	4.2	4.3	1.4	1.9	2.3	2.1
1982-83	-0.9	-1.4	3.4	5.8	0.8	3.0	0.5	3.4	1.6	3.1	2.2
1983-84	-1.0	-0.9	3.1	6.0	0.9	2.9	0.4	2.6	1.5	3.4	2.3
1984-85	-1.3	-1.2	2.3	5.6	0.7	2.8	0.3	3.8	1.0	3.2	1.9

1   The labour force is composed of that portion of the civilian, noninstitutional population aged 15 and over who are employed or unemployed.
SOURCE   Data from Statistics Canada; and calculations from Economic Council of Canada, "base case" solution of the CANDIDE 2.0 model, September 1981.

above population growth rates; however, they will not be strong enough to counter the trend of slowing population growth.

An Occupational Dimension

The occupational dimension of the labour force was obtained by first calculating occupational distributions within age-sex groups from the Labour Force Survey starting in 1975. These distributions were then projected to 1985 as if established trends would continue throughout the period. The occupational proportions were then applied to the labour force projections by age-sex group. The resulting occupational labour force projections are presented at a very broad level, due in no small measure to the nature of the available data, and at the expense of setting aside no less important seasonal and regional aspects.

The major methodological difficulty with this procedure is that the occupational distributions are not the product of supply factors alone but also reflect the influence of demand factors, since they are based upon historical trends. Strictly speaking, therefore, the purist cannot regard the projections as occupational supply. What they do afford us, however, is a set of indicators of occupational tendency, given the changing age-sex composition of the labour force. Even then, care must be exercised in interpreting the results, as changing demand factors combined with occupational mobility will work to modify projections of historical experience.

By and large, the occupational distributions within age-sex groups displayed remarkable stability, with

only a few showing marked trends. It was the under-25 age group that showed the greatest change. This could be expected for a number of reasons. First, the youth group contains only a 10-year age spread, while the other major groups comprise 20-year spreads. Second, this is the new-entry group, where occupational choice is first made; it is probably more sensitive to changing economics than the older more established groups. Finally, this is the group affected by the large gross outflow by the baby-boom generation.

Young men aged 15 to 24 show declining occupational concentration in management, teaching, medical, clerical, sales, and construction occupations, with the largest increase being in the service occupations ("Major Group 61" in the CCDO; see Appendix B for these occupations at the three-digit level). There is a marked decline in the proportion of young women aged 15 to 24 in clerical occupations; smaller declines are noted in the teaching and medical occupations. The largest increase for this group is also in the service occupations, although increases are noted in management and sales as well. The largest decline for men in the 25-44 group is in the proportion in construction occupations, with more modest declines seen in teaching and sales, and with increases in management occupations. Women in that age group show decreases in teaching and increases in management and natural sciences. Men in the 45-64 group show declines in the proportion in sales and clerical occupations and increases in management occupations. Women in that age group are quite stable, with only modest declines in teaching occupations and modest increases in management occupations.

Table 4-12

Distribution of the Labour Force,[1] by Occupation[2] and by Age-Sex Group, Canada, 1975 and 1985

(Per cent)

	15-24				25-44				45-64				Total				Both sexes	
	Men		Women		Men		Women		Men		Women		Men		Women			
	1975	1985	1975	1985	1975	1985	1975	1985	1975	1985	1975	1985	1975	1985	1975	1985	1975	1985
Managerial	0.4	0.3	0.2	0.3	2.8	3.9	0.7	1.5	1.9	2.0	0.4	0.6	5.1	6.2	1.2	2.4	6.3	8.6
Natural sciences	0.5	0.4	0.1	0.1	1.8	2.0	0.1	0.5	0.7	0.6	—	0.1	2.9	3.0	0.3	0.7	3.2	3.7
Social sciences	0.1	0.1	0.1	0.2	0.4	0.6	0.2	0.5	0.1	0.1	0.1	0.2	0.6	0.8	0.5	0.8	1.1	1.6
Teaching	0.2	0.1	0.5	0.2	1.3	1.2	1.6	1.6	0.3	0.4	0.5	0.4	1.8	1.6	2.6	2.2	4.4	3.8
Medical	0.2	0.1	1.0	0.5	0.6	0.6	1.7	2.2	0.3	0.2	0.7	0.6	1.0	0.9	3.4	3.4	4.4	4.2
Artistic	0.2	0.2	0.2	0.2	0.4	0.6	0.2	0.4	0.2	0.2	0.1	0.1	0.8	1.0	0.4	0.6	1.2	1.6
Clerical	1.4	0.9	5.2	3.9	1.6	1.7	5.4	7.3	1.3	0.9	2.6	2.9	4.3	3.4	13.1	14.0	17.4	17.5
Sales	1.7	1.3	1.2	1.2	3.3	2.6	1.3	1.9	2.0	1.4	1.2	1.1	6.9	5.2	3.8	4.3	10.7	9.5
Service	1.8	2.1	2.2	2.8	2.2	2.3	2.1	3.1	2.0	1.6	1.8	2.0	5.9	6.0	6.1	7.9	12.1	13.9
Farming	1.1	0.9	0.2	0.2	1.2	1.5	0.5	0.5	1.5	1.1	0.4	0.4	3.9	3.5	1.1	1.1	4.9	4.6
Fishing	0.1	0.1	—	—	0.1	0.1	—	—	0.1	0.1	—	—	0.2	0.3	—	—	0.2	0.3
Forestry	0.2	0.2	—	—	0.3	0.3	—	—	0.1	0.1	—	—	0.6	0.6	—	—	0.6	0.7
Mining	0.2	0.2	0.2	0.2	0.3	0.4	—	—	0.1	0.1	—	—	0.6	0.7	—	—	0.6	0.7
Processing	1.0	0.8	0.2	0.2	1.4	1.2	0.3	0.4	0.9	0.8	0.2	0.2	3.3	2.7	0.8	0.8	4.0	3.5
Machining	0.6	0.5	—	—	1.2	1.2	0.1	0.1	0.8	0.6	—	—	2.5	2.3	0.2	0.1	2.7	2.4
Fabricating	1.8	1.6	0.6	0.5	3.4	3.4	1.0	1.2	1.9	1.7	0.6	0.5	7.1	6.7	2.3	2.3	9.4	9.0
Construction	1.7	1.1	—	—	3.5	2.6	—	0.1	2.1	1.7	—	—	7.3	5.4	0.1	0.1	7.3	5.5
Transportation	0.8	0.7	—	0.2	2.1	2.1	0.1	0.2	1.1	1.0	0.1	0.1	4.0	3.8	0.1	0.3	4.2	4.1
Material handling	1.0	0.9	0.2	0.1	0.7	0.7	0.2	0.2	0.5	0.3	—	0.1	2.2	2.0	0.5	0.5	2.7	2.5
Other crafts	0.2	0.2	0.1	0.2	0.5	0.6	0.1	0.1	0.4	0.3	0.1	0.1	1.1	1.1	0.2	0.3	1.3	1.4
Miscellaneous	0.3	0.2	0.3	0.2	0.2	0.1	0.2	0.2	0.2	0.2	0.1	0.1	0.6	0.4	0.6	0.5	1.2	0.9
Total	15.2	12.8	12.4	10.8	29.1	29.6	15.9	22.0	18.6	15.3	8.8	9.4	62.9	57.7	37.1	42.3	100.0	100.0

1 Under 65 years of age. No occupational breakdown was done for the labour force aged 65 and over.
2 Two-digit CCDO categories, except for occupations in religion, which were included in the miscellaneous category.
SOURCE Data from Statistics Canada; and calculations from Economic Council of Canada, "base case" solution of the CANDIDE 2.0 model, September 1981.

Table 4-13

Compound Growth Rates of the Labour Force,[1] by Occupation[2] and by Age-Sex Group, Annual Averages, Canada, 1975-80 and 1980-85

(Per cent)

	15-24 Men		15-24 Women		25-44 Men		25-44 Women		45-64 Men		45-64 Women		Total Men		Total Women		Total Both sexes	
	1975-80	1980-85	1975-80	1980-85	1975-80	1980-85	1975-80	1980-85	1975-80	1980-85	1975-80	1980-85	1975-80	1980-85	1975-80	1980-85	1975-80	1980-85
Managerial	-2.4	0.1	9.1	4.0	5.8	6.6	14.9	8.9	3.3	3.2	9.4	4.9	4.3	5.1	12.5	7.3	6.1	5.7
Natural sciences	1.5	0.1	4.5	0.5	4.7	3.8	21.0	12.1	1.8	0.5	9.7	4.2	3.5	2.6	13.1	8.2	4.6	3.5
Social sciences	—	-1.6	9.0	-2.1	9.0	5.3	12.5	8.9	2.2	1.0	5.3	5.1	6.1	3.7	10.0	5.6	7.9	4.7
Teaching	-9.7	-5.5	-8.2	-4.7	1.0	1.6	1.9	3.1	6.3	3.2	1.5	0.9	1.2	1.6	0.3	1.8	0.6	1.7
Medical	-3.4	-3.4	-3.2	-4.8	3.0	2.7	5.3	4.8	-0.8	-1.6	2.1	2.6	0.9	0.9	2.5	2.6	2.1	2.2
Artistic	4.1	—	5.3	-1.5	5.7	7.4	14.3	8.3	1.8	5.6	4.7	5.9	4.4	5.0	9.2	5.0	6.1	5.0
Clerical	0.6	-3.1	1.4	-2.0	2.0	3.4	6.1	5.5	-3.1	-0.2	4.3	3.4	0.1	0.5	4.0	2.7	3.1	2.2
Sales	0.8	-1.3	5.0	-0.6	0.1	0.5	7.3	5.6	-1.2	-1.2	1.4	2.8	-0.1	-0.4	4.8	3.0	1.7	1.0
Service	7.1	2.4	8.6	1.7	2.9	2.9	7.3	5.9	0.7	0.2	3.9	3.1	3.5	2.0	6.8	3.6	5.3	2.9
Farming	1.8	-0.9	4.5	-0.4	1.1	8.0	2.8	4.1	-1.0	-0.5	3.6	3.2	0.5	2.5	3.5	2.8	1.2	2.5
Fishing	10.3	3.3	8.4*	10.8*	9.7	-1.7	32.0*	11.8*	4.2	0.7	32.0*	4.6*	8.3	0.3	30.3*	8.9*	8.9	0.8
Forestry	2.4	2.9	21.1*	2.9*	3.9	5.9	19.1*	11.8*	1.2	0.5	-4.4*	4.6*	2.8	3.9	12.6*	7.2	3.2	4.1
Mining	6.7	0.4	—*	8.4*	5.8	7.0	5.9*	-5.6*	-0.1	1.4	—*	—*	4.7	4.1	7.0*	2.7*	4.7	4.1
Processing	2.6	-1.3	5.3	-0.1	2.1	-0.2	4.9	4.4	1.5	-0.3	2.1	1.2	2.1	-0.6	4.3	2.3	2.5	0.1
Machining	3.1	-0.5	4.8	0.8	3.1	2.9	-2.0	1.8	-1.2	0.4	-2.6	-3.0	1.9	1.5	-0.4	0.5	1.8	1.4
Fabricating	3.1	—	0.8	-0.2	2.8	2.7	4.3	4.5	2.2	0.4	2.2	0.8	2.7	1.4	2.8	2.4	2.7	1.7
Construction	0.8	-3.3	15.5*	5.6	0.7	-1.3	12.0	9.1	0.2	0.6	20.1*	7.0	0.6	-1.2	14.9	7.4	0.7	-1.1
Transportation	2.8	-0.9	9.8	4.0	1.9	3.1	15.9	5.7	2.3	1.3	16.9	3.5	2.2	1.8	15.0	4.9	2.7	2.0
Material handling	3.1	0.1	3.4	-1.6	4.1	1.9	5.1	2.7	-0.3	-1.9	0.8	4.7	2.7	0.4	3.7	1.7	2.9	0.7
Other crafts	3.8	-0.2	7.4	-1.0	2.4	4.9	9.5	9.1	-0.5	1.2	5.7	7.9	1.7	2.8	7.8	5.3	2.7	3.2
Miscellaneous	-4.8	1.3	-3.1	1.8	-6.9	3.2	-2.9	8.2	-7.9	10.9	2.1	7.4	-6.2	4.7	-2.4	5.0	-4.3	4.9
All occupations	2.3	-0.5	3.1	-0.7	2.6	3.0	6.4	5.6	0.6	0.7	3.6	3.1	2.0	1.5	4.7	3.3	3.0	2.2

*The base numbers used to calculate these percentages were very small – less than 2,000 persons in all cases, and less than 1,000 in most cases.

1 Under 65 years of age. No occupational breakdown was done for the labour force aged 65 and over.

2 Two-digit CCDO categories, except for occupations in religion, which were included in the miscellaneous category.

SOURCE Data from Statistics Canada; and calculations from Economic Council of Canada, "base case" solution of the CANDIDE 2.0 model, September 1981.

The changes in the occupational structure of the entire labour force between 1975 and 1985 are rather small (Table 4-12). The largest percentage point changes in the distribution by occupation are the increases in the management and service occupations and the decreases in the construction and sales occupations. The largest changes in the distribution by age-sex group are the previously mentioned declines in the proportions of young workers and older men and the increases in the proportion of women aged 25 to 44.

The combined effect of occupational and age-sex changes can be seen in the change of coefficients from 1975 to 1985. For young men and women, there are declines in most occupations, the notable exception being the service occupations. The increase in the latter results from increases in all age-sex groups, except for men aged 45 to 64; it is concentrated more heavily among women than men, so that the proportion of women of all ages in those occupations rises from 50.9 per cent in 1975 to a projected 56.7 per cent in 1985.

A concern that surfaces fairly frequently is that of the occupational concentration of women in certain occupations. In clerical occupations, for example, women accounted for 75.2 per cent of the total in 1975. As noted earlier, the proportion of women aged 15 to 24 that are in clerical occupations has declined continuously from 1975 onwards. While this might lead one to suspect an overall decline in concentration over the projection period, this is not the case. The occupational distribution of women aged 25 to 44 reveals a virtually constant proportion in clerical occupations. Rapid increases in the labour force of women in that age group, as well as declines among women aged 15 to 24, lead to an even greater concentration of women in clerical occupations over the projection period, reaching 80.3 per cent in 1985. In other words, because of demographic factors, occupational concentration by sex is likely to get worse before it improves.

While there are many other points of interest in Table 4-12, a slightly different perspective may be obtained from Table 4-13, where average compound annual growth rates for the two periods 1975-80 and 1980-85 are given. Note that most of the occupational growth rates in the second period are lower than in the first. This is a reflection of the overall slowing down of labour force growth. The growth rates of the labour force by age-sex group also show a decline, except for men in the 25-44 and 45-64 groups, where higher rates reflect higher growth in the source population; in the latter case, the growth rate of the population is high enough to counter a

decreasing participation rate. The fastest labour force growth in both five-year periods is that of women in the 25-44 group.

The largest growth is expected to be in managerial occupations from 1980 to 1985. Within those occupations, the most rapid labour force growth is expected to be recorded by men and women aged 25 to 44, with all age-sex groups, except young men, expected to experience strong growth. While currently there are shortages in some managerial occupations, the projected growth pattern could potentially cause as many problems as it will solve. The shortages are concentrated in a few detailed occupations in the managerial category and are generally at senior rather than junior levels. The overall strength of the managerial labour force growth could, if it materializes, bring about overcrowding, with all its attendant problems in the career progression of the people in those occupations.

At the other end of the growth spectrum are the occupations in construction, which are projected to decline over the period from 1980 to 1985. Although the female labour force in these occupations is projected to keep on growing, the impact will be very small, since by 1985 only 2 per cent of the construction labour force will be female. The story in construction occupations is that the male labour force is aging. Both the youngest and the prime-age groups show declines, with growth projected only for the 45-64 group. The process of aging can be seen in other occupational categories as well — for example, in machining, which is another male stronghold and is projected to remain so.

In summary, what these tables reflect is the very powerful influence that demographic factors will exert on the labour force. The decline in the younger population, the advance of the baby-boom generation into the prime working age, and the continuing rapid increase in labour force participation by women, accompanied by relative stability in the occupational structure within age-sex groups, all produce the results presented in the tables.

Conclusion

The 1970s was a time of rapid change in the labour force. Large demographic changes in the source population, combined with participation changes, resulted in an accelerating rate of labour force growth during much of the decade. Among men, the participation rate of the youngest group increased, while that of the older men continued its decline. The increases in the female participation rate reflected changes among women in virtually every type of situation. Important factors were the declining fertility rate and the lessening of the inhibiting influence of children on labour market participation.

The labour force of the 1980s will grow at a declining pace, reflecting a marked slowdown in the growth of the source population, with the youth segment actually decreasing. Projected participation rate increases, particularly among the young and among women, aided by the balance of the baby-boom generation moving into prime working years, indicate that the deceleration of the labour force growth will be less marked than that of the source population. Accompanying these changes, however, are likely to be increasing demands for social and labour market policies and programs to accommodate them.

From an occupational viewpoint, if present trends continue, what can be expected in most occupations are declining growth rates, with increasing labour force concentration in managerial and service occupations. The aging of the work force will continue, and it will be more pronounced in occupations with a heavy male concentration. The problem of occupational concentration by sex will worsen in occupations predominantly inhabited by women because of the demographic and participation rate changes and the relative stability of occupational distributions.

We must re-emphasize, however, that our projections of occupational change are based on the continuation of trends established since 1975, not on detailed occupational choice models. Embedded in such trends are a set of economic conditions and market mechanisms, as well as explicit government programs for labour market adjustment. While such trends do not have a life of their own, they do display stability, and this, barring massive sustained change in the economy, permits some short-run predictability, albeit at an aggregate level. The occupational tendency can, and will, be affected by evolving labour market policies and programs; however, much impact remains for the sphere of social and educational policy.

* * * * *

Having presented projections of supply and demand in this and the preceding chapter, what conclusions can now be drawn about labour market developments in the future? A major point to be reiterated is simply that the current state of occupational data and of the forecaster's art does not permit us to pinpoint pressure points at the detailed occupational level. Nevertheless, some general observations can be made.

First, the complexity and dynamism of the market and the different rates of development in its various sectors and segments will inevitably lead to the coexistence of unemployed persons in some locations and vacant jobs in others. Nevertheless it should be borne in mind that behind the bland projections of possible future developments a number of important adjustment mechanisms are constantly at work. Workers and employers adjust their expectations and requirements; people move and train; and governments attempt to assist the process when market forces are sluggish or impeded.

Second, it appears that the forces of demand and supply are strongly interrelated for certain occupational groups. In service occupations, for example, the increasing participation of women in the labour force has meant that many services formerly performed in the unpaid household sector are now entering the market sector of the economy. The demand for these occupations has increased accordingly, and this, in turn, has facilitated the participation of women and young people.

Third, while major imbalances are difficult to identify at the detailed occupational level, one broad area of concern is indicated — that of managerial occupations. Examination of the average annual growth rates for these occupations reveals a deceleration that is, however, more marked on the demand side. This could well mean dashed expectations for many aspiring managers and, at the same time, necessitate innovative employment policies and practices by employing organizations which must tap available talent through the creation of high-level staff positions and advisory functions.

Finally, while the projection exercises of this and the preceding chapter provide useful indications of broad trends in labour market development, it is apparent that finer instruments are required to come to grips with the more detailed aspects of imbalance problems. Accordingly, the next two chapters deal in greater depth with the special problems of skill and job shortages.

5 Skill Shortages

A better understanding of critical problem areas is essential for the design of policies that will be consistent with national economic objectives and effective in carrying them out. Accordingly, in our opening chapter, we emphasized the potential role of labour market policy in the concurrent amelioration of inflation and unemployment. Nowhere is this more evident than in the context of skill shortages. While occasional imbalances between the requirements of the employers and the supply of specific skills are inevitable, their persistence may impede growth, dampen productivity, and limit the expansion of employment. Effective responses will not only address these problems, but they can also, by removing bottlenecks, alleviate inflation at the same time.

Shortages of skilled workers are not a new phenomenon in this country: they have been occurring intermittently, since the Second World War at least. In the years following that conflict and during the post-Korean War period, manpower requirements caused by major economic growth led to significant excess demand, particularly in the trades. A decade later, in its First Annual Review, this Council pointed out that supplies of highly skilled scientific and technical personnel were inadequate for the requirements associated with the advancing technology. It has become apparent that shortages exist again today, and many observers anticipate that this problem will continue, at least on a selective basis, throughout the 1980s.

Although the occupations for which shortages are noted tend to be somewhat similar in every period, today's situation is actually quite different from past occurrences, and perhaps more distressing. Specifically, while the earlier imbalances were dictated by rapid expansion, the current problems have emerged in a very difficult economic climate.

The presence of shortages, at any time, can have unfortunate social and economic implications. Resulting production bottlenecks have the effect of lowering productivity, fueling inflation, and restricting growth – and hence further employment and prosperity. When shortages emerge in times of slow development and high unemployment, as they have done recently, there is cause for additional concern.

Indeed, it is this coexistence of joblessness and shortages that renders the current employment conditions so disturbing. Thus it is appropriate that these two types of imbalances receive attention in a review of the Canadian labour market. Accordingly, this chapter and the next are devoted to skill shortages and unemployment, respectively.

Documenting the Shortages

For the greater part of the 1970s, the problem of unemployment understandably monopolized the attention of labour market observers. Around mid-decade, however, there was, for the first time, some mention of the possibility that labour shortages might emerge during the last 20 years of this century.[1] The basis for this prediction was sound. First, the high rates of labour force growth recorded until then were expected to slow down, once the generation born during the postwar baby boom had entered the work world. And, second, the anticipated rapid technological change seemed to suggest that new and advanced skills would be needed in the upcoming years.

This early perception of impending shortages was very generalized, in that the dimensions of the problem were not well understood. Indeed, they could not be well understood, since the types of information required to document and forecast the imbalances simply did not exist. Nor do they now. As noted on numerous occasions throughout this report, as well as in our previous report on the labour market, the lack of detailed occupational data remains a major obstacle.[2]

Recognizing the informational limitations, the Economic Council addressed the issue of shortages in its Human Resources Survey (HRS), which was carried out in late 1979 and early 1980. Although it cannot be interpreted as an inventory of shortages in

Canada, the survey was unique in that it was nationwide and covered all industries except public administration, forestry, and agriculture. The 1,400 participating establishments generally reflected the geographic and sectoral characteristics of Canadian industry.[3]

In addition to outlining the dimensions of shortages in this country, the Human Resources Survey also sought information from the companies about their efforts to provide the skills they needed, both at the time of the Survey and for the future. Accordingly, data on training, forecasting, and search patterns were gathered. Some of the findings in these areas are presented elsewhere in this Report.

The wide coverage and the representative nature of the sample enable us, then, to use the HRS results with some confidence to paint a "broad brush" picture of the shortage situation. To provide some additional detail, we have also pieced together the findings of a number of unrelated endeavours carried out by a variety of government agencies, industry associations, and local training councils. Although designed to focus on specific occupations, sectors, or regions, together these enquiries have been helpful in further describing the imbalances.

On the basis of the HRS results, it would appear that shortages have, indeed, once again become a reality in this country.[4] Among the participating establishments, 49 per cent reported that during the 1977-79 period they had experienced some hiring difficulties because there were shortages of qualified people. Furthermore, 43 per cent anticipated similar problems from 1980 to 1984.

One would expect the incidence of shortages to vary between different regions of the country, and this is indeed the case (Chart 5-1). Finding the required skills has been, and will continue to be, a greater issue in the rapidly expanding West than elsewhere. Within this region, Alberta is particularly affected: 76.5 per cent of that province's respondents reported past shortages, and 67.7 per cent expected future problems. While the other regions of the country are experiencing relatively slow economic growth, the HRS data indicate that they do nevertheless have selective hiring difficulties.

When considered by industry, shortages of skilled workers are most prevalent in mining and manufacturing (Chart 5-2). In fact, the majority of HRS respondents in both of these sectors reported staffing difficulties in the periods covered by the inquiry. Other surveys have documented the problems in these two industries in some detail. An investigation carried out in 1980 by the Mining Association of Canada, for example, found that 44 of 69 member companies across the country had faced significant

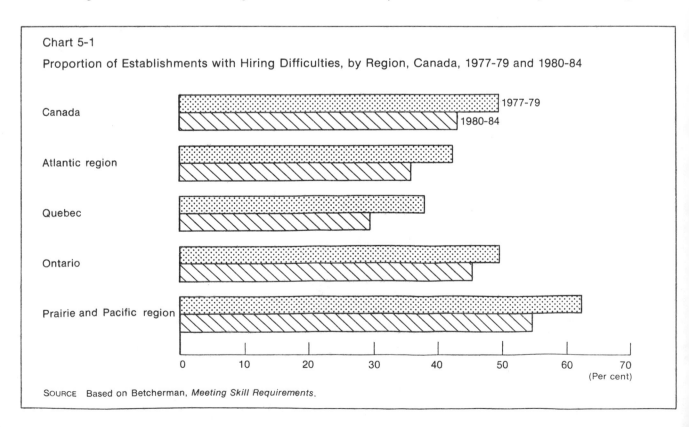

Chart 5-1

Proportion of Establishments with Hiring Difficulties, by Region, Canada, 1977-79 and 1980-84

SOURCE   Based on Betcherman, *Meeting Skill Requirements*.

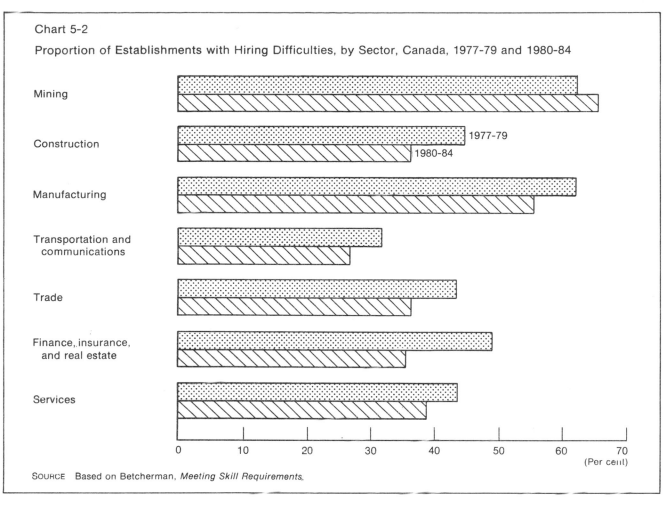

Chart 5-2

Proportion of Establishments with Hiring Difficulties, by Sector, Canada, 1977-79 and 1980-84

SOURCE Based on Betcherman, *Meeting Skill Requirements.*

difficulty in hiring skilled workers during the preceding year.[5] And in a 1979 study of over 1,000 Ontario manufacturers, half of the respondents reported that they were currently experiencing shortages. Moreover, most of the employers planning future expansion believed that recruitment would be a problem.[6]

Although the Human Resources Survey and other sources indicate that shortages are not as widespread in the other sectors of the economy, a more detailed breakdown does locate additional problem areas. Some of these — for example, construction in Western Canada — can be circumscribed regionally, while others are isolated in subindustries with distinctive skill requirements. Examples are information and communication services, health, air transportation, and business services.

Which occupational skills are associated with shortages of labour? According to the HRS data, hiring difficulties have been, and will continue to be, most prevalent for processing and, to a lesser degree, managerial and professional positions. These two categories, together, represent approximately 60 per

cent of the shortage-related vacancies reported by the survey respondents (Table 5-1). To put this figure into perspective, only 40 per cent of the country's employed labour force falls into one or the other of these occupational groups.

Table 5-1

Distribution of Job Vacancies,[1] by Occupation, Canada, 1977-79 and 1980-84

	1977-79	1980-84
	(Per cent)	
Managerial and professional	16.8	20.2
Clerical	5.4	6.6
Sales	6.0	5.1
Service	7.6	4.8
Primary	8.8	13.4
Processing	42.1	40.5
Construction trades	8.0	4.8
Other trades, crafts	5.2	4.7
Total	100.0	100.0

1 Estimated data from the Human Resources Survey.
SOURCE Betcherman, *Meeting Skill Requirements.*

Processing, by itself, accounts for the greatest share of hiring difficulties. This category consists of occupations involved with machining, product fabricating and repairing, and a variety of other tasks associated with transforming raw materials into semi-finished and finished goods. The critical problems within this group concern the skilled manufacturing trades.

A number of empirical inquiries have confirmed the undersupply of these highly trained blue-collar workers.

• The Human Resources Survey found that shortages were cited more often for the following five trades – machinery mechanics, machinists, motor vehicle mechanics, welders, and tool-and-die makers – than for any other occupation in the entire labour market.

• A 1979 study carried out by the Machinery and Equipment Manufacturers' Association of Canada reported that 86 per cent of its member companies surveyed were experiencing difficulties in obtaining journeymen. Machinists and fitters/millwrights headed the list of trades in demand.[7]

• Over 70 per cent of the "hard-to-fill" vacancies found by the Mining Association survey involved the electrical, millwright, heavy duty mechanic, welder, and diesel mechanic trades.

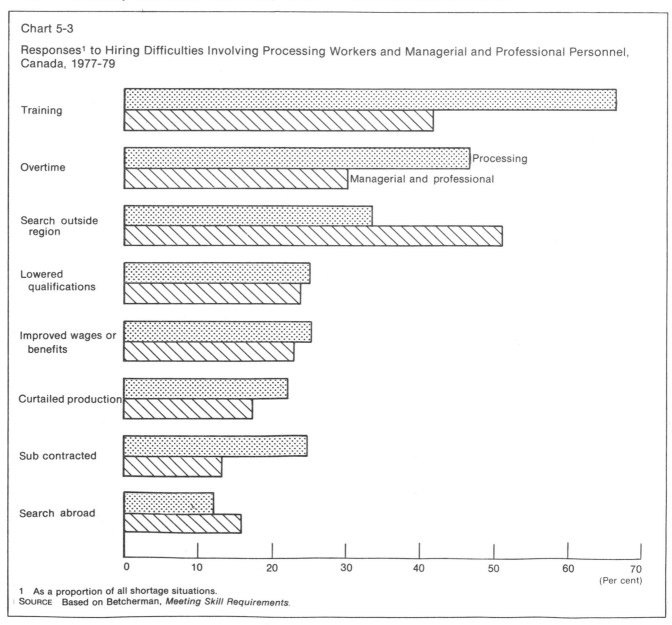

Chart 5-3

Responses[1] to Hiring Difficulties Involving Processing Workers and Managerial and Professional Personnel, Canada, 1977-79

1   As a proportion of all shortage situations.
SOURCE   Based on Betcherman, *Meeting Skill Requirements*.

• Two provincial inquiries – one in Ontario (mentioned above) and the other in British Columbia[8] – observed significant numbers of job openings for a number of trades.

In the category of managerial and professional personnel, shortages are most critical in the scientific and engineering fields. Specific problem areas are those involving virtually all types of engineers, computer programmers and analysts, and engineering technicians and technologists. And while such imbalances are already prominent, they may well become even more so in the rest of the 1980s and in the 1990s. Undoubtedly, the continuing diffusion of electronics-based technology and the growing emphasis on research and development will contribute to a rising demand for appropriately trained personnel. Similar pressures can be expected to come from the mega-projects and other energy-related activities.

Although difficulties in meeting skill requirements are greatest for processing and managerial and professional personnel, it is evident that shortage problems are not limited to those two categories. Occupations involved in the primary industries are also characterized, to some extent, by excess demand, and plans for expansion are expected to exacerbate some of these imbalances. Shortages exist as well within the construction trades, particularly in the western provinces. And although the HRS data suggest that these problems will diminish in the 1980-84 period, this may be largely a reflection of the uncertainty about the future that construction firms in the West faced at the time of the survey. Indeed, other sources of information have pointed to the likelihood of a continuation of some shortages in the construction trades.[9]

What is the effect of shortages on Canadian companies? To gain some understanding of this issue, the Human Resources Survey asked the participating firms to indicate what actions they took in response to hiring difficulties. Their replies show that the adjustment strategies they used depended very much on company characteristics, most notably organization size. Faced with hiring problems, the large establishments participating in the survey were able to cope more effectively by searching further afield, paying more overtime, subcontracting more frequently, and improving wages and benefits more often than small establishments. In contrast, the least desired response to shortages – cutting production – was twice as common among firms with fewer than 50 employees as among those with more than 500 workers.

The outcome of a hiring difficulty also depends on the kinds of skills that are in short supply. The response patterns characterizing the adjustment of HRS firms to shortages of processing workers, on the one hand, and managerial and professional personnel, on the other, were quite different (Chart 5-3). With respect to the former, training was the dominant solution. Most establishments, though, were less able to develop managerial and, particularly, professional and technical skills through training; accordingly, there was a greater tendency to rely on extended search patterns to meet these skill requirements.

Explaining the Shortages

The factors underlying the emergence of labour shortages at the present time must also be understood. It is important to recognize at the outset that the current problems have arisen during a period of slow economic growth. This stands in contrast to earlier bouts of shortages when, at the risk of over-simplification, the imbalances could be explained, to some extent anyway, by the sheer volume of industrial activity, which periodically outstripped the capacities of the labour force.

Certain robust segments of the labour market notwithstanding, this is not the case today. The current shortages cannot simply be attributed to the magnitude of the demand for labour. Rather, to use the jargon of economists, the problem is one of allocation – in other words, one of matching people and jobs. When attempting to explain existing shortages, considerable emphasis must therefore be placed on factors associated with the supply of workers.

Immigration

The historical influence of immigration on the Canadian reality cannot be overstated. The social and cultural fabric of our society has been aptly described as a mosaic of heritages transported from other lands. In an economic sense, too, immigrants have played a role of enormous significance. Indeed, much of our growth can be attributed to the efforts of the men and women who have emigrated to Canada from abroad.

During certain periods, in particular, the number of immigrants and their contribution to economic development have been remarkable. In the first 15 years of this century, for example, Canada received close to three million people, many of whom were to take part in the opening up of the West. And, in many respects, the industrial progress of the post-Second World War era has depended heavily on the skills of the nearly five million people who have come to this country since 1945.

Recent evidence underlines this former reliance on immigrants. Census data on tool and die makers for example, indicate that since 1941 an ever smaller proportion of the workers in this occupation have been Canadian-born. In fact, by 1971, 54 per cent of them had immigrated from other countries.[10] A survey of 61 Ontario companies in 1976-77 found that only 27 per cent of the skilled labour force was born in Canada.[11] Two other inquiries observed that the majority of highly skilled tradesmen in metal machining had been trained outside Canada.[12]

In the 1970s, however, more restrictive policies inspired by slow economic growth and high unemployment resulted in a decrease in the influx of immigrants. This trend embedded a shrinking contribution of external sources to Canada's labour supply (Chart 5-4). While immigrants destined to the labour force numbered 106,083 in 1974, the figure for 1978 was only 35,211. To illustrate this another way, in the earlier year, this flow represented nearly 28 per cent of the overall labour force growth; by 1978, that share had dwindled to 8 per cent (Chart 5-5).

A more detailed look at the data from the 1970s shows that the reduction in the number of immigrant workers occurred in virtually every occupational category. In particular, this was the case for those

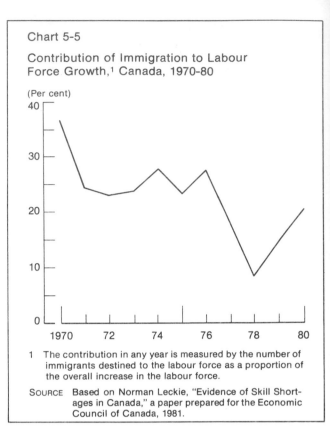

Chart 5-5

Contribution of Immigration to Labour Force Growth,[1] Canada, 1970-80

(Per cent)

1   The contribution in any year is measured by the number of immigrants destined to the labour force as a proportion of the overall increase in the labour force.

SOURCE   Based on Norman Leckie, "Evidence of Skill Shortages in Canada," a paper prepared for the Economic Council of Canada, 1981.

groups that are now most strongly beset by skill shortages (Table 5-2). The two critical processing categories – product fabricating and repair, and machining – experienced crests in 1974 and then underwent significant annual declines. The high-shortage professional group – sciences and engineering – exhibited a similar pattern, although its peak occurred one year later.

Towards the end of the 1970s, as it became more and more apparent that certain imbalances were becoming critical, admissions of immigrants destined to high-shortage occupations in the labour force increased. If historical experience is a guide, further activity in this direction can be anticipated. Indeed, Canada has always reacted to domestic manpower difficulties by priming the immigration pump. During each period of the postwar era that was characterized by shortages, the flow of foreign workers rose dramatically (Chart 5-6).

While immigration remains an important source of skilled labour, a rapid escalation would be an unlikely response to our current and projected shortages. In the first place, many of the scientific, technical, and trades skills in short supply here are also in demand in many other countries. Thus recruitment in these occupations tends to be very competitive. And, unfortunately, the relative attractiveness of Canada

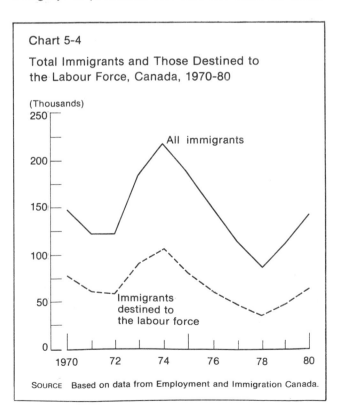

Chart 5-4

Total Immigrants and Those Destined to the Labour Force, Canada, 1970-80

(Thousands)

All immigrants

Immigrants destined to the labour force

SOURCE   Based on data from Employment and Immigration Canada.

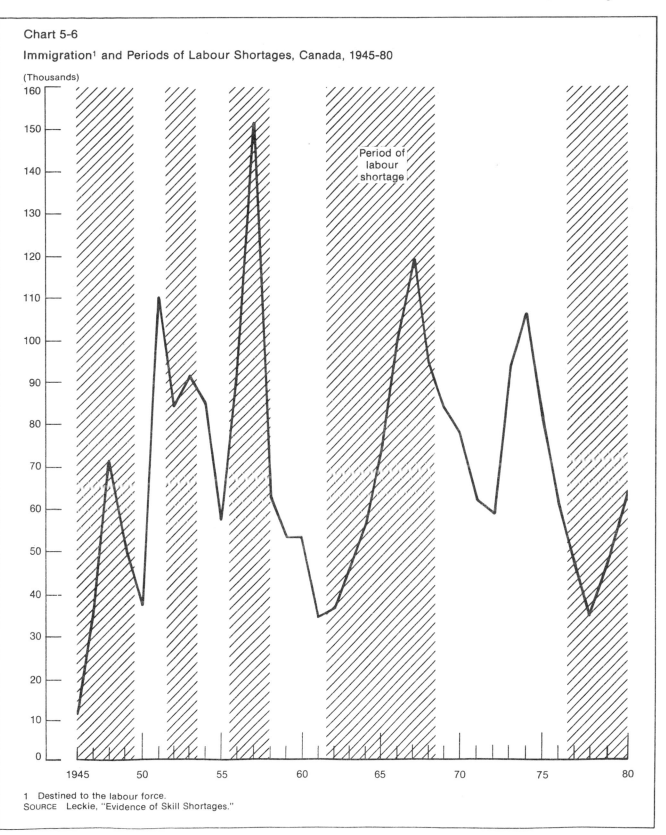

Chart 5-6

Immigration[1] and Periods of Labour Shortages, Canada, 1945-80

(Thousands)

Period of labour shortage

1   Destined to the labour force.
SOURCE   Leckie, "Evidence of Skill Shortages."

Table 5-2

Immigrants Destined to the Labour Force, Selected
High-Shortage Occupations, Canada, 1973-80

	Product fabricating and repair	Machining	Sciences and engineering
	(Thousands)		
1973	13.4	5.5	7.4
1974	15.5	7.6	8.7
1975	11.9	5.2	8.9
1976	8.4	3.0	5.6
1977	6.2	2.2	4.2
1978	4.1	1.7	3.0
1979	7.2	2.3	3.5
1980	10.3	2.9	5.0

SOURCE   Based on data from Employment and Immigration Canada.

has been eroded somewhat. Particularly in comparison with the Western European countries that have been the traditional sources of our skilled labour, we no longer enjoy the wage and standard-of-living advantages that we once did.

Developing Skilled Canadians

As the immigration tap was turned down during the 1970s, Canadian employers had to adjust their human resources practices. Obviously, less dependency had to be placed on foreign supplies and, according to the HRS data, this did indeed occur. Only 7.5 per cent of the participating establishments in 1979-80 identified other countries as an important source of skilled labour. Even when faced with hiring difficulties, the vast majority of the HRS firms did not search outside Canada.

Naturally, the reduced access to foreign supplies of tradesmen and other needed workers has heightened the importance of developing occupational skills within Canada, through training and education. Yet, for a variety of reasons, including our historical dependency on immigration, this domestic capability has been limited. While we shall return, in Chapter 8, to the problems associated with vocational skill development, a quick review might contribute to the present discussion.

For the past 20 years, governments have poured a great deal of money into technical and vocational training. Federal initiatives alone now involve annual expenditures of over $800 million. These endeavours, however, have not been able to generate all of the skills needed for the labour market. In the first place, accurate forecasts of these requirements have been hindered by occupational data shortcomings. Moreover, the programs have never really focused specifically on meeting demands for labour. Rather, they

have attempted to pursue this goal along with others; unfortunately, in the process, none of the objectives have been served optimally.

Industry, too, must take some responsibility for developing vocational skills. Conditioned by plentiful immigration flows and a universal education system, however, Canadian companies have relied on "buying" rather than "breeding" skilled workers. With access to these supplies, firms have not given labour the same consideration that other investments receive. According to the results of the Human Resources Survey, comprehensive and systematic personnel forecasting is too often ignored. Moreover, the survey results strongly suggest that firms underinvest in vocational development. The majority of respondents provided some training, but only one in five conducted programs of more than one year's duration.

Apprenticeship, which represents the primary means of fostering many of the high-level, blue-collar skills that are currently in short supply, has never flourished in this country. Only 16 per cent of the HRS respondents reported this type of training. And the relative incidence of apprentices in Canada is very low, particularly in comparison with many Western European countries (Table 5-3).

Underlying Canada's poor record regarding apprenticeship and other forms of vocational training is a socio-cultural perspective that glorifies professional, white-collar careers and places less value on blue-collar occupations, even those of a highly skilled nature.[13] This strong societal preference, reinforced through a heavily subsidized and academically oriented school system, has made trades and crafts

Table 5-3

Incidence of Apprenticeship Training
in Selected Countries, 1974

	Apprentices	
	Number	Proportion of total civilian employment
	(Thousands)	(Per cent)
Austria	164	5.4
Canada[1]	67	0.7
France	197	0.9
Germany	1,130	5.2
Italy	670	3.6
Switzerland	143	4.9
United Kingdom (1971)	463	2.1
United States	291	0.3

1   Excluding Quebec.
SOURCE   Organisation for Economic Co-operation and Development, *Policies for Apprenticeship* (Paris: OECD, 1979).

an unlikely training choice for young Canadians. Indeed, in the absence of a heritage based on the contribution of the master craftsman, vocational education such as apprenticeship began in Canada as a welfare policy; while this perception has changed somewhat, apprenticeship still has not completely escaped this stigma.

Occupational Wages

Decreasing flows of immigrants and the problems associated with the domestic development of vocational skills must both figure prominently in explaining the selective shortages that have emerged in this country. There are other factors, however, that appear to have contributed, albeit less directly, to the current imbalances.

One such determinant has been the occupational wage structure. Compensation, of course, plays a central role in the allocation of labour, as earning levels constitute an essential mechanism for the matching of people and jobs. And empirical evidence, some of which is presented in Chapter 7, suggests that the relative wage levels of many currently shortage-ridden occupations have declined over the past decade. This is most apparent in the case of many highly skilled trades, which have experienced narrowing pay differentials with respect to both the national average and the rates for unskilled jobs.

It would seem reasonable to assume that this compressing trend has contributed to the current shortages. Most occupations now in short supply require lengthy and costly instruction periods; thus people are not likely to undergo such training unless they perceive the material reward to be worthwhile. The decline in relative wages, then, would act as a deterrent against entry into such occupations.

Mobility Barriers

Mobility, or the movement of qualified workers to available jobs, can at times play an important allocative role in the labour market. Recently, this mechanism has become particularly relevant in light of the rapid economic expansion in Western Canada, where the attendant employment growth could not be accommodated entirely by the region's own labour force.

It is evident from even the most casual observation that this situation, coupled with the slack labour market in Eastern Canada, has resulted in a significant westward movement of workers. There are, however, some factors that may have constrained additional mobility even more, thus contributing to the imbalances noted previously.

One of these is the cost associated with relocation. Admittedly, during the past decade, the western provinces have experienced wage gains relative to the rest of the country; in fact, workers in Alberta and, above all, British Columbia earn more than Canadians in general. Whether or not this compensatory advantage, though, is enough to offset the rising costs of living – particularly for housing – in the West is certainly a question that merits close attention. Furthermore, there are often considerable social adjustments involved in relocating that, while defying precise accounting, cannot practically be ignored.

In addition to these economic and social costs, barriers to mobility can also result from regulatory practices that may, in some cases, inhibit skilled workers from utilizing their qualifications. Occupational regulation through licensing, certification, and registration is generally defended as a means of protecting the public interest with respect to the quality of service and safety. An unanticipated consequence of this activity, however, can be the creation of entry barriers that restrict labour supply.

In considering worker mobility in Canada, there is the added dimension of jurisdictional authority accorded to the provinces and territories for occupational regulation. There are at present 12 different sets of legislated arrangements pertaining to the training, standards, and accreditation of controlled skills.

A recent report by this Council concluded that for the professions and white-collar occupations, specifically, regulation was in need of reform. Although entry barriers, themselves, were not seen as a major source of problems, the restrictions imposed by provincial differences in licensing practices were recognized.[14]

With respect to the skilled trades, significant interprovincial variation is evident. For example, as of 1980, there were 153 different provincial apprenticeship training programs in Canada. Only 11 were offered throughout Canada, but 101 were provided in only one or two jurisdictions. There is an interprovincial certification program, however, that, to some extent, does minimize obstacles stemming directly from licensing *per se*. Rather more serious mobility barriers appear to result from large jurisdictional differences in the quality of training in the skilled occupations.

Conclusion

The shortages currently being experienced in Canada are particularly notable in light of their occurrence during a period of high aggregate unemployment. There is significant economic growth in Western Canada, and, as one would expect, the problems associated with unmet labour demand are greatest in that region. Evidence gathered from a number of sources, including our Human Resources Survey, points, however, to the presence of selective shortages in other parts of the country as well.

Nationally, the most critical shortage-related problems involve the scientific, technical, and trades occupations. While, historically, there has been significant reliance on immigration to meet Canada's needs in these areas, the decline of supplies from this source in recent years has increased the importance of developing the required skills domestically. Unfortunately, though, Canada has not been up to the task. Industry has underinvested in human resources, and the public training and education systems have not been responsive to the needs of the labour market.

Other factors, too, seem to have played a part in the emergence of the present shortages. In particular, the glorification of professionalism, occupational wage differentials, and barriers to mobility have been discussed. Not mentioned but perhaps worthy of future analysis is the importance of effective management in the utilization of human resources.

Turning to the responses needed to adjust to the shortages, it must be recognized that, in the foreseeable future, immigration is unlikely to play as significant a role in labour supply as it has in the past. Accordingly, the focus must be on Canada's domestic capability to develop needed skills. Initiatives by all parties involved are necessary in order to increase the activity in the private sector and to make government programs more responsive to market conditions.

Once skills are developed, steps must be taken to facilitate the movement of trained workers to the jobs available. Indeed, the importance of this mechanism is likely to be heightened in the 1980s as a consequence of the sheer volume of economic activity anticipated in sparsely populated areas of the country. While there may inevitably be barriers to mobility in the form of personal and social costs, there is no need for others that are institutionally created. Any regulation of occupations that results in supply constraints must be examined carefully; if public protection can be guaranteed in other ways, these regulations should be reformed.

The shortages also suggest the need for superior forecasting of labour market conditions. Particularly crucial are regional projections of demand and supply disaggregated along the occupational dimension. As noted above, however, a number of hurdles must be cleared before reaching this target. The most fundamental, perhaps, is the lack of information from which stock imbalances could be calculated.

Clearly, the current shortages attest to the enormity of the task of producing the skills required by the Canadian labour market. A number of factors point to the possibility of further and more substantial dislocations in the upcoming decade. First, in many critical trades, numbers are likely to be depleted by the high retirement rates caused by an aged work force. Second, the magnitude and unique nature of the employment demands associated with the huge energy projects planned in the western provinces and in the Territories must be recognized. Third, significant labour market adjustments may be necessary as a consequence of the industrial changes stemming from international economic developments. Finally, technological advances – the diffusion of microelectronics, in particular – appear likely to continue to affect occupational demand. Undoubtedly, these factors will require major adaptations during the 1980s.

6   Unemployment and Labour Market Turnover

Unemployment is another classic example of the dilemma of problem identification facing policy makers, to which we alluded at the beginning of the preceding chapter. While the Canadian labour market as a whole may be said to work reasonably well, unemployment remains a severe social and economic ailment. It is for this reason that this Council has, over the years, investigated the phenomena underlying the official unemployment figures. In that context, our research shows that, contrary to the widely held view, most unemployment is not essentially a short-term, turnover phenomenon. A crucially important corollary of this demonstration is that policies framed on the basis of an imperfect diagnosis of the problem are likely to constitute inappropriate treatment.

As shown earlier (Chart 2-2), the rate of unemployment rose significantly in the 1970s in a number of western industrialized countries. This development touched off a wide-ranging examination of the nature and significance of unemployment, especially in the United States, and engendered a body of economic literature generally considered as representing the "dynamic" or "turnover" view of labour markets. This analysis focuses on the flows between the three states of the labour force – namely, employment, unemployment, and non-participation ("not in the labour force"). Purposely or not, the work of the turnover school has contributed to a benign view of unemployment that tends to de-emphasize its economic and social costs.

While it does not share this view, the Economic Council itself pioneered the flow analysis of labour markets in Canada, in its 1976 report on *People and Jobs*.[1] Major research undertaken more recently provides fresh insight into the process of unemployment in Canada, suggesting a general scarcity of jobs that is particularly reflected in long spells of unemployment and leads to economic and social waste.

The Turnover View

The labour market figures that are made public each month represent what could be described as "snapshots" showing the number of persons in different labour force states at a particular point in time. Based upon its monthly survey of the labour force, Statistics Canada classifies the working-age population (aged 15 and over) as being either "in the labour force" or "not in the labour force." The labour force itself is divided into those who are employed and those who are unemployed.[2] This categorization of the labour market, frozen at an instant in time, is known as the "stock" concept. It forms the basis of traditional discussions of the unemployment problem.

Yet the stock figures – the pool of the unemployed, for instance – are subject to constant change through inflows to, and outflows from, the various labour force states. In the early 1970s, economists began to realize that a better understanding of the nature of unemployment could be gained by focusing on those flows that occur not at a particular instant in time but over a period of time – the so-called "dynamic" movements. To continue with the earlier metaphor, they have found it useful to look not only at "snapshots" of the labour force but also at a "moving picture" of the continuous flows of people into and out of jobs.

Following this lead, we pointed out in *People and Jobs* that the net changes in stock figures between two points in time are dwarfed by the gross flows that occur over the same period. A more recent picture – that for January and February 1981 (Table 6-1) – conveys the same message. Between these two months, the number of the unemployed decreased from 945,000 to 928,000 – a drop of only 17,000. Behind this net change were large flows, however: some 367,000 joined the pool of the unemployed (152,000 who were formerly employed and 215,000 who were not in the labour force), while 399,000 persons "flowed out" (225,000 who became employed and 174,000 who left the labour force).

The proponents of the turnover view emphasize that, seen in this perspective, unemployment is a state through which a large number of labour force participants pass and that, consequently, its burden is shared by a large proportion of the work force. From the observed brevity of completed spells of

Table 6-1

Labour Market Stocks and Flows, Canada, January-February 1981

	(Thousands)	Employed	Unemployed	Not in labour force
			Labour market status in February	
			(Thousands)	
Labour market status in January				
Employed	10,462	10,115	152	195
Unemployed	945	225	546	174
Not in labour force	6,758	238	215	6,305
Total working-age population in January	18,165	10,578	913	6,674
Net increase between January and February	27	5	15	8
Working-age population in February	18,192	10,583	928	6,682

SOURCE   Gross flow data provided by Statistics Canada.

unemployment, they argue that persons out of work can find jobs quickly and that only limited hardship is imposed by unemployment. Finally, since the groups with high unemployment rates also have high turnover rates – that is, a greater likelihood of becoming unemployed – some turnover theorists maintain that unemployment is caused by worker behaviour that generates unstable job-holding patterns. As these workers also experience shorter durations of unemployment than others, it is concluded that jobs are readily available for those who want them:

> [The] picture of a hard core of unemployed persons unable to find jobs is an inaccurate description of our economy and a misleading basis for policy. A more accurate description is an active labor market in which almost everyone who is out of work can find his usual type of job in a relatively short time. The problem is not that these jobs are unavailable but that they are unattractive. Much of the unemployment and even more of the lost manpower occurs among individuals who find that the available jobs are neither appealing in themselves nor rewarding as pathways to better jobs in the future.[3]

In a nutshell, unemployment is viewed by the turnover school as primarily "frictional" (because of the time involved in moving from one job to another) or "voluntary" (because workers choose not to accept the jobs that are available). This conclusion has led many labour market analysts to suggest that appropriate measures to reduce unemployment should focus on facilitating rapid job search and increased job holding, rather than on increasing the number of available jobs.

The Components of the Unemployment Rate

Does the turnover characterization of the labour market apply to Canada? Until recently, the lack of

data hindered the analysis of labour market turnover in this country. A comprehensive look at the flow-vs.-duration question is now possible, however, thanks to the body of gross flow data that has recently been made available to us by Statistics Canada.

The unemployment rate in any month has two components: the proportion of people who become unemployed during that month (the "incidence" of unemployment) and the average duration of their unemployment spells.[4] This is illustrated by the following equation:

unemployment rate[5] = incidence x duration
(in months)

The usefulness of this equation stems from the fact that it enables policy makers, when diagnosing unemployment, to know the relative contributions of its two components. These relative contributions are shown in Table 6-2, from which three major conclusions are derived.[6] First, higher unemployment rates are associated with a higher incidence of unemployment. Second, the demographic groups with higher unemployment rates are often without work for shorter periods. Taken together, these two findings suggest that the primary explanation for a high unemployment rate in any group comes from the greater likelihood of its experiencing a bout of unemployment rather than from the length of that unemployment spell, once it occurs. Finally, the average duration of unemployment is relatively brief – close to two months for teenagers, for example – and it does not exhibit much variation among demographic groups.

The structure of unemployment rates by region also suggests that higher rates are associated with a higher incidence (Table 6-3). In this case, however, a higher incidence is not, generally speaking, compen-

Table 6-2

Selected Unemployment Indicators, by Demographic
Group, Canada, 1980

	Unemployment rate		Spells of unemployment	
	Actual	Calculated	Incidence	Duration[1]
	(Per cent)		(Per cent)	(Months)
Men				
15-19	17.1	16.2	8.0	2.0
20-24	11.5	11.0	4.2	2.6
25-44	5.2	5.2	1.9	2.8
45-64	4.2	4.4	1.7	2.6
Average	6.9	6.8	2.7	2.5
Women				
15-19	15.3	13.6	7.1	1.9
20-24	10.7	9.6	4.2	2.3
25-44	7.0	6.4	3.0	2.2
45-64	5.8	5.8	2.5	2.3
Average	8.4	7.7	3.6	2.2
Overall average	7.5	7.1	3.1	2.3

1 Completed spells.
SOURCE   Estimates by the Economic Council of Canada based on gross
flow data provided by Statistics Canada; and Statistics
Canada, *The Labour Force*, December 1980.

sated by a shorter duration. In fact, compared with
the Canadian average, each region with a lower
unemployment rate not only benefits from a lower
incidence but also experiences shorter-duration
unemployment. Differences in the rates of unemployment, therefore, are also associated with differences
in duration in the same direction.[7] In the Prairie
provinces, for example, the incidence of unemployment is about 70 per cent of the Canadian average,
while duration is 78 per cent. For Quebec, the

Table 6-3

Selected Unemployment Indicators, by Region,
Canada, 1980

	Unemployment rate		Spells of unemployment	
	Actual	Calculated	Incidence	Duration[1]
	(Per cent)		(Per cent)	(Months)
Atlantic region	11.2	10.7	4.6	2.3
Quebec	9.9	9.9	3.7	2.7
Ontario	6.9	6.6	2.9	2.3
Prairie region	4.3	3.9	2.1	1.8
British Columbia	6.8	5.6	2.7	2.0
Canada	7.5	7.1	3.1	2.3

1 Completed spells.
SOURCE   Estimates by the Economic Council of Canada based on gross
flow data provided by Statistics Canada; and Statistics
Canada, *The Labour Force*, December 1980.

proportions are 21 and 15 per cent, respectively,
above the Canadian average. This suggests that, in
addition to incidence, the variability in the duration of
unemployment provides an important explanation of
the structure of regional unemployment rates.

The role of the incidence and duration of unemployment may vary, depending upon economic
conditions – that is, depending upon the degree of
tightness of the labour market. Although the gross
flow data at our disposal (for the years 1976 to 1980)
do not provide much variation in economic climate,
we use the years 1976 and 1978, which exhibit the
greatest divergence in unemployment rates, to
examine the role of incidence and duration in explaining this change (Table 6-4). It can be seen that close
to 70 per cent of the change is attributable to differences in duration. This is less true of the younger
groups, for most of which both the incidence and
duration of unemployment spells are of roughly equal
importance.[8] This indicates that duration cannot be
ignored when we examine the nature of unemployment.

Table 6-4

Contribution of the Incidence and Duration of
Unemployment to the Change in the Unemployment
Rate, by Demographic Group, Canada, 1976-78

	Increase in unemployment rate	Contribution of:	
		Incidence	Duration
	(Percentage points)	(Per cent)	
Men			
15-19	1.2	52.0	48.0
20-24	1.3	58.2	41.8
25-44	0.7	27.6	72.4
45-64	1.2	23.4	76.6
Average	0.9	31.7	68.3
Women			
15-19	2.3	74.0	26.0
20-24	1.8	48.0	51.0
25-44	0.9	-16.8	116.8
45-64	1.0	14.7	85.3
Average	1.2	26.6	73.4
Both sexes			
15-19	1.7	65.9	34.1
20-24	1.5	52.1	47.9
25-44	0.8	17.2	82.8
45-64	1.0	18.6	81.4
Overall average	1.0	30.5	69.5

SOURCE   Estimates by the Economic Council of Canada based on gross
flow data provided by Statistics Canada.

The Duration of Unemployment

The traditional measure of average unemployment duration has some shortcomings. Indeed, this seemingly simple concept is, in practice, very complex to measure. If each unemployment spell could be "tracked" from beginning to end, it would be easy enough to compute an average for complete unemployment spells that would be a true indicator of the actual unemployment experience. The data published by Statistics Canada, however, are based on monthly labour force surveys of individuals who, when surveyed, are unemployed and may continue to be. In other words, the surveys take a "snapshot" of unemployment spells that are "in progress." Respondents can indicate how long they have been unemployed, but not how long they will remain out of work. Thus the official figures tend to underestimate the duration of completed unemployment spells, but they may also overestimate it because of the so-called "length bias": the longer one's unemployment spell, the greater one's chance of being included in the survey and, *pari passu*, the greater the estimate of average duration. Also to be considered, however, are spells of very short duration (lasting only a few weeks) that start and end between two successive surveys and thus are not captured at all by them. Overall, then, the official data on average duration tend to overstate the actual measure, and they should therefore be treated with caution.

Using a concept that relates the chances of escaping from unemployment (by finding a job or by dropping out of the labour force) to the duration of unemployment,[9] we have derived the estimates of completed spells and compared them with .the "in progress" measure published by Statistics Canada (Table 6-5). It is immediately obvious that the figures published by Statistics Canada overstate the average duration of completed spells of unemployment by more than 50 per cent in most years. The average duration of a completed spell is, in fact, quite brief.

Table 6-5

Average Duration of In-Progress and Completed Spells of Unemployment, Canada, 1976-80

	1976	1977	1978	1979	1980
	(Months)				
In-progress spells[1]	3.2	3.4	3.6	3.4	3.4
Completed spells	2.1	2.3	2.3	2.2	2.2

1 The duration in months was obtained by dividing the duration in weeks by 4.33.

SOURCE   Statistics Canada, *Labour Force Annual Averages, 1975-1978,* Cat. 71-529, and *The Labour Force,* various issues; the data on completed spells are estimates by the Economic Council of Canada based on gross flow data provided by Statistics Canada.

The Concentration of Unemployment

While the figures just cited indicate that the average unemployment spell is short, it is nevertheless possible that much of joblessness may be concentrated in long spells. To see the importance of this point, consider the following example. Suppose that each month 10 unemployment spells lasting one month and one spell lasting 12 months begin. The total unemployment represented by the 11 spells will then be 22 months. While the average duration of unemployment is only two months, more than half of all the unemployment (about 55 per cent) will be accounted for by the spell lasting 12 months. At the same time, 10 out of 11 (91 per cent) spells will be only one month long. The remaining 9 per cent of the spells thus account for 55 per cent of the total unemployment. This is what we mean by concentration of unemployment in long spells.

Our work shows that approximately 55 per cent of unemployment spells in 1980 ended within one month (Table 6-6). The long spells – those exceeding six months' duration – accounted for a disproportionate share of total unemployment. This phenomenon happens, obviously, because an unemployment spell of six months, for example, contributes six times more to unemployment than a spell that lasts only one month. Our findings reveal that the *number* of spells lasting longer than six months represent only 4.9 per cent of all spells but 21 per cent of the total unemployment experienced in Canada. What is more revealing is that spells exceeding three months account for 45 per cent of total unemployment. The importance of these figures can be understood intuitively by considering the fact that if all unemployment spells in 1980 exceeding three months, are not counted, then the observed unemployment rate would have been reduced in a proportion of some 45 per cent; in other words, it would have been

Table 6-6

Observed and "Normal" Unemployment Spells and Total Unemployment, by Duration of Spell, Canada, 1980

	Observed	"Normal"
	(Per cent)	
Spells		
Ending within 1 month	55.3	43.0
Exceeding 3 months	16.4	18.5
Exceeding 6 months	4.9	3.4
Total unemployment		
More than 3 months	45.0	42.4
More than 6 months	20.6	12.3

SOURCE   Estimates by the Economic Council of Canada based on gross flow data provided by Statistics Canada.

4.1 per cent instead of the 7.5 per cent actually observed.

It is worth noting that the proportion of unemployment contributed by long spells is consistently larger than would be expected if all job seekers had the same, unchanging chances of finding work. In other words, even if all job seekers were alike in all important respects and thus had the same chances of finding work, some would remain unemployed longer than others if jobs were relatively scarce, because "some people's names just don't get drawn in the job lottery." The long-term unemployment generated under these conditions could, therefore, be regarded as "normal." Our findings suggest that the observed contribution of long-term spells is higher than "normal" (as just defined) by about 67 per cent for 1980 (20.6 compared with 12.3). Thus a major aspect of the concentration of unemployment in long spells is that the latter contribute more to unemployment than could be expected under "normal" circumstances.

One reason for the concentration of unemployment in long spells could simply be that job seekers are not all alike and do not all have the same probability of escaping unemployment. For example, worker behaviour may differ according to demographic (age-sex) characteristics. Nevertheless, when we examine separately workers in several different demographic categories, there is still evidence of significant concentration of unemployment in long spells for each of the groups examined. In fact, when several other characteristics of job seekers are also taken into account, there remains a disproportionate amount of long-spell unemployment. These results can be attributed to the fact that the chances of finding employment worsen as the duration of unemployment increases.

The concentration of unemployment in long spells is one indication of the difficulty in finding jobs. Our work shows that these problems are more severe for men than for women — and more so for prime-age men (aged 25 to 44) than for others. In 1980, about 32 per cent of total unemployment among prime-age men took the form of spells that exceeded six months (55 per cent for spells lasting more than three months). Compared with the "normal" concentration in long spells, however, the observed data show large variations between demographic groups: concentration is generally greater for adults than for youths, and it is especially significant for women aged 45 to 64 and for men aged 20 to 24.

Other sources of information on unemployment also suggest a high incidence of long-term unemployment. The Labour Force Tracking Survey (LFTS), conducted in 1978 by the Department of Industry,

Trade and Commerce, focused on communities with special unemployment problems. The results should therefore not be taken to apply to Canada as a whole.[10] Each participant in the survey was asked to recall his/her labour force experience over the five years preceding 1978. Each unemployment episode that was recorded (except the last one in some cases) had been completed — i.e., the respondent had found new employment. It is interesting to note that short spells are relatively insignificant in this set of data (Table 6-7). Spells lasting up to three months represent only 32 per cent of all spells and account for only 9 per cent of total unemployment. Long-term unemployment spells (lasting more than six months), on the other hand, represent more than one-third of all spells and account for more than two-thirds of total unemployment.

Table 6-7

Distribution of Spells and Total Unemployment, by Duration of Spell, Canada, 1973-78

	Spells of unemployment	Total unemployment
	(Per cent)	
1 month or less	5.9	0.8
2 months or less	19.0	4.0
3 months or less	31.6	9.2
6 months or less	62.3	32.4
9 months or less	81.3	56.0
More than 9 months	18.7	44.0
Total	100.0	100.0

SOURCE Estimates by the Economic Council of Canada based on Department of Industry, Trade and Commerce, Labour Force Tracking Survey, 1978.

We conclude from the foregoing that while the unemployment picture is characterized by large flows into and out of joblessness, its burden is borne by a small group of the unemployed. This group contributes disproportionately to the unemployment rate recorded by Statistics Canada. Its share is even more conspicuous in communities with serious unemployment problems.

The Role of Aggregate Demand Conditions

While long spells of unemployment play an important role in the measurement of total unemployment and the rate of unemployment, our work also indicates that the frequency of long spells is closely related to demand conditions in the economy. The first effect of declining demand for labour is the curtailment of new hirings, which causes the average duration of unemployment to lengthen. Reductions in staff levels, which contribute to an increase in the incidence of unemployment, occur only later. The impact of cyclical factors on the duration of unemployment is one indication of how job scarcity affects the unemployment rate.

The gross flow data at our disposal, which cover the years 1976 to 1980, do not permit a direct analysis of the impact of the business cycle on unemployment duration. It is possible to obtain an indirect assessment, however, by comparing labour markets with significantly different rates of unemployment – those of the different provinces, for example – although such comparison should take into account the structural differences between these markets.

Keeping this caveat in mind, the five regions of Canada exhibit very different patterns with respect to this situation (Table 6-8). The greatest contrast is given by the comparison between Quebec and the Prairie provinces. The average duration of completed spells is about 40 per cent higher in Quebec. Also, the burden of long-term unemployment is much more

pronounced in that province than in any other region: 7 per cent of all spells last more than six months in Quebec, representing 27 per cent of total unemployment in that province; the corresponding figures for the Prairie provinces, at the other extreme, are 2 per cent and 10 per cent, respectively – i.e., about three times less than in Quebec. All the other regions lie between these two cases, Ontario being very close to the Canadian average. Relative to Ontario, the Atlantic provinces appear to be in a better position than Quebec, although this is primarily because they have a higher rate of withdrawals than does Ontario (Table 6-9).

Recently, the Council had the occasion to look extensively at the Newfoundland labour market,[11] and the message there was consistent with our findings here: the duration of unemployment, especially when it lasts more than three months, is an important indicator of job scarcity. In regions where jobs are plentiful, long spells contribute only a limited amount to total unemployment; this contribution is disproportionate in areas where jobs are scarce.

Table 6-8

Average Duration of Unemployment Spells, and Proportion of Unemployment Spells and Total Unemployment, by Spell Length and by Region, Canada, 1980

	Atlantic region	Quebec	Ontario	Prairie region	British Columbia	Canada
	(Months)					
Average duration of spells						
Completed	2.2	2.5	2.2	1.8	1.9	2.2
"Indomitable job seeker"	5.0	5.3	4.3	3.4	3.7	4.5
	(Per cent)					
Spells exceeding:						
3 months	16.9	21.0	16.4	10.0	11.8	16.4
6 months	4.6	7.2	4.8	2.1	3.3	4.9
Total unemployment due to spells exceeding:						
3 months	44.3	52.8	44.8	30.7	36.8	45.0
6 months	18.4	27.0	20.2	9.9	15.7	20.6

SOURCE   Estimates by the Economic Council of Canada based on gross flow data provided by Statistics Canada.

Table 6-9

Distribution of Unemployment Spells, by Outcome and by Region, Canada, 1980

	Atlantic region	Quebec	Ontario	Prairie region	British Columbia	Canada
	(Per cent)					
Spells ending in:						
Employment	48.3	50.0	58.5	62.7	60.8	55.8
Withdrawal from the labour force	51.7	50.0	41.5	37.3	39.2	44.2
Total	100.0	100.0	100.0	100.0	100.0	100.0

SOURCE   Estimates by the Economic Council of Canada based on gross flow data provided by Statistics Canada.

Multiple Spells of Unemployment

So far, we have focused on the incidence of long-term unemployment as manifested in a single spell. Multiple spells, which are experienced by a fairly large proportion of labour force participants, represent a different dimension of the concentration of unemployment. The data about single spells therefore understate the extensiveness of unemployment for these people.

The Annual Work Pattern Survey (AWPS) conducted by Statistics Canada provides one source of data for assessing the incidence of repeat spells of unemployment. In the 1980 survey, some 16 per cent of the people who were unemployed at any one point in 1979 experienced at least two spells that year (Appendix Table D-1).[12] As the period of observation lengthens, the incidence of repeat spells increases. The LFTS results suggest that, over a period of five years, close to 35 per cent of those surveyed experienced more than one unemployment spell. Again, this latter figure does not apply to the Canadian labour market as a whole; it is presented here only to underscore the pervasiveness of multiple spells of unemployment.

These findings indicate that repeat unemployment spells must be considered when assessing the severity of unemployment for those who experience it. The number of weeks of unemployment during a year, without regard to the number of spells, is one indicator of this problem. Viewed in this perspective, the data from the AWPS show that 45 per cent of total unemployment in 1979 was borne by individuals who were without work more than six months and that 16 per cent of those with some unemployment were searching for work that long (Appendix Table D-2). An even higher 36 per cent were unemployed for more than three months, contributing about three-quarters of the total recorded unemployment for 1979. At the other extreme, one-third of those who experienced some unemployment were out of work for one month or less; they accounted for only 6 per cent of total unemployment. It is clear that the turnover view has focused on this latter category and underemphasized the case of severe unemployment.

Unemployment and Withdrawals from the Labour Force

The significance of extensive unemployment makes it apparent that development of appropriate policies to curtail unemployment in general requires as precise a definition of the "at risk" category as possible. As we shall see, the identification of individuals and groups experiencing long-term unemployment is inextricably linked with a proper understanding of withdrawals from the labour force.

The "Discouraged Job Seeker" Phenomenon

This question arises because the dividing line between being unemployed and being outside the labour force is, at best, very fuzzy. The distinction hinges on whether or not a person is actively "looking for work," and that in itself is an ambiguous phrase. An unemployed person may cease to actively look for work while still wanting a job, on the perceived assumption that jobs are not available. This circumstance is often described as the "discouraged worker" phenomenon, although it might be more apt to say "discouraged job seeker." Official estimates of unemployment exclude such persons; thus the recorded duration of unemployment for them would also be underestimated. Consider another situation in which an unemployed person may stop searching for a day or for a week, possibly waiting for employer responses before resuming the search. Some economists argue that the effect of such withdrawal spells, which are quite common, is to reduce the average duration of unemployment spells while increasing their incidence. In reality, however, these people are experiencing extensive unemployment. For this reason, the term "joblessness" is often preferred as a measure of the burden of unemployment. In both of the examples cited above, the incidence of withdrawals from the labour force leads to an underestimation of the job-finding difficulty that is implied by the average duration figures, especially for some demographic groups.

A large proportion of all unemployment spells (about 44 per cent in 1980) terminate not in employment but in exit from the labour force (Appendix Table D-3). If all unemployment spells ended only in employment (i.e., if there were no labour force withdrawal), the average unemployment spell would last much longer (close to 4.5 months). This concept of duration applies to the so-called "indomitable workers" (or "job seekers"), who leave unemployment only when they find a job. The duration of unemployment for these job seekers is almost twice as high as that reported in Table 6-5; the differences between the two sets of figures show the importance of withdrawals from unemployment to "not in the labour force."

The foregoing analysis documents one way in which labour force withdrawal data may understate the significance of long-term unemployment. To the extent that discouraged workers are not counted among the unemployed, they create a further problem for policy makers when they stream back into the labour market at the hint of an improvement in job

Table 6-10

Average Duration of Unemployment Spells, and Proportion of Unemployment Spells Ending in Withdrawal from the Labour Force, by Age Group and by Sex, Canada, 1980

| | Age group | | | | | | |
	15-19	20-24	25-44	45-64	Women	Men	Both sexes
	(Months)						
Average duration of spells							
In-progress[1]		2.9*		3.7	4.4**	3.3	3.5	3.4
Completed	1.9	2.4	2.4	2.3	2.0	2.4	2.2
"Indomitable job seeker"	4.5	4.2	4.4	4.7	4.9	4.1	4.5
	(Per cent)						
Spells ending in withdrawal from the labour force	52.5	36.7	40.9	46.1	52.7	36.4	44.2

*Average duration for the group aged 15 to 24.
**Average duration for the group aged 45 and over.
1   The duration in months was obtained by dividing the duration in weeks by 4.33.
SOURCE   Estimates by the Economic Council of Canada based on gross flow data provided by Statistics Canada; and *The Labour Force*, December 1980.

prospects. Under these conditions, while additional employment is generated, the rate of unemployment may not decline. For these reasons, it is important to know what proportion of the labour force withdrawals could be regarded as a manifestation of discouragement.

At one extreme, all exits from the labour force could simply be regarded as voluntary decisions unrelated to labour market pressures – for example, to look after one's family. At the other extreme, they could be viewed as stemming from discouragement. Under the first assumption, the average duration of unemployment would range between 2 and 2.5 months; under the second assumption, it would increase to a range of between 4 and 5 months (Table 6-10).

Unfortunately, the nature of withdrawal spells and the motivations that lie behind withdrawal behaviour are not properly understood. While job seekers are likely to spend quite a bit of time looking for work before being driven out of the labour market by poor job prospects, noneconomic factors may tend to make them leave much sooner. Considering, therefore, only those withdrawal spells that occur after three and five months of unemployment, alternatively, we are able to derive a range of estimates for discouraged workers. Our work suggests that in 1980 up to 20 per cent of all unemployment spells ending in withdrawal represented discouragement after three months; the corresponding figure for withdrawals after five months of search was 9 per cent (Table 6-11). This range was equivalent to between 106,000 and 225,000 persons a month, on average. If these had been added to the number counted as unemployed that year, the unemployment rate would have ranged between 8.4 and 9.4 per cent, instead of the official 7.5 per cent figure. An earlier study by the

Council estimated that the number of discouraged workers in March 1978 was 244,000.[13] Not unexpectedly, the estimate for 1978 is higher than that for 1980, because employment prospects in 1978 were the poorest in the last decade, and discouragement is naturally sensitive to employment conditions. Under the conditions prevalent in 1980, it would be safe to estimate the number of discouraged workers at 150,000 – approximately midway in the range mentioned above. This figure is somewhat higher than the number of persons (111,000) who indicated to Statistics Canada in March 1980 that they wanted to work but were out of the labour force because they believed that jobs were not available.[14]

Table 6-11

Distribution of Unemployment Spells Ending in Labour Force Withdrawal, by Duration of Spell and by Sex, Canada, 1980

	Men	Women	Both sexes
	(Per cent)		
Duration			
1 month or less	45.7	55.3	50.7
Between 1 and 3 months	30.5	28.6	29.5
Between 3 and 5 months	11.9	9.2	10.5
More than 5 months	11.8	6.9	9.2
Total	100.0	100.0	100.0

SOURCE   Estimates by the Economic Council of Canada based on gross flow data provided by Statistics Canada.

The notion that at least some withdrawal spells represent discouragement behaviour stands out clearly in Table 6-9. In a buoyant labour market, where jobs are relatively plentiful, one would expect most unemployed persons to be able to find work and that spells ending in labour force withdrawal would be at a minimum and due, in large measure, to personal reasons. These expectations are supported by our data. Thus, in the Prairie region almost two-thirds of the unemployment spells eventually end with a job; the balance end in withdrawal. In contrast, less than half of the unemployment spells in the Atlantic provinces end in jobs. As expected, our estimates point to a more pronounced incidence of withdrawals in regions with a poor employment climate. Indeed, they show that the disparity in regional unemployment rates is even worse than that indicated by the published data: the addition to the unemployment rate attributable to the discouragement factor is larger in the Atlantic provinces and in Quebec than in the Prairie region, Ontario, and British Columbia (Appendix Table D-4).

Discouragement Among Women and Youths

Regarding the impact that labour force withdrawals have on the demographic groups, recent debate has focused on two groups — women and the young. Women currently constitute 40 per cent of the labour force; and, as we have seen earlier, this proportion will continue to grow throughout the 1980s. Since the unemployment rate for women is higher than that for men, upward movement of the aggregate unemployment rate may be in the offing. The share of youths (aged 15 to 24) in the labour force is about 27 per cent. Even though that proportion is likely to diminish marginally during the 1980s, the fact that their unemployment rate in the mid-1970s was 2.8 times as great as that for adults makes them an important concern for public policy.

More than half (53 per cent) of all the unemployment spells experienced by women terminate in withdrawal from the labour force rather than in transition to jobs — a proportion that is much higher than that for men (Table 6-10). It is often argued that the higher rates of exit from the labour force exhibited by women reflect a lack of commitment to the labour market. The proportion of exits occurring within the first month of unemployment, for example, is larger for women than for men (Table 6-11). Thus the importance of noneconomic factors in withdrawals from the labour force appears to be much higher for women than for men. However, using the alternative criteria for measuring discouragement mentioned above (i.e., after three and five months of job search), it is apparent that, relative to their number in the work force, women experience greater difficulties in the labour market, and this is reflected in a relatively higher degree of discouragement (Appendix Table D-5). It seems appropriate to conclude that official statistics significantly understate the severity of unemployment by ignoring its hidden forms and that

this understatement is relatively more acute in the case of women. If this bias were corrected, the published figures on the duration of unemployment would be much higher, as would those relating to the incidence of long-term unemployment.

Similar conclusions are obtained when we look at the youth labour market. The problems of youth unemployment are often discussed for the group aged 15 to 24. A distinction must be made, however, between the labour market experience of those aged 15 to 19 and those aged 20 to 24 (Table 6-10). Withdrawal rates are much higher for teenagers than for young adults or, indeed, for other age cohorts. For this reason, their duration of completed spells of unemployment is very brief — less than two months. At the other extreme (the "indomitable job seeker" case), the average duration for teenagers is among the highest. Avoiding these extremes, we have calculated, on the same bases as described above, a range of estimates for discouraged job seekers by age and sex groups (Appendix Table D-5). As in the case of women, the relative impact of discouragement on the unemployment rate is greater for younger participants in the labour force.

Discouragement and Long-Term Unemployment

The proportion of unemployment that is attributable to long spells is one measure of the concentration of unemployment. Earlier, by comparing this statistic for various demographic groups, we were able to obtain a measure of their relative state of disadvantage. We now propose a more direct approach. Conceptually, we can look at the total volume of long-term unemployment (LTU) and disaggregate it into the shares that each group contributes. The share of any group in LTU can then be compared with its share of the labour force. Women, for example, make up about 40 per cent of the labour force. If their share of LTU is greater, they will appear to be at a relative disadvantage. Also at issue, of course, is the measurement of LTU itself. As we have stressed above, taking account of withdrawals from the labour force significantly changes the volume and composition of LTU.

These two elements are brought together in Charts 6-1 and 6-2, and in Table 6-12. Each chart presents the same type of information: the external circle (labeled A) shows the shares in the labour force of the various groups considered; the inner circle (labeled C) presents the shares of LTU accounted for by the various groups, directly derived from the observed figures (i.e., without considering hidden unemployment in the form of labour force withdrawals); the intermediate circle (labeled B) presents the share of LTU when the discouraged-worker component of labour force withdrawal spells is taken into account.

Chart 6-1 illustrates our basic finding that the discouragement-augmented measure (B) significantly alters the relative impact of LTU on the various labour force groups. Women, for example, account for 29 per cent of LTU as directly observed, but this share is much larger (42 per cent) if hidden unemployment is included. Contrariwise, the men's share of LTU decreases sharply from 71 to 58 per cent, somewhat below their share of the labour force.

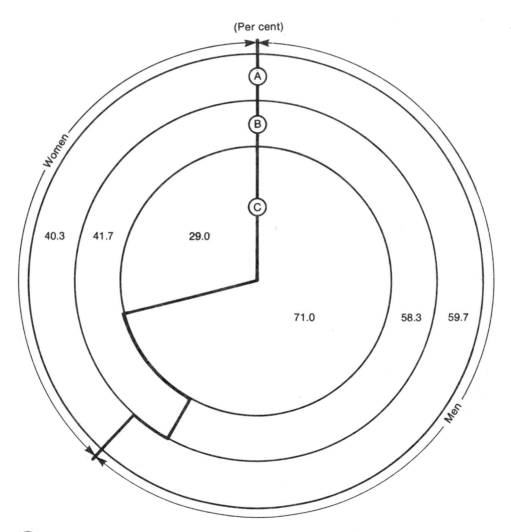

Chart 6-1

Distribution of the Labour Force and of Long-Term Unemployment (Alternatively Defined), by Sex, Canada, 1980

(Per cent)

40.3   41.7   29.0   71.0   58.3   59.7

(A) Total labour force aged 15-64

(B) Long-term unemployment, including job seekers discouraged after three months of search

(C) Long-term unemployment (more than six months)

SOURCE   Estimates by the Economic Council of Canada based on data from Statistics Canada.

This general point is also apparent from the disaggregation of data by age groups. Consider the case of prime-age males (aged 25 to 44), as shown in Chart 6-2. The observed data indicate that their share in LTU is 34.6 per cent, but this share drops to 24.6 per cent when the discouraged-worker effect is taken into account. In general, the inclusion of hidden unemployment increases the share in LTU for each age group among women and among men, for teenagers and older workers (aged 45 to 64).

Chart 6-2

Distribution of the Labour Force and of Long-Term Unemployment (Alternatively Defined), by Demographic Group, Canada, 1980

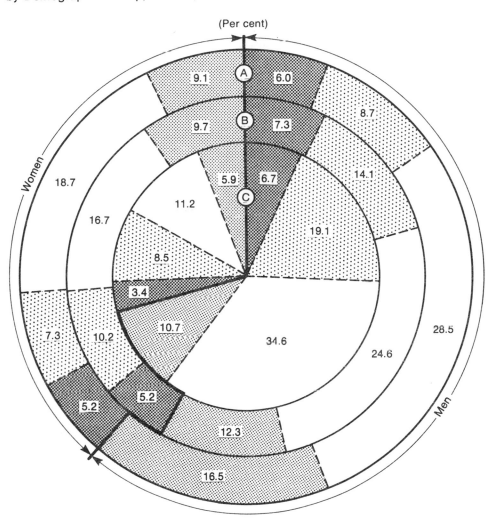

(A) Total labour force aged 15-64

(B) Long-term unemployment, including job seekers discouraged after three months of search

(C) Long-term unemployment (more than six months)

- 15-19 age group
- 20-24 age group
- 25-44 age group
- 45-64 age group

SOURCE   Estimates by the Economic Council of Canada based on data from Statistics Canada.

Table 6-12

Distribution of the Labour Force and of Long-Term Unemployment[1] (Alternatively Defined), by Region and by Sex, Canada, 1980

| | Atlantic region | | Quebec | | Ontario | | Prairie region | | British Columbia | | |
	Men	Women	Men	Women	Men	Women	Men	Women	Men	Women	Canada
Labour force	4.9	3.0	15.8	9.9	22.1	15.8	10.5	6.9	6.7	4.4	100.0
Long-term unemployment[1]	7.3	2.7	34.6	14.5	23.0	9.7	2.2	1.1	2.8	2.1	100.0
Long-term unemployment, including job seekers discouraged after three months	7.2	4.7	30.4	20.8	16.1	12.6	1.8	1.5	2.3	2.5	100.0

1   More than six months.
SOURCE   Estimates by the Economic Council of Canada based on gross flow data provided by Statistics Canada.

From the foregoing we conclude that the measure of long-term unemployment that is relevant for policy purposes should include rather than ignore the discouragement effect. The message from Chart 6-2 is that young adults, whether men or women, represent by far the most disadvantaged category: their share in the discouragement-augmented LTU is much greater than their share in the labour force. In addition, older women and male teenagers are also at a relative disadvantage.

Additional direction for targeting job creation policies is suggested by Table 6-12, which illustrates the regional pattern of extended unemployment in relation to labour force shares. Long-term unemployment, as augmented by discouragement, is concentrated by far in Quebec (especially for women) and, to a lesser extent, in the Atlantic region. Ontario, the Prairie provinces, and British Columbia, on the other hand, exhibit shares of long-term unemployment that are lower than the corresponding shares of the labour force. As expected, the Prairie region has the greatest relative advantage in this respect.

To conclude, we re-emphasize the crucial significance of labour force withdrawals for an understanding of the economic hardship implied by unemployment and for the framing of labour market policies. The flows into unemployment and the duration of unemployment spells cannot be properly assessed without a fuller understanding of labour force withdrawals.

Who Are the Long-Term Unemployed?

In the absence of more precise information on job discouragement, we use data from the LFTS to examine the likelihood that particular groups of job seekers are among those encountering spells of unemployment exceeding six months in duration. A special statistical technique called "logit analysis" was used to determine the probability of extended unemployment. The results, presented in Appendix Table D-6, show that relative to the reference category of prime-age males, all other age-sex groups exhibit greater probability of being in the "at risk" category. Thus youths of either sex are more likely to experience long spells of unemployment than prime-age males. Women, especially those in the 20-and-over age group, are at a relatively greater disadvantage. Our results also show that, other things being equal, being married reduces the chances of long-term unemployment, especially for men. As is generally expected, higher levels of education and training each reduce the likelihood of extended unemployment.

Among the variables representing the influence of labour market conditions on the probability of long-term unemployment, the occupational classification that unemployed workers had in their previous jobs is not statistically significant. The direction of the influence of these factors is as expected, however: the risk of long-term unemployment tends to be less for white-collar than for blue-collar occupations. On an industry basis, relative to construction – where seasonality often generates extended unemployment – employees in both manufacturing and the trade, finance, and public administration sector have less chance of being at risk when they do become unemployed. The province of residence of job seekers has a high level of statistical significance. Relative to the Ontario reference group, unemployed individuals in Newfoundland, New-Brunswick, and Quebec are at a disadvantage, while those in British Columbia and in Manitoba are in a favourable position. Union membership is another facet of the market structure. Our results suggest that union membership lessens the likelihood that long spells will be experienced. Possible reasons for this are the availability of union hiring halls and informal networks of job information, the existence of recall provisions in union agreements, and so on.

Several behavioural factors may also account for long-term unemployment. High and inflexible wage expectations are one such factor that we have examined. Our evidence, however, points to a negative relationship between higher expectations – using post-unemployment wages as a proxy – and longer spells. Factors that reduce the cost of job search may also lengthen the period of search. This interpretation is supported by the highly significant result for the unemployment insurance variable. Finally, because a part-time job would cushion the financial loss incurred during an unemployment spell, job seekers could be induced to search for longer periods. As expected, those who obtain part-time jobs exhibit a greater likelihood of experiencing long unemployment spells.

These results provide some indication of the characteristics of job seekers who experience long spells of unemployment. As mentioned earlier, our data are drawn from a special survey of local communities that were experiencing severe unemployment difficulties. In addition, the persons surveyed had to rely on their memories of labour market experiences going back five years from the time of the survey. These limitations are not serious for our purposes, however, since we focus precisely on those groups who experience long-term unemployment and labour force withdrawals caused by discouragement. Nevertheless, caution should be used when extending these results to Canada as a whole.

One source of information that is Canada-wide in nature does support some of our findings: Statistics Canada's Survey of Consumer Finances provides considerable detail on the family and personal characteristics of the individuals surveyed. For the unemployed, the total number of weeks of unemployment during a year are recorded, regardless of the number of spells. Persons with six months of unemployment during a calendar year are now regarded as being in the long-term category. In the aggregate, some 29 per cent of the unemployed men and 32 per cent of the unemployed women experienced total unemployment in excess of six months during 1977 (Table 6-13).

Table 6-13

Proportion of Men and Women Unemployed More than Six Months, by Selected Characteristics, Canada, 1977

	Men	Women
	(Per cent)	
Number of unemployment spells		
1	25.9	28.8
2	38.5	44.2
3 or more	32.3	42.4
Age		
15-19	30.2	25.0
20-24	29.6	26.0
25-44	25.7	33.9
45-64	34.3	39.2
Household status		
Head	26.9	29.0
Wife	. . .	34.1
Other	34.4	27.2
Census family size		
1 person	28.5	25.0
2 persons	29.7	32.1
3 persons	28.2	30.4
4 persons	24.8	32.3
5 persons or more	33.1	37.0
Years of education		
No schooling or elementary	35.2	39.7
9-10 years elementary and secondary	31.0	36.1
11-13 years elementary and secondary	25.5	29.4
Some postsecondary	27.5	26.2
Postsecondary certificate or diploma	23.3	32.2
University degree	20.1	18.7
Occupation		
Never worked before[1]	41.9*	53.7
Last worked more than 5 years ago[1]	85.9*	57.7
White-collar	29.3	28.8
Blue-collar	28.2	38.3
Industry		
Never worked before[1]	41.9*	53.7
Last worked more than 5 years ago[1]	85.9*	57.7
Goods producing	28.6	34.7
Services	28.5	29.4
Weekly wages and salaries[2]		
Less than $200	25.0	25.9
$200 – 399	23.0	28.5
$400 – 499	28.7	28.5*
$500 – 699	32.0	61.0*
$700 and over	57.0	61.3*
All persons unemployed more than six months	29.1	31.7

*Based on a small sample.

1 The same sample was used for occupation and for industry, as for all the other characteristics in the table. For each of these two categories, therefore, the proportions of the long-term unemployed who had never worked before or who had not worked for more than five years are also the same.

2 Annual wages and salaries, divided by the number of weeks worked as collected by the Survey. This provides only a proxy variable for average weekly wages and salaries because of conceptual and methodological problems.

SOURCE Statistics Canada, Survey of Consumer Finances, 1978.

For men, those least likely to experience extended unemployment are those aged 25 to 44. Among women, the incidence of long-term unemployment increases with age, and the under-25 group is less likely to undergo long-term unemployment than young men of the same age group. Older women are more likely than men in the same age categories to experience long spells of joblessness. Teenagers and young adults endure, more often than others, a higher incidence of shorter spells; thus their probability of extended unemployment over a year is increased by adding up the multiple spells. Heads of families, whether male or female, are less likely to suffer extended unemployment than other members of the family.[15] Family size does not appear to be related to the incidence of extended unemployment, except possibly for families with five or more persons; this last case is likely related to the presence of young adults.

The influence of education is, perhaps, the most clearly identifiable: the lower the level of education, the higher the incidence of long-term unemployment. This may result both from the job instability characteristic of persons with lower levels of education and from the difficulties that these people may encounter in finding a job once they become unemployed.

The data on occupation reveal no significant difference between blue- and white-collar occupations for men. For women, however, the higher incidence of extensive unemployment in blue-collar jobs is noteworthy. These features are also reflected in data disaggregated by industry: for men there is hardly any difference between goods- and service-producing industries, but for women a significantly larger proportion in the goods-producing industry suffer from unemployment exceeding six months' duration. The most significant finding from the occupation and industry disaggregation pertains to the case of new entrants (those who never worked before) and re-entrants (those who return to the labour force after an absence of more than five years). Both groups, whether male or female, are significantly overrepresented among the long-term unemployed and present a formidable challenge for labour market policies. The plight of these people is even worse if their educational attainment is low.

Finally, the incidence of long-term unemployment appears to be greater for persons who had weekly wages of $500 or more before becoming unemployed than for individuals who had lower weekly rates of pay (in 1977 dollars). This somewhat surprising result may originate from the fact that at lower rates of pay it is perhaps easier to find alternative employment, even though career prospects in these jobs may not be bright. Of the unemployed women with weekly pay

in excess of $500, some 61 per cent are in the extended unemployment category. The availability of unemployment insurance benefits ($147 a week in 1977, the year of the survey), which makes extended job search less costly, may be a partial factor here. It is especially appealing for married women with earning spouses, and this may explain the higher-than-average incidence of long-term unemployment in this group (see data on household status in Table 6-13). A different explanation, especially for men in the 45-to-64 group with weekly wages of $700 or more, may lie in the possible demand/supply mismatch for these people.[16]

Repeat Spells of Long-Duration Unemployment

While recognizing the significance of long spells of unemployment, some labour market observers attach little policy relevance to it on the grounds that persons suffering from such unemployment are not easily identifiable. It is no doubt true, as we have demonstrated above, that there are people who experience long spells of unemployment in each demographic group and in all parts of Canada, although we have also found that some groups and regions suffer more than others. For this reason alone, long-term unemployment should therefore be used as a criterion in the design of job creation programs. Furthermore, our work indicates that people who have already experienced one long spell of unemployment are more likely to experience further long spells. This finding needs to be spelled out in greater detail.

Using data drawn from the LFTS (1978), it is possible to follow, over a five-year period, the labour force history of individuals represented in this survey (Appendix Table D-7). In particular, persons experiencing two, three, four, or five spells of unemployment can be examined as separate groups. Consider the group with two unemployment spells and, within that group, those whose first spell was long (more than 26 weeks) and those whose first spell was "short" (26 weeks or less). The likelihood that the second spell would be long was greater if the first spell was long than if it was short. While only a minority in each group experienced extended unemployment in the second spell, it is clear that the chances of undergoing long spells was greater if the first spell was long. The same pattern can be seen for groups of individuals with three, four, or five spells.[17]

Conclusion

The findings presented in this chapter point out conclusively that extended unemployment spells, while experienced by a small group of the unemployed, contribute a disproportionate amount of unemployment in Canada. There are also strong indications that the extent of long-term unemployment is closely related to job availability in the economy. In regions where jobs are relatively plentiful, there is less long-term unemployment than elsewhere. Although some groups of job seekers are more prone to undergo long spells, all age-sex groups experience some concentration of unemployment. Even prime-age men, supposedly the group with the best job prospects, are no exception. The relative scarcity of jobs, then, is a general phenomenon, and job creation should be accorded first priority for labour market policies. The incidence of long-term unemployment could be used as a major consideration in the design of such policies, especially since people who experience one long spell are more likely than others to repeat such spells.

To sum up, we feel that the Canadian labour market, which is highly dynamic and has otherwise performed reasonably well, somehow fails to provide jobs for a number of people who then suffer from extended unemployment. While programs that focus on the short-run, turnover variety of unemployment may be of some usefulness, an emphasis on long-term unemployment will be more likely to curtail the extent of joblessness in the long run. Because the number of people who suffer from extended unemployment is quite small, it should be easier to develop intensive and carefully targeted programs to enhance their employment prospects. Such action would not only have a greater impact on the unemployment rate, but it would also be consistent with the equity concerns of Canadians.

7 Adjustment Processes and Policies

In the preceding chapters, we examined the supply of, and demand for, labour and the problems of skill shortages and unemployment that occur when supply and demand are imperfectly balanced. In practice, of course, they are never precisely matched, and so the labour market is always reacting and adjusting to changing circumstances. This complex and dynamic process of adjustment involves a host of economic, social, and political factors affecting the attitudes and behaviour of workers, employers, and governments, whose activities shape the course of wages, employment, and the output of the economy. The process is one of constant action and reaction in which the forces of demand and supply, in the tangible form of people and jobs, are reconciled in the pursuit of that efficient allocation which promotes employment, productivity, and incomes.

Some appreciation of the variety and complexity of the relevant factors is gained when one bears in mind that the adjustment process is one in which the characteristics of people — age, sex, education, skills, location, employment experience, attitudes, and wage aspirations — must be matched with such job features as pay, working conditions, and skill requirements. Clearly, information is the essential lubricant of this mechanism, since responses in any or all of these variables may be needed to enhance the speed and ease with which the adjustment mechanism operates. As far as wages are concerned, for example, both parties to the employment contract may need to "test the waters" before setting, and resetting, their remuneration goals. If location is the source of mismatch, workers may have to absorb moving expenses, while employers may have to help defray such costs. Where skill levels are the critical issue, responses may be required of employers to provide, and of workers to obtain, the necessary training.

For a variety of reasons, however, such adjustment responses may not so easily be brought into play. Ties of culture and language may impede geographical mobility, for example; age and sex may preclude access to certain occupations; and attitudes and values — and, in some cases, downright discrimination — may impose further restraints on the labour market. Because the unaided market may in certain instances fail to adjust with optimum ease and speed, governments may be called upon to assist the process. Thus training programs may be required to provide skills in the types and quantity that more nearly match employers' needs. Mobility grants or incentives may help to reconcile locational mismatches. Job creation programs may improve the sheer numerical availability of jobs. Unemployment insurance benefits may subsidize the extent and intensity of job search. And counselling, placement, and job-listing services may improve the information necessary for successful search by both workers and employers.

Comprehensive treatment of these adjustment mechanisms and policies would go far beyond the scope of this report, but we are able to raise some questions and bring fresh evidence and analysis to bear on a number of topics. In the present chapter we look at the process of job search, wage differentials, nonpecuniary aspects of remuneration, mobility, and job creation. Manpower training is also a major area of concern, one with which we deal in the next chapter.

The Process of Job Search

In recent years labour market analysts, when attempting to gain fresh insights into the unemployment problem, have devoted a good deal of attention to the process by which individuals search for jobs. This Council undertook some research in this field in the early 1970s;[1] but since that time the bulk of the theoretical and empirical work has taken place in the United States. Now, however, we are fortunate in having access to a body of recent Canadian analysis[2] that lends some new perspectives to this subject.

The first point to be noted is the sheer magnitude and extent of the job search process: fully one out of ten Canadian labour force participants at any point in time is a job seeker. Search activity takes place irrespective of socioeconomic characteristics; even 3 per cent of the employed workers, on average, are looking for a new job. This is consistent with the view that labour market search not only involves the allocation of unemployed workers to vacant jobs but also leads to improvement in allocative efficiency when employed workers move to jobs that fit their skills and ambitions more closely. Indeed, evidence

Table 7-1

Distribution of Unemployed Job Seekers and of the Total Labour Force, by Selected Characteristics, Canada, 1977

	Unemployed job seekers	Labour force
	(Per cent)	
Sex		
Men	55.7	61.9
Women	44.3	38.1
Total	100.0	100.0
Age		
15-19	25.1	11.1
20-24	25.1	15.8
25-44	34.2	45.0
45-64	15.3	26.4
65 and over	0.3	1.7
Total	100.0	100.0
Education		
No schooling or elementary	19.8	17.8
High school (some or completed) and some postsecondary	68.5	60.8
Postsecondary certificate or diploma	7.6	11.6
University degree	4.0	9.8
Total	100.0	100.0
Occupation		
White-collar		
Managerial and professional	6.2	21.2
Clerical, sales, and service	39.9	41.1
Blue-collar		
Primary occupations, mining, and processing	12.7	12.8
Fabricating	9.7	9.1
Construction	11.8	7.3
Transportation	8.5	8.0
Unspecified[1]	11.1	0.5
Total	100.0	100.0
Industry		
Agriculture and other primary industries	5.3	7.2
Manufacturing	19.6	19.6
Construction	12.4	7.1
Transportation	5.5	8.3
Trade and finance	19.2	22.6
Community, business, and personal services, and public administration	30.2	34.8
Unspecified[1]	7.8	0.4
Total	100.0	100.0

1 Failed to specify industry and/or occupation.
SOURCE Abrar Hasan and Surendra Gera, "Aspects of Job Search in Canada," Economic Council of Canada Discussion Paper 156, March 1980.

suggests that about two-thirds of all employed searchers seek higher wages, better hours or working conditions, and/or better promotion opportunities. Furthermore, the phenomenon of on-the-job search is quantitatively important in Canada, since over a quarter of a million people, or more than 25 per cent of all job seekers, are in this category. They are obviously a source of competition to the unemployed job seekers, and their activities affect both wages and the duration of unemployment spells.

When unemployed job seekers are considered, we see that women account for roughly 44 per cent of the searcher population, thus being significantly overrepresented in relation to their proportion in the labour force (Table 7-1). Teenagers and young adults are also overrepresented in the searcher category, as are searchers with an educational attainment of secondary schooling or less. White-collar occupations account for 46 per cent of all searchers – a proportion significantly lower than their corresponding share of the labour force.

A useful way to study the data on unemployed job seekers is to divide them between the formerly employed and those who were not in the labour force. The former group can be split into job leavers and job losers, while the latter is traditionally divided into new entrants and re-entrants. Data on these flows for the period 1975-78 in Canada and the United States are provided in Table 7-2. Although there are some differences between the U.S. and Canadian definitions of the various categories, they are probably not important enough to significantly affect the differences between the figures for the two countries.

The important point to note is that although 40 to 50 per cent of the unemployed job seekers in Canada had lost their jobs, a very substantial proportion had left jobs voluntarily or had come back into the labour market after a period of absence. The voluntary leaver category appears substantially larger in this country than in the United States, reflecting, perhaps, the greater opportunity to search for more productive jobs that is afforded by a more generous UI system.

With respect to the duration of search, our data underline the familiar theme of the turnover literature – namely, that demographic groups with high unemployment exhibit a shorter duration of unemployment. Teenagers, for example, display a greater-than-average concentration in the one-to-four-week duration category and are relatively less concentrated in the 27-week-or-more category (Table 7-3). As pointed out in Chapter 6, however, these unemployment duration figures do not represent all periods of "joblessness." In other words, the people who leave the labour force are not counted as unemployed, even though they are, literally, without a job.

Table 7-2

Unemployment Rate, and the Distribution of the Unemployed, by Status,
Canada and the United States, 1975-78

| | | Unemployment rate | Distribution of the unemployed | | | | |
			Job leavers	Job losers	Entrants	Reentrants	Total
			(Per cent)				
1975	Canada	6.9	27.8	39.4	5.8	26.7	100.0
	United States	8.5	10.3	55.7	10.3	23.7	100.0
1976	Canada	7.1	24.5	45.0	5.6	24.9	100.0
	United States	7.7	12.2	49.7	12.1	26.0	100.0
1977	Canada	8.1	22.9	48.6	5.6	22.8	100.0
	United States	7.0	13.0	45.3	13.7	28.1	100.0
1978	Canada	8.4	22.9	48.4	5.8	22.7	100.0
	United States	6.0	14.1	41.5	14.3	30.0	100.0

SOURCE   Hasan and Gera, "Aspects of Job Search in Canada."

How productive is the search process? Our results indicate that a number of factors determine successful job search, as measured by higher wages. First, those who quit their jobs, whether men or women, made wage gains, on average, while those who were laid off suffered a loss. This result is consistent with the idea that persons who quit their employment are likely to have better market information, and to be more confident about it, than those who lose their jobs. The latter experience difficulty because layoffs generally take place in unfavourable market conditions and because a laid-off worker may, rightly or wrongly, be perceived by recruiting firms as being somewhat undesirable. Note also that among both the quits and the layoffs, women did less well than men, on average.

Next, it appears that the productivity of the search varies over time. The search yields wage gains for those seekers who find jobs within 15 weeks. Beyond that point, however, while men may continue to experience gains, women suffer losses. This is consistent with the fact that men and women generally operate in different markets: women who are able to exploit the relatively new opportunities for well-paying jobs terminate their search early; if unsuccessful, however, they must accept lower-paying jobs. Male job seekers operating predominantly in the "primary" segment of the market, which is characterized by higher wage levels, higher skills, and greater stability, have more opportunities for improving their wages, but find that early acceptance of a job offer could jeopardize better opportunities that turn up after a more extensive search.

Studies on job search in Canada do confirm that job seekers appear to behave as though following a "strategy" that weighs the relative benefits and costs

of further search. They do this in the belief that they will land an offer that is more attractive financially, compared with their current wages. Note, also, that there is some evidence that job seekers lower their wage expectations marginally during the search process.

Wage Adjustments

The "prices" that characterize the worker and the job are a crucial element in the mechanism by which labour demands and supplies are reconciled. Employers typically have some concept of what a particular job, appropriately defined, is worth to them. Workers, similarly, keep in mind a concept of remuneration that is consistent with their abilities and aspirations. An important part of the adjustment process is therefore the constant "resetting of sights" by employers and employees. While wages do appear to increase faster in times of general prosperity and productivity growth it is often contended that they are "sticky" downwards. In this regard, however, our analysis of the unemployed in communities that experienced plant closure or production cutbacks during the period 1973-78 shows that workers do tend to make marginal downward adjustments in their asking wage as the duration of unemployment increases. Furthermore, their responsiveness to labour market conditions is demonstrated by the fact that: first, 40 per cent of those sampled expressed a willingness to accept a lower wage; and, second, 62 per cent of the men and 48 per cent of the women looked for work in industries other than their own. Roughly comparable figures apply to searches in alternate occupations.

Wages are, of course, a very important determinant, not only of the general decision to participate in the labour force but, more specifically, of the choice

Table 7-3

Distribution of Unemployed Job Seekers, by Duration of Search and by Selected Characteristics, Annual Averages, Canada, 1977

	Duration of job search (in weeks)				
	1 to 4	5 to 10	11 to 26	27 and over	Total
	(Percentage of unemployed job seekers)				
Sex					
Men	29.2	24.3	31.7	16.4	100.0
Women	30.7	23.4	29.8	16.7	100.0
Age					
15–19	35.9	25.6	27.2	11.2	100.0
20–24	30.8	25.4	31.2	16.1	100.0
25–44	27.5	23.4	31.4	17.8	100.0
45–64	21.9	20.9	34.5	22.7	100.0
65 and over	--	--	--	--	100.0
Education					
No schooling or elementary	25.0	21.8	33.2	20.0	100.0
High school (some or completed)					
and some postsecondary	30.4	24.3	29.8	15.5	100.0
Postsecondary certificate or diploma	30.8	23.9	29.2	16.1	100.0
University degree	30.6	26.4	29.4	13.7	100.0
Occupation					
White-collar					
Managerial and professional	30.9	24.0	27.9	16.8	100.0
Clerical, sales, and service	29.6	23.6	30.3	16.6	100.0
Blue-collar					
Primary occupations, mining,					
and processing	27.8	22.8	33.1	16.3	100.0
Fabricating	25.6	22.1	34.1	16.1	100.0
Construction	28.6	25.1	31.9	14.8	100.0
Transportation	26.5	24.5	31.1	17.6	100.0
Industry					
Agriculture and other					
primary industries	28.5	23.7	34.2	13.9	100.0
Manufacturing	25.3	22.9	33.3	18.5	100.0
Construction	28.1	25.5	31.9	14.6	100.0
Transportation	26.7	23.5	30.7	19.3	100.0
Trade and finance	29.0	23.6	30.9	16.6	100.0
Community, business, and					
personal services,					
and public administration	31.0	23.7	29.2	16.0	100.0
Province					
Newfoundland	23.5	21.7	31.7	22.4	100.0
Prince Edward Island	27.5	25.0	40.0	15.0	100.0
Nova Scotia	25.6	22.2	32.8	20.0	100.0
New Brunswick	22.8	21.6	35.0	21.9	100.0
Quebec	26.2	22.1	32.4	19.5	100.0
Ontario	30.2	25.5	29.5	14.9	100.0
Manitoba	35.4	27.5	28.8	8.8	100.0
Saskatchewan	40.6	25.6	26.3	9.4	100.0
Alberta	51.2	26.1	11.5	5.2	100.0
British Columbia	31.5	24.7	29.9	14.8	100.0
All unemployed job seekers	29.3	23.8	30.5	16.3	100.0

SOURCE   Hasan and Gera, "Aspects of Job Search in Canada."

of occupation. This particular role of wages is especially important in this study, since shrinking occupational pay differentials have been cited as one cause of the hiring difficulties encountered by Canadian employers in recent years. Workers are not attracted to highly skilled occupations that fail to offer suitable levels of compensation for the extra time spent in training, and shortfalls will result. It is instructive, therefore, to see whether there has been a secular pattern of wage compression that has eroded skill premiums and exacerbated the skill shortage problem.

Strictly speaking, two types of wage differentials are crucial to the question of occupational choice. For not only do individuals compare the salaries of a range of occupations (the starting salaries, for example, or the average salaries, for various jobs); they also consider the likely course of remuneration *within* a particular occupation: How long is the training period before one starts to make "good money," for example, or what are the prospects for rapid advancement? The relevant data, therefore, deal with both inter- and intra-occupational differentials over time.[3]

The evidence is somewhat inconclusive (Table 7-4). Most intra-occupational differentials, with the exception of those for chemists, seem to be at, or below, their level in the early 1970s, most having peaked in mid-decade and having declined thereafter. If the salary spread is viewed as a rough indication of the "growth opportunities" within these highly-skilled occupations, the evidence could suggest that career prospects have generally become rather less attractive. Even this conclusion, however, could be reached only with caution. The narrowing may occur because entry-level salaries have risen faster than those for the higher echelons. The key question, then, is whether compression in one occupation has occurred because the higher levels have lost ground vis-à-vis other occupations.

In order to measure inter-occupational differentials, we have calculated the hourly wage rates of some higher-skilled (Table 7-5) and some lower-skilled occupations (Table 7-6) as a percentage of the national rate for the years 1971 to 1979. As expected, the higher-skilled occupations command rates of pay that are generally in excess of the Canadian average, while the lower-skilled wages are below the average. What is more interesting, however, is that over time the higher-skilled occupations have shown constant or decreasing rates relative to the Canadian average, whereas the lower-skilled occupations have displayed increasing rates: on balance, the skill differential has been compressed.[4]

Among the higher-skilled positions, computer programmers, who have experienced shortages of late, show a marked tendency towards declining relative wage rates; between 1971 and 1979, their margin over and above the national average rate was cut in half. Computer operators exhibit a similar, though less pronounced, pattern. In the blue-collar trades, the picture is the same. The relative wages of tool and die makers and of maintenance plumbers have declined, though the rates for electrical repairers, maintenance carpenters, maintenance pipefitters, and first-class stationary engineers have generally kept even with the Canadian rate. These are some of the very trades identified as being in short supply by our Human Resources Survey.[5]

Another way of looking at skill differentials is to measure the gap between the pay rates for a range

Table 7-4

Intra-Occupational Pay Differentials,[1] Selected Professions, Canada, 1969-80

	Number of levels[2]	1969	1970	1971	1972	1973	1974	1975	1976	1977	1978	1979	1980
						(Per cent)							
Chemist	4	..	..	..	..	78.3	..	78.1	..	81.2	99.4	92.2	91.3
Engineer	6	127.7	..	..	126.2	127.9	137.8	124.3	125.1	126.6	129.3	127.2	124.0
Physical scientist	5	..	..	..	..	..	134.5	130.4	117.7	122.4	115.0	117.7	118.3
Computer systems administrator	5	..	..	..	122.0	129.0	127.6	125.6	118.9	129.7	127.6	127.3	122.1
Draftsperson	7	..	..	129.8	120.1	124.1	125.0	118.8	125.9	99.4	124.2	124.2	121.0
Electronic technician and technologist	7	..	..	..	..	103.8	120.2	111.2	113.7	116.7	108.0	128.7	98.8
Buyer and purchasing agent	5	..	..	..	..	106.4	..	104.0	..	88.0	..	83.7	88.1
Financial administrator	5	..	..	..	114.8	113.0	105.0	101.7	101.4	104.8	92.8	94.8	101.1
Information officer	7	..	..	..	..	233.5	..	205.6	..	200.7	..	212.8	213.5
Economist and statistician	4	..	..	109.9	105.9	119.7	114.3	103.1	95.2	100.9	92.6	99.2	100.4

1 For each occupation, the difference between the top-level and entry-level annual salaries, taken as a percentage of the entry-level annual salary. A figure of 100 per cent would imply that the top-level salary is exactly double the entry-level salary.
2 Data are collected at detailed levels within the various occupational classes surveyed.
SOURCE Based on data from the Pay Research Bureau of the federal government's Public Service Staff Relations Board.

Table 7-5

Hourly Wage Rates Relative to the National Average,[1] Selected Higher-Skilled Occupations,[2] Canada, 1971-79

	1971	1972	1973	1974	1975	1976	1977	1978	1979
					(Per cent)				
Computer programmer	131.9	128.8	123.4	122.6	117.1	115.1	114.1	117.3	115.4
Nurse, general duty	96.5	94.0	95.2	101.4	103.0	107.3	104.8	106.3	103.8
Computer operator	102.1	95.8	93.8	94.3	91.8	88.9	86.9	88.5	89.4
Tool and die maker	124.5	113.1	113.1	115.9	111.2	108.2	110.0	111.5	110.9
Machinist, maintenance	113.3	110.4	108.4	110.7	108.4	107.1	106.8	108.7	108.7
Welder, maintenance	108.9	107.7	109.9	114.0	111.3	111.1	110.3	111.2	110.7
Electrical repairer	116.1	115.0	115.4	118.4	115.4	113.7	113.2	114.4	114.6
Motor vehicle mechanic	100.6	100.7	107.0	111.7	110.1	108.5	107.1	105.4	102.7
Millwright	108.2	107.5	112.9	116.9	113.0	111.9	112.2	114.7	114.5
Carpenter, maintenance	103.7	101.4	102.5	104.3	103.2	103.4	103.7	102.7	102.5
Pipefitter, maintenance	115.7	116.8	115.2	120.1	114.6	113.7	114.0	116.0	115.2
Plumber, maintenance	111.2	110.3	107.2	107.0	108.3	107.0	106.1	107.6	108.2
Stationary engineer	105.2	103.6	104.8	107.7	106.5	105.1	105.3	105.5	106.3
National hourly wage rate	$3.71	$4.02	$4.35	$4.83	$5.65	$6.44	$7.06	$7.43	$8.07

1   The average hourly wage of each occupation as a proportion of the national hourly wage rate, which is given a value of 100. The national hourly wage rate is calculated as follows: the average weekly wages and salaries (as collected by the Employment, Payrolls and Manhours Survey, Statistics Canada) are divided by the average weekly hours (as compiled by the Labour Force Survey, Statistics Canada).
2   Higher-skilled occupations require more than one year of specific vocational preparation (training), as defined in the CCDO manual.
SOURCE   Based on data from Labour Canada and Statistics Canada.

Table 7-6

Hourly Wage Rates Relative to the National Average,[1] Selected Lower-Skilled Occupations,[2] Canada, 1971-79

	1971	1972	1973	1974	1975	1976	1977	1978	1979
					(Per cent)				
Typist	64.2	64.0	63.1	66.8	66.0	65.8	66.6	69.1	67.7
Accounting clerk	85.1	81.4	78.8	81.5	78.1	76.5	75.7	78.5	80.2
Bank teller	..	..	..	..	..	56.1	55.4	61.9	66.3
Duplicating machine operator	..	..	..	..	75.4	70.3	71.9	74.7	74.6
Keypunch operator	72.8	72.0	71.9	74.1	73.6	72.3	72.8	73.7	73.4
Telephone operator	65.1	63.7	64.5	67.9	66.1	65.2	65.9	72.4	68.1
General office clerk	80.2	81.2	78.6	80.9	77.6	76.9	77.0	78.3	78.9
Sales clerk	89.1	89.1	91.9	96.7	94.6	95.3	96.6	92.6	96.9
Waiter	42.0	42.0	43.6	46.3	45.5	44.3	43.5	42.8	40.5
Janitor	72.2	69.8	68.8	73.3	73.2	73.7	72.3	76.4	75.8
Sewing machine operator	54.0	52.9	55.1	58.7	57.7	57.2	56.8	58.2	57.9
Labourer, non-production	81.8	79.5	79.0	80.4	81.9	81.9	83.6	82.8	84.1
Truck driver, light	82.0	81.8	81.5	84.9	85.6	82.8	83.1	83.0	83.5
National hourly wage rate	$3.71	$4.02	$4.35	$4.83	$5.65	$6.44	$7.06	$7.43	$8.07

1   The average hourly wage of each occupation as a proportion of the national hourly wage rate, which is given a value of 100. The national hourly wage rate is calculated as follows: the average weekly wages and salaries (as collected by the Employment, Payrolls and Manhours Survey, Statistics Canada) are divided by the average weekly hours (as compiled by the Labour Force Survey, Statistics Canada).
2   Lower-skilled occupations require one year or less of specific vocational preparation (training) as defined in the CCDO manual.
SOURCE   Based on data from Labour Canada and Statistics Canada.

of relatively skilled jobs and those for one unskilled job (Table 7-7). Once again, a degree of compression is observed. Several occupations exhibit a few years of widening differentials followed by a decline, and the differential is generally narrower at the end of the decade than at the beginning.

The role of trade unions in wage adjustment is, of course, not negligible. It is also a complicated one. Evidence based on the distinction between unionized and nonunionized workers suggests that the effect of unions has been to accelerate the compression of differentials inasmuch as, for every skilled job listed,

Table 7-7

Inter-Occupational Pay Differentials[1] between Selected Skilled and Unskilled Occupations,
Canada, 1971-79

	1971	1972	1973	1974	1975	1976	1977	1978	1979
					(Per cent)				
Carpenter, maintenance	126.8	127.5	129.6	129.7	126.0	126.3	124.1	124.0	121.8
Electrical repairer	142.0	144.6	146.0	147.3	140.9	138.8	135.4	138.2	136.2
Pipefitter, maintenance	141.4	146.8	145.7	149.4	139.9	138.9	136.4	140.1	136.9
Plumber, maintenance	136.0	138.6	135.6	133.2	132.2	130.7	126.9	130.0	128.6
Tool and die maker	152.2	142.1	143.1	144.2	135.7	132.1	131.6	134.7	131.8
Millwright	132.2	135.1	142.8	145.5	137.9	136.7	134.2	138.5	136.1
Machinist, maintenance	138.5	138.7	137.1	137.7	132.4	130.8	127.7	131.3	129.2
Welder, maintenance	133.1	135.4	139.0	141.8	135.8	135.6	131.9	134.3	131.6
Stationary engineer, 1st class	151.0	153.8	152.4	154.7	150.5	146.2	143.9	138.4	138.8
Labourer, nonproduction (average hourly wage rate)	$3.04	$3.20	$3.44	$3.88	$4.63	$5.27	$5.90	$6.15	$6.79

1 The average hourly wage of each skilled occupation as a proportion of the average hourly wage of a nonproduction labourer. A figure of 100 per cent would imply pay equality between a skilled and an unskilled occupation.
SOURCE   Based on data from Labour Canada.

Table 7-8

Union/Nonunion Inter-Occupational Pay Differentials[1] between Selected Skilled and Unskilled Occupations,
Canada, 1974-79

	Union status[2]	1974	1975	1976	1977	1978	1979
				(Per cent)			
Tool and die maker	Unionized	142.7	132.8	128.8	129.4	132.3	128.7
	Nonunionized	153.1	150.6	147.9	152.2	153.2	158.2
Machinist, maintenance	Unionized	135.1	129.4	127.3	125.4	128.3	126.5
	Nonunionized	144.8	141.5	142.1	141.0	141.3	145.8
Welder, maintenance	Unionized	139.8	132.7	132.1	129.8	132.2	128.3
	Nonunionized	145.3	147.9	148.7	144.8	144.3	150.3
Electrical repairer	Unionized	142.8	136.3	134.0	131.7	135.1	132.3
	Nonunionized	161.2	159.4	157.1	154.2	155.3	155.7
Millwright	Unionized	142.3	133.7	132.1	130.9	135.2	132.9
	Nonunionized	151.9	154.6	154.2	149.2	154.6	150.2
Carpenter, maintenance	Unionized	128.1	123.8	124.6	123.0	124.3	121.2
	Nonunionized	135.1	132.7	131.9	134.6	130.0	130.0
Pipefitter, maintenance	Unionized	144.9	134.3	133.7	132.0	135.9	132.5
	Nonunionized	162.2	166.9	159.7	162.2	164.1	163.1
Plumber, maintenance	Unionized	128.9	128.4	126.4	123.3	127.0	125.4
	Nonunionized	146.0	143.0	145.6	148.3	144.5	144.5
Stationary engineer, 1st class	Unionized	147.3	142.9	138.6	135.0	128.9	130.4
	Nonunionized	180.2	180.0	181.0	192.2	173.9	180.5
Labourer, nonproduction (average hourly wage rate)	Unionized	$4.03	$4.80	$5.50	$6.11	$6.37	$7.03
	Nonunionized	$3.41	$4.00	$4.43	$4.76	$5.10	$5.51

1 The average hourly wage of each skilled occupation as a proportion of the average hourly wage of a nonproduction labourer, for unionized and nonunionized workers. A figure of 100 would imply pay equality between a skilled and an unskilled occupation.
2 Unionized (nonunionized) status implies that more (less) than 50 per cent of the workers in the respective occupations within a particular firm are represented by a bargaining unit.
SOURCE   Based on data from Labour Canada.

Table 7-9

Interprovincial Migration Flows,[1] Annual Averages, Canada, 1961-71 and 1971-80

	In-migration		Out-migration		Net migration	
	1961-71	1971-80	1961-71	1971-80	1961-71	1971-80
	(Thousands)					
Newfoundland	7.7	11.4	11.1	12.5	-3.5	-1.1
Prince Edward Island	3.7	4.6	4.3	3.9	-0.6	0.7
Nova Scotia	22.1	24.0	26.5	22.7	-4.4	1.3
New Brunswick	18.5	20.9	23.0	18.4	-4.5	2.5
Quebec	41.4	32.2	55.7	56.6	-14.3	-24.4
Ontario	104.2	95.7	80.7	102.7	23.6	-7.0
Manitoba	27.4	27.0	33.8	34.5	-6.4	-7.5
Saskatchewan	22.8	26.6	35.2	29.4	-12.4	-2.8
Alberta	52.0	81.5	49.0	61.7	3.0	19.8
British Columbia	62.0	73.7	42.7	54.8	19.3	18.9

1 Including adults and children.
SOURCE Employment and Immigration Canada, *Labour Market Development in the 1980s* (Ottawa: EIC, July 1981).

the skill differential is clearly lower among unionized workers (Table 7-8).

Labour Market Mobility

In an analysis of imbalances and the adaptation of demand and supply, the question of mobility is obviously of interest, particularly in a country where vast, immobile resource-related projects require large numbers of workers of various skills. The traditional view of interprovincial migration in Canada is that British Columbia, Alberta, and Ontario attract workers from Quebec and the Atlantic provinces and that such movements generally reflect the structure of provincial unemployment rates.

This situation has changed substantially in recent years, however. In the 1970s, five provinces experienced net in-migration (Table 7-9). The case of Alberta is well known, but three Maritime provinces (Prince Edward Island, Nova Scotia, and New Brunswick) also experienced net in-migration, largely as a result of large return flows, while Ontario became a net loser. At first glance, these developments are somewhat strange, since the structure of provincial unemployment rates has not changed appreciably. The report of the Employment and Immigration Canada Task Force suggests that relative rates of employment growth, rather than unemployment rate differentials among the provinces, are a primary determinant.[6] Our own report on the Newfoundland economy indicates that migration decisions in that province are profoundly affected by government social programs (including unemployment insurance),[7] although some argue that unemployment insurance encourages mobility by furnishing recipients with the financial springboard to more distant

job opportunities.)[8] To sum up, mobility rates, calculated as the sum of entries and exits divided by the population, are lower at the end of the decade than at the beginning for all provinces except Alberta (Table 7-10). Quebec and Ontario, moreover, appear to have relatively immobile populations compared with the rest of Canada.

Table 7-10

Interprovincial Mobility Rates,[1] by Province or Territory, Canada, 1970-71 and 1979-80

	1970-71	1979-80
	(Per cent)	
Newfoundland	4.3	4.1
Prince Edward Island	7.1	6.0
Nova Scotia	6.0	5.0
New Brunswick	6.6	5.1
Quebec	1.8	1.3
Ontario	2.8	2.4
Manitoba	6.4	6.1
Saskatchewan	6.9	5.6
Alberta	7.0	8.8
British Columbia	5.7	5.2
Yukon and Northwest Territories	21.3	21.2

1 Entries and exits as a percentage of population.
SOURCE Jeanine Perreault and Ronald Raby, "Recent Developments in interprovincial Migration in Canada and Possible Scenarios for the 1980s," *Demographic Trends and Their Impact on the Canadian Labour Market*, proceedings of a workshop (Ottawa: Statistics Canada, and Employment and Immigration Canada, 1981).

This perception is erroneous, however, inasmuch as it fails to take into account intraprovincial migration flows. In a recent DREE study that specifically takes account of migration within provinces, Quebec and Ontario no longer show the lowest mobility rates (Table 7-11). Indeed, the proportion of overall

Table 7-11

Total Mobility Rates and the Contribution of
Interprovincial Migration, Canada, 1971-76

	Total mobility rate[1]	Interprovincial migration as a proportion of total migration[2]
	(Per cent)	
Atlantic region[3]	18.0	24.7
Newfoundland	16.8	31.9
Prince Edward Island	20.2	42.2
Nova Scotia	18.7	35.7
New Brunswick	17.7	34.9
Quebec	20.0	12.1
Ontario	21.3	16.3
Prairie region[3]	22.3	22.9
Manitoba	19.0	46.2
Saskatchewan	23.8	39.1
Alberta	23.3	31.0
British Columbia	26.7	18.0
Yukon	40.5	82.3
Northwest Territories	33.6	73.2
Canada	21.3	20.7

1 The migrant population between 1971 and 1976 divided by the total population in 1971.
2 The interprovincial migration divided by the total migration between 1971 and 1976.
3 When grouping the provinces, intraregional migration cancels out, and the interprovincial proportion is accordingly diminished.
SOURCE Based on Department of Regional Economic Expansion, "Migration Patterns in Canada," Ottawa, May 1979.

migration accounted for by interprovincial movements gives an indication of the openness of provincial labour markets. On this basis, Ontario, Quebec, and British Columbia appear to be less open, and the remaining provinces more open, than the Canadian average. In fact, while labour demand in certain provinces, such as those of the Prairie region, may appropriately be satisfied in a pan-Canadian market, the evidence suggests that other provinces find that, for reasons of size or culture, their main response is much more localized. The people of Quebec, for example, are as mobile, overall, as the people of most other provinces, but it is clear that the anglophones make up the bulk of the interprovincial migrants, while 96 per cent of francophone migrants move only within their province (Table 7-12).

Barriers or impediments to mobility are an important consideration and may take a variety of forms.[9] The costs of uprooting home and family to move to a distant location are obviously a financial and psychological deterrent that is exacerbated if employers' assistance to migrants is subject to tax, if living costs are higher in the new area, if jobs for other family members are scarce, or if the migrant worker must, in effect, maintain two homes. For the host company and area, the costs of creating or expanding a social infrastructure may be prohibitive. Artificial barriers may take the form of variations in licensing or certification between provinces, of the kind that skilled tradesmen and those in some professional occupations find troublesome. Furthermore, the nontransferability of certain work-related benefits, like pensions and various kinds of insurance, may pose impediments to movement. Finally, as mentioned earlier, there is evidence that government programs themselves may well discourage geographical mobility.

Information

Earlier in this chapter, we referred to information as the essential lubricant for the market adjustment mechanism. Knowledge of the whereabouts, quantity, quality, availability, and remuneration of people and

Table 7-12

Total Migration, by Mother Tongue and by Type of Migration, Quebec, 1971-76

	External migration				Internal migration		Total Quebec migration	
	In-migration[1]		Out-migration					
	Number	Per cent	Number	Per cent	Number	Per cent	Number	Per cent
Anglophones	41,450	50.1 / ...	94,006	64.6 / 44.6	116,595	11.0 / 55.4	210,601	17.5 / 100.0
Francophones	36,723	44.3 / ...	41,075	28.2 / 4.3	911,525	86.1 / 95.7	952,600	79.1 / 100.0
Others	4,659	5.6 / ...	10,401	7.1 / 25.1	31,080	2.9 / 74.9	41,481	3.4 / 100.0
Total	82,832	100.0 / ...	145,482	100.0 / 12.1	1,059,200	100.0 / 87.9	1,204,682	100.0 / 100.0

1 Figures represent migrants coming into Quebec from outside; consequently they are not included in the total migration originating in Quebec.
SOURCE Based on DREE, "Migration Patterns."

jobs is absolutely vital to the effective decisions of countless workers and employers on whom the allocation process depends. For example, the high school student who contemplates a variety of career prospects must contend with an accumulation of social values that overglamourize white-collar occupations. The married woman entering (or re-entering) the labour market after some years of concentrating on family responsibilities may find the range of available opportunities severely limited. The middle-aged worker in a "steady" job who is laid off because of technological change or slumping markets faces the prospect of having to pick up new skills or to relocate, or both. The native Canadian faces a labour market fraught, in addition to the usual problems, with those of access and assimilation. For their part, employers anxious to exploit new and rapidly unfolding opportunities frequently have labour requirements that are highly specific as to skills, locations, and hiring. Finally, various companies, and governments at all levels, must wrestle with the range of labour market contingencies associated with the enormous projects that are expected to exploit the country's natural resource endowments in the coming decade. The critical requirement that is common to all of these situations is information.

It is curious, therefore, that the information issue is frequently neglected or ignored by observers of the labour market, and particularly by those who frame its policies. This is partly due, we believe, to a tendency to regard the information question as the dull exercise of collecting and processing facts and figures to be released in statistical documents that are dull reading at best, incomprehensible at worst, and seemingly far removed from the real-life day-to-day decisions of people in the "real" world of work. Programs to retrain laid-off workers or to move them to regions with abundant jobs seem, by contrast, more exciting and so much more practical.

Although inherently unappealing in themselves, data are nevertheless essential to wise policy decisions. The information must be regular, consistent, timely, and sufficiently detailed to permit the kind of analysis on which the more attractive work of policy formulation can be based. And it is precisely this consideration that underlies our concern over the state of Canadian labour market information. It is our contention that there are important data gaps and deficiencies in dissemination and analysis.

We have seen in earlier chapters some of the enormous difficulties encountered in attempting to analyse the demands and supplies of labour by occupational type and in making projections for the future. Our labour market data on occupations are, at the moment, quite inadequate — derived primarily from a decennial census but required to shed light on circumstances that change substantially from year to year. The demise of the Job Vacancy Survey leaves us without important information on a major aspect of labour demand and skill shortages. And while our own work on labour force dynamics provides insights into the question of flows, this country has not since the mid-1960s had a regular and consistent body of information on turnover.[10]

The upshot of all this is that the many potential users of occupational data and projections are at present ill-served. Job seekers and employers can avail themselves of the Canadian Occupational Forecasting Program (COFOR), for example, but quite apart from the methodological and data problems alluded to in Chapter 3, its projections are intermittent at best. The first results were released in 1976, giving projections to 1982, while the most recent were released in 1981 for the period to 1985. Moreover publication of the more short-term Forward Occupational Imbalance Listing (FOIL), designed to provide CEIC program managers with two-year imbalance projections on a quarterly basis for use in placement, counselling, training, mobility and immigration programs, has been discontinued.[11] It is understood, however, that this latter program is being substantially regenerated and will resume in 1982.

As far as analysis is concerned, while a number of government departments and agencies (the most prominent of which are Statistics Canada, Labour Canada, and Employment and Immigration Canada) do produce a variety of regular statistical reports, research documents tend to appear in a somewhat haphazard or piecemeal fashion. Canadian universities, research institutions of various types, and employer and labour associations also undertake valuable analytical work that tends to reflect current interests or needs, but it is largely unconnected and may even be characterized by some duplication. There is no bureau of labour market research of the kind recently established in Australia, for example, nor the rich blend of research and practical assistance to industry that characterizes Britain's Institute of Manpower Studies. Though Laval University's *Relations Industrielles* continues to provide an important medium for labour economic research, Canada is generally lacking in such journals. And while a number of magazines, such as *Worklife*, have attempted to fill the gap left by the ill-fated *Labour Gazette*, Canada does not afford many opportunities for the nonacademic analyst to become informed of labour market developments and issues.

In our discussion so far we have referred chiefly to the acquisition, processing, dissemination, and analysis of data that may be used to improve our understanding of how labour markets work and the effectiveness of the process by which decisions are made concerning policies and programs. But the direct exchange of information among economic agents is also of crucial importance, and it is the focus of one of our major labour market institutions – namely, the Canada Employment Centres (CEC). A recent CEIC study presents some interesting findings on this operation:[12] it appears that 62 per cent of registered job seekers get no job referral and only 18 per cent are actually placed. An opinion survey conducted by Goldfarb Consultants in 1980 found that over 50 per cent of the users thought the CEC did a poor or "only fair" job of helping people to find work. About 59 per cent said the CEC would not be one of their main job-seeking avenues.

From the employer side, the attitude expressed by one in ten was that the service was only a "last resort" to fill immediate vacancies. On the other hand, 60 per cent of those who did use the service reported favourable experience. The CEC fills, on average, about 78 per cent of the job orders it receives, and 70 per cent of the referrals are made within a few days of receiving the job orders. It appears, however, that unfilled vacancies often arise because appropriate referrals are not available. As for helping to reduce search time, there is evidence suggesting that compared with other job seekers, CEC clients found jobs in three to four weeks sooner. But the best people are naturally placed the fastest; and, as noted above, only 18 per cent of CEC clients are actually placed, regardless. There is no discernible wage advantage to being placed through the CEC offices. Finally, the range of occupations served is somewhat limited: close to two-thirds of all CEC placements are in clerical, sales, service, and construction occupations; very few placements are made in managerial occupations or in jobs in the primary and transportation sectors.

Nonwage Factors in the Employment Contract

Earlier, we considered the role of wages in the allocation of labour resources. It has long been understood, however, that the nonpecuniary aspects of jobs may also exert tremendous influence on the matching process. Indeed, the "father" of economics, Adam Smith, formulated a theory of wage differentials that explicitly takes into account differences in the "agreeableness" of various jobs.

The importance of such nonwage aspects derives from several considerations. First, they crucially affect the relative attractiveness of various jobs and thus the allocation of labour. Second, there is growing evidence that more and more people are concerned not just with monetary returns but with job satisfaction and fulfilment, and that such concerns will continue to be important in the future. Third, from a policy standpoint there is increasing acceptance of the view that improvement in the physical and psychological conditions of work, as well as in the pecuniary rewards, is an appropriate goal in itself. And, finally, there are strong suggestions that the attainment of this goal may have highly salutary effects on productivity, in particular, as well as on other areas such as turnover, absenteeism, and industrial disputes.

There is, of course, a long tradition of payment in kind, which in modern guise is revealed in sophisticated employment contracts involving a complicated package of not only wages and leisure but also fringe benefits, such as life, health, and unemployment insurance; stock options; and pension entitlements. The physical conditions of work may also be an important component of the total reward system. We have come a long way from the dark, satanic mills of the Industrial Revolution, but extremes of temperature, problems of lighting, noise, and ventilation, and the hazards of machinery and toxic chemicals are still a major concern for many Canadians. Increasingly, also, we are becoming aware of the mental and emotional consequences of work-place stress in a variety of fast-paced, high-pressure positions in modern society. An important part of the adjustment process, therefore, consists in eradicating or ameliorating the distasteful aspects of various occupations. Increasing attention has also been given recently not only to removing the negative features of the overall employment package but also to accentuating its positive contributions to the psychic well-being of workers.

The concept of work humanization is not new, of course, and it is broad enough to encompass the goals of centuries of philanthropy, political reform, and the unceasing struggle of labour organizations. Moreover, there is a long tradition of a "human relations" approach to organization management. The appearance of what is now known as "the quality of working life movement" can be traced to all of these developments.[13] It stems from a reaction to the dire consequences, for the human psyche, of the minute fragmentation of jobs into repetitive tasks that is associated with the scientific management approach to work design. It is an outgrowth of efforts to avoid the mind-numbing and soul-destroying regimen of the assembly line, so strikingly evoked by Charlie Chaplin in *Modern Times*. Some of the earliest, now-famous, research on quality of working life (QWL) demonstrated the favourable effects on communications, work relations, and productivity of certain types of work organization in the British coal mines. The research of Eric Trist and Fred Emery, among others, demonstrated the effectiveness of "autonomous work groups" (in today's parlance) that, within broad constraints, set their own objectives and their own pace, organize their own work teams, and assume responsibility for the quantity and quality of their output. One of the major steps in the evolution of the QWL movement was the spread of consultative, co-operative, participative, and co-deterministic modes of labour-management relations in Scandinavia and Western Europe generally in the 1960s.

Two important pillars of QWL emerged in this process. The first may be loosely associated with the term "industrial democracy," which is concerned largely, if not exclusively, with the structure of work-place relationships.[14] The spectrum of such relationships runs all the way from a system in which owners and/or managers wield total power over work-place decisions (slavery in the antebellum South is an example) through collective bargaining to the *Mitbestimmung* system of co-determination in Germany and outright worker ownership of factories in Illyria (Yugoslavia).

The second pillar is the concept of "socio-technical design," which starts from the principle that, rather than erect a technology consisting of scientifically sophisticated physical capital components to which human inputs are required to adapt (with whatever consequences!), these inputs (and their attendant requirements) should be built in from the start. An important premise is that the production process can be served by a variety of equally efficient configurations of input combinations and organization. In socio-technical design, the traditional view of a single, "best" process, uniquely determined by the sheer sophistication of physical technology and capital inputs, is considered myopic: industrial engineering tends to be much more glamorous than personnel management, but neglect of the latter may lead to turnover, absenteeism, work slowdowns or stoppages, grievances, strikes, and poor workmanship. These, in turn, may nullify the potential of even the most dazzling equipment.

In Canada the QWL movement is gaining momentum. Awareness of demographic shifts in the work force that have deeply affected work attitudes and values, coupled with technological and institutional changes that have altered the whole meaning of work, has caused Canadians to ponder the lessons to be learned from the experience of other countries. While the problems of wholesale application of foreign systems to Canada are evident, the drawbacks of the present confrontational mode of industrial relations in this country are no less apparent. Furthermore, concern about slower productivity growth has led some to seek solutions not in traditional sources of growth, such as the quantity and quality of physical and human capital, but in changes in the organizational structure of work. This could lead, through the chain of job satisfaction and motivation, to improvements in output and to less turnover, absenteeism, and even time lost in industrial disputes.

Already a number of QWL initiatives are under way in a variety of Canadian organizations, from food processing to forest products, from textiles to oil refining, from chemicals to public service. The record is still mixed. In particular, it is apparent that no single model will prove to be the panacea and that existing approaches must be modified and adapted to the particular circumstances and needs of Canadian organizations. There is hope, however, that careful adaptation of this type, along with meticulous monitoring and evaluation, may in certain instances have highly beneficial results not only for productivity but also for worker satisfaction and fulfilment.

The interest shown in such ventures by Canadian governments is apparent in the form of the Ontario QWL Centre in Toronto and the federal QWL Unit in Ottawa. Both have been promised substantial funding and are engaged in the business of educating and informing Canadian business, labour, and governments. The Ontario centre has established a multipartite body representing various interest groups; it sends its representatives to the work place to provide information and advice and, where appropriate, to aid in designing programs. In the federal sphere a number of programs have been initiated in various departments, including Statistics Canada, the Treasury Board, the Department of the Secretary of State, Canada Post, and Revenue Canada.

Thus, in the context of labour market adjustment, QWL is a force to be reckoned with. It has grown rapidly in recent years and may no longer be regarded as a trifling fad, although its shape and extent in this country are still somewhat unprecise. Given the labour market prospects outlined earlier in this report, along with the continuing concern about productivity, we may expect to see more of this particular institutional adaptation to changing circumstances.

Job Creation Programs[15]

Many of the government programs designed to aid the operation of the labour market in the last two decades have been focused primarily on the supply side; training, mobility, and immigration programs are examples of this trend. More recently, however, faced with stubborn unemployment and traditional demand management policies that have been hampered by sensitive inflationary forces, governments have increasingly sought alternatives in the form of direct job creation programs in the public and private sectors. Such measures have been varied and ubiquitous. Their common aim is to stimulate employment in an effort to reduce the unemployment rate. It is argued that it is less costly to stimulate employment by such measures than by tax cuts or government spending hikes; that by reducing labour costs these measures may be less inflationary than equally costly alternative employment-creating measures; and that this effect can be still further enhanced if subsidies are targeted to areas and groups with a relatively low inflationary impact.

But in terms of the adjustment process, how are such policies justified? The answer seems to depend on a number of factors. The first is closely associated with the diagnosis of the unemployment problem: while many of the unemployment spells in Canada are of the short-spell turnover variety that can be addressed by measures to improve the matching process, a good deal of total unemployment involves much longer periods of joblessness for particular groups for whom the sheer existence of jobs is the overriding problem. Second, and inextricably related, is the concern over whether recourse to conventional macroeconomic instruments to ease the problem of job availability would lead to unacceptable inflationary consequences. Third, while the long-term joblessness is borne by relatively few people, there is an important equity dimension to the unemployment problem that suggests the need for an approach that is more finely targeted than aggregate monetary and fiscal measures.

Given these considerations, it is the targeted nature of job creation programs that is the crucial aspect of their raison d'être. If such programs employ persons who, because of various disadvantages, have experienced special difficulty in finding and holding jobs, then not only is the potential output of the economy increased but, because the wage demands of such persons are comparatively less inflationary, the increase in employment need not threaten price stability. Taxpayers may benefit from the taxes paid by newly hired workers and from the reduction in transfer payments. Direct job creation programs in the private sector may actually exert downward pressure on prices by reducing total labour costs. Finally, of course, selective job creation, by tilting the composition of employment towards the target group of low-skill workers, reduces inequality in the distribution of income – a legitimate goal in itself.

The economic case for direct job creation programs can also be seen from a microeconomic standpoint. In a complex labour market, there is a well-recognized array of factors that constrain purely economic forces and lead to disincentives and allocative distortions. Some, like die-hard social

conventions or downright bias and discrimination, tend to place certain labour force groups at a hiring disadvantage. Others, like minimum wages and unemployment insurance, are put in place for very good reasons of their own and could not, therefore, be easily removed. What such factors do, however, is drive a considerable wedge between employers' conceptions of the gross wage they must pay some individuals and the expected productivity of the latter. The case for job creation programs (of which wage subsidy is the clearest example) is therefore one of efficiency: by closing the apparent gap between wages and productivity a distortion is corrected and an allocative failure removed. But equity, too, is served as the position of the target groups is improved.

Canadian governments, both federal and provincial, have experimented with a variety of job creation programs (see Appendix Table E-1). At the federal level, initiatives for the private sector included the Job Experience Training Program (JETP), which operated from 1977 to 1979 and was designed to offer summer jobs to young people having difficulty integrating into the work force. The Employment Tax Credit Program (ETCP), begun in 1978, was a temporary wage subsidy scheme, offering tax credits of up to $2.00 an hour for "incremental" employees who worked full-time for at least three months. Initially designed to create 50,000 jobs a year, the ETCP was discontinued in March 1981. A new wage subsidy program for the disadvantaged was introduced the following month. It provides a subsidy on a decreasing scale (85 per cent, 50 per cent, and 25 per cent) for three phases of 13, 26, and 26 weeks respectively – 65 weeks in all.

Public service employment (PSE) programs in Canada have been in vogue since the early 1970s, and approximately $2.5 billion has been spent on them. Their objectives have been many: to increase employment in general, and for youths, native Canadians, and the handicapped in particular; to improve the future earning potential and employability of these people; and to produce a more equitable income distribution. The winter of 1971-72 saw the introduction of what was perhaps the best-known of all the federal PSE measures – the Local Initiatives Program (LIP). A labour-intensive, winter-season, community involvement program, LIP paid the local going wage rate and served an average of over 50,000 clients a year. Its average annual expenditure was close to $140 million until it was phased out in 1977. It was superseded by a year-round program called "Canada Works," which funds incremental local employment on nonprofit community services that enhance the skills of the participants. It has provided 208,000 jobs so far, at a cost of $680 million. The Local Employment Assistance Program

(LEAP) was designed to create long-term employment for the chronically unemployed. Its target groups include women, youths, native people, the handicapped, welfare recipients, and ex-convicts; its clients number close to 9,000 annually. About 30,000 jobs a year are created under the auspices of the Young Canada Works (YCW) program, a summer employment measure aimed at students and costing between $40 and $50 million a year. It replaces the former Opportunities for Youth (OFY) program, which was discontinued in 1975/76. There are a number of other minor community development and/or summer programs as well.

The important question, of course, is how successful such programs have been. A number of factors affecting performance are common to programs in both the public and the private sectors. First, there is the net employment effect, which is a difficult factor to evaluate because of the possible displacement effects (i.e., a reduction in employment elsewhere as a result of the job creation program) and, in the case of the public sector, because of fiscal substitution (where public agencies substitute subsidies for some percentage of their normal payroll costs, thus freeing up funds to be used to retire debt, reduce borrowing, reduce taxes, or increase other expenditures). Second, there is the question of how well such programs compare with other means of creating employment. Third, there is the assessment of their efficiency in terms of the benefits and costs to society, which should, ideally, take account of interrelationships with other government programs of regional employment stimulus, for example, that may be complementary or conflicting. And there is the question, often overlooked, of possible long-run distortions if job creation programs impede technological change, for example, or subsidize inefficient organizations. Finally, and almost inextricably related, is the contributions they make to specific societal goals, such as the reduction of inflation and the pursuit of equity.

Looking first at the private-sector programs, as exemplified by the Employment Tax Credit Program (ETCP), our results indicate that the incremental gain in employment was between 20 and 37 per cent. There are no other Canadian estimates available with which to compare these figures, but U.S. estimates for the New Jobs Tax Credit Program are in the 20 to 30 per cent range; U.K. estimates are around 40 per cent, and a French study places the net employment impact at between 15 and 40 per cent. If we use the lower figure (20 per cent) for the ETCP the net annual cost per job is $17,500, while the higher (37 per cent) figure yields an average cost of only $9,500. As far as the composition of labour demand is concerned, ETCP participants appear not to differ significantly

from a CEIC comparison group in terms of any major characteristic (such as age, sex, education, or unemployment insurance benefits) except for duration of unemployment, which was greater for program participants. Finally, the ETCP attracted mainly small firms: about 77 per cent of the participating enterprises employed fewer than 20 people, and these accounted for 41 per cent of all ETCP hirings.

In sum, while the potential employment effect of private-sector job creation programs is considerable, displacement effects in practice may be important, with the possible windfalls to employers amounting to between 63 and 80 per cent of the entire subsidy, in the case of the ETCP.

The prominent community-service nature of many PSE ventures suggests that the displacement effects are unlikely to be large. Our estimates of the fiscal-substitution effect, however, range between 50 and 70 per cent, close to those obtained in a comparable U.S. study in 1975. Using these figures our estimate of the average person-year cost of net PSE jobs is about $14,000; on this basis alone, expenditures on PSE programs are likely to have a greater direct employment impact than equivalent fiscal stimulus through general government expenditures, since GNP per person employed was $23,000 in 1978. In addition, further employment is created through PSE programs because of the multiplier effects from the income of the participants. Compared with conventional aggregate demand stimulus as an employment-generating instrument, public-service employment is therefore faster, more direct, and more cost-effective; it can be targeted more finely; and, because it reduces transfers and increases tax revenues, it is less detrimental to the budget deficit.

The social benefits and costs of Canadian PSE programs have not been comprehensively assessed. Indeed, society's preference for the provision of public jobs rather than transfer payments, the dignity and self-esteem that such jobs afford to the participants, and the income redistribution effects of the programs, while important benefits, are practically unquantifiable. Experience in the United States strongly suggests that PSE programs, by virtue of their ability to focus on particular target groups, are less inflationary than conventional fiscal policy. This targeting capability in itself is enough to recommend PSE measures as a way of promoting the objectives of distributional equity.

Conclusion

In this chapter we have examined some of the factors that play a role in the process of labour allocation. This complex and dynamic process is, as we have emphasized, one of unceasing adjustment to the push and pull of myriad forces. A few of the important adjustment mechanisms were selected for discussion.

Our studies of job search have shed some light on the process by which workers, both employed and unemployed, seek jobs in the light of their assessment of the costs (pecuniary and psychic) of further search and of the benefits anticipated in terms of wage gains. It is from the job search perspective that a rather neglected aspect of the unemployment insurance system emerges: in certain circumstances, the ability to search longer, instead of accepting the first job offer that comes along because of sheer economic necessity, may yield a more productive outcome in the matching of job requirements with worker capabilities.

The wage responsiveness of economic agents is a crucial aspect of adjustment, and it has been illustrated here with reference to career choice and occupational wage differentials. Our work has shown that the compression of skill differentials can be related to shortages. Mobility is expected to be an important factor in a future Canadian labour market characterized by new growth poles in relatively isolated areas. Our figures show the changing pattern of migration in recent years and reveal considerable differences in the "openness" of provincial labour markets.

While the monetary aspects of labour market transactions are of major concern, it was pointed out that a wide range of nonwage aspects also play a critical role. The development and potential of the quality of working life and its relevance to the Canadian scene were accordingly discussed.

Finally, since the sheer enormity and complexity of its task causes the unaided market mechanism to perform less than perfectly on occasion, it has long been considered appropriate to take auxiliary action in the form of government programs. These are many and varied, and in this chapter we have considered only two. Having identified information as the essential lubricant of the adjustment mechanism, we reported some of the results of an analysis of the performance of the federal government's CEC system, which processes information in providing counselling and placement services.

The other policy intervention discussed was that of direct job creation. Such measures in Canada, as in many other countries, became prominent during the last decade as an alternative to the traditional aggregate demand policies used to alleviate unemployment in the inflation-prone economies of Western Europe and North America. We have concluded that while direct job creation programs have a potential for timely employment stimulus that may be quantitatively effective compared with traditional measures, the question of the net increment to employment creation is critical in both public- and in private-sector measures. On balance, perhaps the most attractive feature of the programs is the fact that they can be finely targeted to particular areas and groups, with consequent benefits in terms of distributional equity and the avoidance of inflation. Unquantifiable socio-psychological benefits to workers may, in the long run, be of great importance too.

The development of vocational skills is one of the central features of any industrialized economy. While there is disagreement regarding the exact nature of the link between training and education, on the one hand, and productivity and socioeconomic mobility, on the other, it is generally conceded that they are related. All other things being equal, a labour force that is highly skilled will outperform one that is not.

Governments have become closely involved in the business of developing vocational abilities, and Canada takes a back seat to no other nation in that respect. In fiscal 1980/81, for example, the training programs of the federal government alone accounted for expenditures of over $800 million, which, on a per capita basis, placed Canada among the world's leaders. Despite the magnitude of this effort, however, it has become evident that serious shortages of manpower have endured. As a result the current approach needs to be seriously reconsidered. Indeed, the federal government has recently announced its intention to introduce wholesale changes in the national training effort.

The changing economic context makes this a propitious moment to cast a critical eye at the public policies and programs directed towards developing vocational skills. First, the existing government efforts were instituted, for the most part, in the late 1960s and early 1970s when economic growth was rapid and public sector expansion seemed unlimited. These conditions have changed notably. In addition, demographic, social, and economic factors are inducing marked shifts both in the composition of the labour force and in the types of skills required.

Given our focus on imbalances in this report, our review of training will highlight its usefulness in the reduction of bottlenecks. While it would clearly be unreasonable to expect Canada to anticipate, and prepare for, all impending labour demands, the existence of skill shortages within the present context of high unemployment constitutes compelling evidence that this country faces a serious problem regarding the development of the skills required by the labour market.

A concern for vocational training and education, however, must extend beyond their contribution to economic development and performance. It is also essential to consider the importance of training in improving the prospects of those who experience difficulties in the labour market. Indeed, a major emphasis of this report is that governments must play a critical role in improving the employment prospects of *all* Canadians.

Thus the development of vocational skills can serve both the promotion of economic efficiency and the pursuit of a more equitable society. In devising policy prescriptions, however, recognition of the distinctiveness of these two objectives is, in our view, of paramount importance. Efficiency and equity considerations, while not totally unrelated, are exclusive enough to warrant quite different program arrangements.

Should Governments Be Involved?

The appropriate role for governments in the development of vocational skills is a highly contentious and important question. Indeed, although the federal government and the provinces are both heavily involved in manpower training, there have been numerous questions raised about the suitable division of responsibility between the public and private sectors. This is clearly shown by much of the testimony presented to the recent Parliamentary Task Force on Employment Opportunities for the '80s.

The controversy over this issue can be traced to differences in ideological outlook and to different impressions of how the economy works. It must also be viewed within the context of the recent soul-searching on the part of the public, politicians, and others regarding the social and economic implications of government intervention for the operation of the economy.[1] In light of the recent and widespread perception of failures in our public training system, it is not surprising that this aspect of government involvement has not escaped such doubts.

Those who maintain faith in the market argue that, although it operates imperfectly at times and under severe strain, it can nevertheless be relied upon to follow the right "instincts." With respect to the question of "externalities," which often enters into the arguments in favour of government intervention, the market itself does accommodate the problem to some extent. Thus a trainee typically shares with his/her employer some of the costs of training by accepting lower wages during the training period. The more generally applicable – and, therefore, "portable" – the training, the greater the trainee's share of the cost. And if the trainee does move to another employer, the latter may compensate him/her by paying a sufficiently attractive wage.

The case against government involvement asserts that the market generally leads towards efficient adjustments and solutions, while public intervention offers no such assurances. This view holds that governments, unconstrained by considerations of competition or profit, have a propensity to erect self-serving bureaucracies that are more officious than efficient, more flaccid than flexible, and characterized more by excess than by success. Hence if there is to be a role for government in the training field, it should be as "facilitator" rather than as "decision maker." It is highly inappropriate, this argument contends, to place decisions about curriculum design, course duration, or selection of trainees in the hands of bureaucrats who have never set foot into a shop, let alone assessed its manpower needs.

The case for government involvement in manpower training has at its core the notion that, in the absence of government aid, the free market would fail to yield the required quantity or quality of training. From the individual's point of view, uncertain future prospects make it difficult to anticipate labour demand and to borrow to finance training. Externalities, too, constitute a commonly heard argument. The reluctance of industry to provide training stems from the fact that although the employer would invest in developing the abilities of his/her employees, those abilities would remain the property of the latter. If the trainees move to another organization, therefore, the employer loses his/her investment: the benefits are reaped by persons *external* to the enterprise. In view of such risks, the employer may be reluctant to invest in training; as a result, too little may be undertaken for the economy as a whole.

Closely allied to this argument is the suggestion that training confers on society as a whole important benefits that are not restricted to the narrower purview of the individual employer. For example, the advantages of a well-trained and flexible work force that can adapt smoothly to technological change or to the competitive rigours of shifting patterns of international trade are enjoyed by the nation as a whole in a way that is analogous to services like defence, justice, and education. The narrow focus of individual entrepreneurs could lead, however, to less training than would the view encompassing the much broader benefits of training for society. Thus far-sightedness – including, in principle at least, concern for future generations – would render governments more likely to invest in the future and offset the "defective telescopic faculty" of individuals.[2]

Another argument for intervention rests with the belief that only government can ensure fulfilment of certain equity objectives in the economy. If, on equity grounds, we felt that incomes should be redistributed, we might accordingly wish to redistribute the ownership of human capital by subsidizing vocational training. Of course, the question of income redistribution could be addressed directly by transfer payments, but training might receive greater public support for a number of reasons. First, there might be more widespread political acceptance of a policy designed to "help people help themselves" through the medium of work, as opposed to one that might encourage dependence. Second, training and/or work experience programs are, ideally, an investment: an initial outlay could yield a stream of benefits thereafter. With transfer payments, on the other hand, successive outlays would be required if income redistribution were to be maintained. Hence training might simply be less costly.

Essentially, then, the proponents of government involvement argue that the unaided labour market encounters impediments to optimal resource allocation; this, in turn, gives rise to structural unemployment and inflationary, growth-inhibiting bottlenecks. Their contention appears to rest on two types of observations about real-life labour markets. First, because of the sheer magnitude of the stocks and flows involved, the pace of change, and the complexity of the requirements of people and jobs, the task of matching them efficiently is enormous. Second, in addition to the inevitable imperfections of information, the allocation process is also impaired by a broad array of artificial impediments – based on age, sex, ethnicity, limited entry to occupations, and barriers to geographical mobility – that require public policy attention.

Despite the arguments of those against intervention, the case for government involvement on a selective basis is persuasive, on balance. In the first place, there is something to the externalities argument: Canadian employers are often heard to say that it is too costly to train people who are going to move to other companies. While there is also wide-spread evidence of the sharing of training costs between employers and employees, it would seem reasonable for government to become involved, particularly with respect to the kind of training that is most generally applicable and therefore risky for individual firms. This is particularly important for small and medium-sized firms, where the greater part of employment growth is now occurring. Second, it is clear that Canadians favour income redistribution and want their governments to maintain a wide variety of equity-oriented policies and programs. The potential for manpower training to serve as a redistributive device would thus appear to make it a logical candidate for government involvement. Also, within the existing context of maladjustment in the Canadian labour market, there is a need for the kind of assistance that might improve the efficiency of the allocative process and thus help to realize the goals of price stability, full employment, and income growth. An improved training system must play an important part in this process. Some government involvement in such arrangements might well be advantageous in the future, as the sharp shifts in industrial structure, changing patterns of international competitiveness, and rapid technological development will place a premium on a well-trained and adaptable work force.

The Evolution of the Federal Role

The question of responsibility for training in Canada is complicated by the intricacy of federal-provincial jurisdictions. The stake of the provinces stems from the constitutional delegation to them of matters pertaining to education, whereas authority for national economic development was granted to the federal government. Both levels therefore maintain that they have legitimate interests in the training field. While the question of the primary constitutional responsibility is one to be determined by legal experts, what is critical from the point of view of the observer is the recognition of this collision between jurisdictions. Any recipe for formulating training policies in this country will inevitably involve some degree of struggle and negotiation between Ottawa and the provinces.

In the nineteenth century, public involvement in the arena of training was essentially limited to modest provincial support for apprenticeship and vocational education. The federal presence originated with legislation in 1912, and it continued throughout the next half-century with the introduction of a number of bills intended to stimulate vocational schooling. It was not until 1960 and the passage of the Technical and Vocational Training Assistance Act (TVTA), however, that the federal government assumed a major role.

A glance at federal expenditures clearly illustrates the change in magnitude. Under the various training Acts that were in effect before 1960, Ottawa contributed a total of $110 million; in contrast, this amount climbed to $850 million during the six years of TVTA. The new Act was also more sweeping in coverage than its predecessors. Not only did it extend existing federal support of institutional training, apprenticeship, and training of the unemployed, but it also introduced a matching-grant formula in a number of new areas, such as retraining of the labour force, training of the disabled, and training development.

While these operational programs represented a new level of federal involvement in vocational skills development, TVTA will be remembered mainly for its capital grants provision, which eventually accounted for 70 per cent of all expenditures made under the Act. During the 1960s, this program played a major role in the phenomenal growth of education institutions, particularly those in the field of vocational training. The effects of the resulting expansion of public training facilities have been felt ever since.

By the mid-1960s, the federal government had become concerned about various aspects of TVTA, particularly its shared-cost format.[3] In response to this dissatisfaction, it devised a new approach that was to form the basis for the Adult Occupational Training Act (AOTA).[4] This legislation, enacted in 1967, constituted a radical departure from earlier initiatives. First, it shifted the fiscal arrangements from a shared-cost funding approach to one in which Ottawa, in effect, purchased training services. And, second, AOTA altered the existing federal-provincial training relationship, enabling Ottawa to achieve more visibility and control.

Activity under AOTA includes both institutional and industrial training. The former is provided under the Canada Manpower Training Program (CMTP), while the latter operates through the Canada Manpower Industrial Training Program (CMITP) and Critical Trades Skill Training (CTST). Both in terms of expenditures and number of trainees, the overall effort is dominated by the institutional initiative (see Chart 8-1).

Under CMTP, the federal government "buys" seats in provincial education and training institutions. Because the persons using these places are generally referred through Canada Employment Centres, the vast majority are from the ranks of the jobless. In fact, during the 1979/80 fiscal year, 86.3 per cent of the trainees who began courses under CMTP were either unemployed or not in the labour force prior to

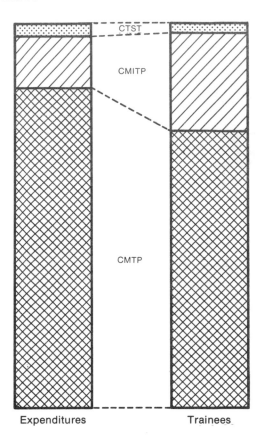

Chart 8-1

Distribution of Expenditures and Trainees under the Adult Occupational Training Act, Canada, 1980/81

Expenditures   Trainees

CTST – Critical Trades Skill Training.
CMITP – Canada Manpower Industrial Training Program.
CMTP – Canada Manpower Training Program.

SOURCE   Based on data from Employment and Immigration Canada.

orientation classes for people without recent employment experience (Job Readiness Training); and adjustment courses for workers experiencing particular problems (Work Adjustment Training).

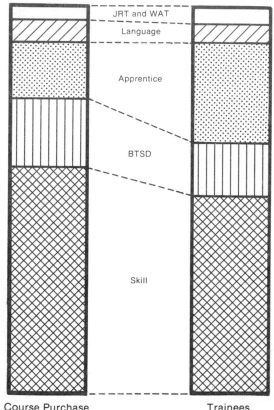

Chart 8-2

Distribution of Course Purchase Expenditures[1] and Trainees under the Canada Manpower Training Program, Canada, 1979/80

Course Purchase   Trainees
Expenditures[1]

JRT – Job Readiness Training.
WAT – Work Adjustment Training.
BTSD – Basic Training for Skill Development.

1   Represents the amount spent by Employment and Immigration Canada on the purchase of training services from provincial institutions, private schools, and industry.

SOURCE   Based on data from Employment and Immigration Canada.

training. In addition to paying for the actual training, Ottawa provides allowances for the trainees (or, if they are eligible, unemployment insurance benefits) and contributes to other expenses associated with dependant care, commuting, and living away from home. By law, CMTP courses can last no longer than 52 weeks.

Different types of institutional programs are available within CMTP (see Chart 8-2). These include the development of specific vocational skills (Skill Training); the classroom component of provincial apprenticeships; academic upgrading (Basic Training for Skill Development); language training for immigrants;

Under both of the industrial training initiatives (CMITP and CTST), the federal government reimburses employers for certain costs incurred in providing on-the-job instruction, following agreement between both parties. With a 52-week course ceiling, CMITP is targeted towards the development of lower-level skills. Participating employers may be reimbursed for direct training costs, such as instructors' salaries and expenses, training aids, and course fees. Trainee wages, too, are covered to some degree under CMITP; the extent of repayment varies according to the characteristics of the trainee. In particular, the reimbursement scale is designed to provide incentives for employers to train the unemployed or workers whose jobs are threatened, women destined to nontraditional jobs, and workers with "special needs."

The CTST initiative, introduced during 1979/80, is intended to assist employers in training workers in skilled trades that are persistently in short supply. In design, CTST is very similar to CMITP. Employers are reimbursed for training costs, as well as all or part of the trainees' wages. This program differs, however, in the duration of the assistance provided. In order to address higher-level skills, this program offers financial support for up to two years. In its initial year of operation, less than $1 million was spent on 500 trainees under CTST. A significant expansion was planned for 1980/81, with $30 million budgeted for 7,500 trainees.

In addition to authorizing the federal government to purchase training services, AOTA also provides for a Manpower Needs Committee (MNC) in every province, to assess labour requirements and recommend training plans and priorities.[5] Each MNC consists of senior officials from both levels of governments. Supporting these committees are a number of training or technical subcommittees, which tend to be staffed by project managers and specialists from both levels of government and, in some cases, from the education system.

Particularly in recent years, the training programs offered under AOTA have been criticized extensively. While many problems have been cited, the most obvious failure of the system has been its inability to produce the skilled workers needed for the economy. Critics of AOTA point out its lack of responsiveness to changes in labour market conditions and contend that bottlenecks have persisted and that economic growth and stabilization have been impeded considerably. The cost of Ottawa's training activities has been climbing towards the $1 billion mark, yet this grand-scale effort has been unable to redress the critical labour imbalances that we face.

As a result of these developments, the federal government recently announced plans to replace AOTA and its programs with new legislation. We will return to this proposal later in this chapter, but, as we shall see below, it is clear that the training system must be focused more closely on labour demand.

Vocational Training

The relatively weak responsiveness of the training system to labour demand has been the result of at least two factors. In the first place, it is not clear that the central objective of publicly sponsored training – specifically, the AOTA programs – has been to meet the needs of the market. And, second, even if that were the primary goal, the data needed to forecast those needs accurately have been inadequate.

Information Shortcomings

Let us look first at the information issue. Manpower programs, in general – and training initiatives, in particular – require detailed and forward-looking occupational data. As the Economic Council wrote in its Eighth Annual Review, this is indeed a formidable task:

> Data are required on labour demand and supply, with considerable detail on both occupation and geographical areas. Further, since the aim of manpower policy is to anticipate, and therefore prevent, structural maladjustments in the labour market, what is really required is highly detailed prospective information – i.e., projections of manpower needs by occupation and area, together with projections of supply from training institutions and other sources.[6]

The Council went on to note that, despite great efforts, many data problems remained unresolved. That is still true today. The information needed to implement responsive programs is still unavailable – a situation that undoubtedly affects the training decisions made at all levels from Ottawa down to the Canada Employment Centres.

Data shortcomings render the identification of imbalances in this country an extremely problematic exercise. Not only are there the usual problems associated with "looking ahead," but there are also, as we noted in Chapters 3 and 4, basic deficiencies with respect to current detailed occupational information. The paucity of data on training in industry is a glaring example of this – one that is particularly germane to this chapter.

Within the context of effective public training policy, information on skill development in the private sector would seem indispensable on at least two counts. First, the recipients of training in industry should be considered in the identification of imbalances. Second, if an essential reason for public intervention is to provide for training that would not otherwise be carried out, it would seem reasonable for private-sector activity to be taken into account by government decision makers.

Risks are involved, then, in instituting government programs without greater knowledge of the training effort in industry.[7] In fact, the data gathered by our own Human Resources Survey (HRS) suggest that public initiatives — notably those under AOTA — are directed precisely towards those types of training which employers are likely to carry out on their own. In other words, rather than complement the training activity within industry, government programs often displace private efforts.

According to the HRS results, while 60 per cent of the participating establishments reported some skill development activity, most of them provided short-term training only. In fact, no more than 20 per cent of the firms sampled had instituted programs of at least one year's duration.[8]

The picture painted by the Human Resources Survey, then, is that employers are quite willing to undertake training that lasts for brief periods of time; they are far less likely, however, to carry out protracted development programs. Obviously, the greater cost associated with the latter type of training is an inhibiting factor. One would therefore expect government assistance to be particularly important in the decision of firms to institute long-term programs; and, according to the HRS results, this is indeed the case. Despite the fact that public initiatives are oriented towards brief periods of support, the presence of some government funding was over three times greater in 1980 for programs lasting 52 weeks or longer than for those lasting less than one month (Chart 8-3).

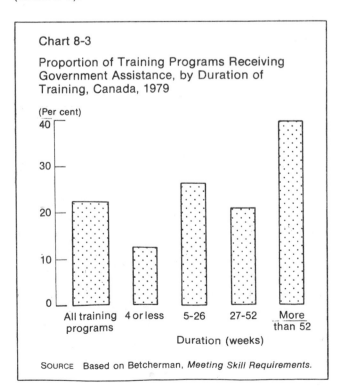

Chart 8-3

Proportion of Training Programs Receiving Government Assistance, by Duration of Training, Canada, 1979

(Per cent)

All training programs / 4 or less / 5-26 / 27-52 / More than 52

Duration (weeks)

SOURCE Based on Betcherman, *Meeting Skill Requirements.*

The propensity of employers to carry out short-term training certainly casts doubt on the brief-duration emphasis of AOTA, since much of the training that has been supported by public funds would likely have been undertaken even if such assistance had been unavailable.

An Unsteady Focus

Another shortcoming of public training initiatives has been that the programs have not been focused exclusively, or even primarily, on this sort of objective. The AOTA programs have tried to serve both efficiency and equity considerations; and, at least as far as market-oriented training is concerned, this has posed problems.

The rhetoric accompanying the inception of AOTA suggested that the new Act was geared, first and foremost, to the development of a productive labour force. Initially, emphasis was placed on the link between the nation's economic success and the vocational skills of its people. Later, this priority on the growth objective shifted somewhat towards stabilization and then, towards equity. In the past few years, the emphasis seems to have reverted to efficiency goals.

It may well be that the multiple, and sometimes changing, orientations of AOTA have limited its effectiveness in pursuing *any* of its goals. Because AOTA was designed with the objectives of equity and efficiency both in mind, it was not tailored, in effect, to treat either one optimally. In other words, although equity and efficiency considerations are somewhat interrelated, they are perhaps exclusive enough to warrant quite different policy prescriptions.

This is evident when public initiatives are evaluated on the basis of their responsiveness to labour demand. From an efficiency point of view, the volume of training should be positively linked to labour demand. This, of course, is predicated on the fact that economically active areas have the greatest need for skilled workers. Examination of the geographical distribution of AOTA-sponsored activity shows, however, that a disproportionate amount of training under the federal government programs has occurred in those parts of the country which exhibit relatively poor employment prospects (Table 8-1). The Atlantic provinces, for example, accounted for only 7.6 per cent of the country's employment in 1979 and for only 7.1 per cent of the increase in jobs during the preceding half-decade. Yet, during 1979/80, that region had 13.4 per cent of AOTA's trainees. Similarly, Quebec's share of the overall training effort was greater than its employment and growth would seem to warrant. In comparison, Ontario and the four western provinces accounted for over two-thirds of Canada's jobs and for more than three-quarters of the recent employment growth, but for only 55 per cent of the trainees.

Table 8-1

Distribution of Employment, Employment Growth, and AOTA Trainees,[1] by Region, Canada, 1975 to 1980

	Employment, 1979	Employment growth, 1975-79	AOTA trainees, 1979//80
	(Per cent)		
Atlantic region	7.6	7.1	13.4
Quebec	25.1	15.5	31.3
Ontario	38.6	39.8	27.0
Prairie region	17.8	25.2	16.1
British Columbia	10.9	12.4	12.2
Canada	100.0	100.0	100.0

1 Trainees starting in 1979/80 under the Adult Occupational Training Act.
SOURCE Based on data from Employment and Immigration Canada; and Statistics Canada, *Historical Labour Force Statistics - Actual Data, Seasonal Factors, Seasonally Adjusted Data, 1980* (Ottawa: Supply and Services Canada, 1980).

To some extent, then, AOTA has been aimed at reducing regional disparities. The problem with this strategy is that in those parts of the country where training activity is disproportionately great, there are few opportunities available for those who complete the programs.[9] So, "if the jobs aren't there, what's the point of training?"

Clearly, an important point is that the AOTA programs have been used in an attempt to address unemployment, which is particularly high in the Atlantic provinces and Quebec. In fact, a very high proportion of all AOTA trainees have been drawn from the ranks of the jobless. This is particularly true on the institutional side, which accounts for almost three-quarters of the overall effort (Table 8-2).

Table 8-2

Distribution of Full-Time AOTA Trainees,[1] by Prior Labour Force Status and by Type of Training, Canada, 1979/80

	Type of training	
	Institutional	Industrial
	(Per cent)	
Prior labour force status		
Unemployed	72.3	43.7
Not in labour force	14.0	8.6
Employed	13.7	47.7
Total	100.0	100.0
Number of trainees	176,483	83,334

1 Trainees starting in 1979/80 under the Adult Occupational Training Act.
SOURCE Based on data from Employment and Immigration Canada; and Statistics Canada, *Historical Labour Force Statistics – Actual Data, Seasonal Factors, Seasonally Adjusted Data, 1980* (Ottawa: Supply and Services Canada, 1980).

Linking AOTA to equity considerations through its function of "soaking up unemployment" does impede the efficiency of the programs and, more particularly, their responsiveness to the demand for labour. Not only has the distribution of training been inversely

Table 8-3

Distribution of Employment, Job Vacancies, and AOTA Trainees,[1] by Occupation, Canada, 1977 to 1980

	Employment, 1979	Job vacancies,[2] 1977-79	AOTA trainees, 1979/80	
			CMTP skill training	CMITP
		(Per cent)		
Managerial and professional	22.9	16.8	10.5	9.1
Clerical	17.1	5.4	24.7	8.5
Sales	10.4	6.0	1.4	6.6
Service	12.9	7.6	9.7	6.1
Primary	6.4	8.8	6.6	5.5
Processing	15.8	42.1	28.1	44.2
Construction trades	6.4	8.0	10.1	6.3
Other trades, crafts	8.1	5.2	8.9	13.7
Total	100.0	100.0	100.0	100.0

1 Trainees starting in 1979/80 under the Adult Occupational Training Act; CMTP: Canada Manpower Training Program; CMITP: Canada Manpower Industrial Training Program.
2 Estimated data from the Human Resources Survey.
SOURCE Data from Statistics Canada, Economic Council of Canada, and Employment and Immigration Canada.

related, to some extent, to regional patterns of economic activity and hence to the needs of the market, but the strong orientation of AOTA towards alleviating unemployment has not facilitated the development of those skills which are in greatest demand.

The skill training provided under AOTA has not met the more critical occupational demands. As can be seen in Table 8-3, this is particularly true for the CMTP activities. Using data from our Human Resources Survey to identify the occupational dimension of labour demand, it is obvious, for example, that there has been an institutional overemphasis on clerical training. On the other hand, market conditions would seem to suggest the need for more skill training courses in the managerial, professional, and processing categories.

The lack of responsiveness of the AOTA programs is even greater when one considers the 52-week limit placed on training assistance in both the CMTP and CMITP. This is particularly significant, since labour demand tends to be greatest for middle- and high-level skills, which require rather lengthy periods of instruction.

The New Federal Proposal

In January 1982, the Minister of Employment and Immigration unveiled a new proposal, known as the National Training Plan. Presumably, this proposal will act as the basis for discussion in federal-provincial training negotiations. While not all of the details of the new policy have been spelled out publicly, it is clear that its primary intent is to make government efforts more responsive to the needs of the labour market.

In pursuing this objective, Ottawa proposes to shift its training dollars away from lower-level skills — for which there are few apparent job opportunities — towards middle- and high-level skills, for which the demand is greater. To this end, the federal government proposes to finance the capital and start-up costs of new facilities designed to provide training in occupations where shortages exist. Current public programs would also be modified to reflect the new orientation. Greater emphasis would be placed on industrial training, particularly for high-demand skills, while institutional instruction would be cut back somewhat. Moreover, funding for the latter would become more closely tied to anticipated job prospects. It should be pointed out that, in addition to changing the mix of industrial, institutional, and skill-

level programs, the National Training Program would also result in a substantial regional shift in activity towards the West, where employment growth is most rapid.

This initiative represents the first major policy reform in the training area in 15 years. In the opinion of many observers, this reform is long overdue. The federal proposal constitutes a recognition of the failure of existing arrangements to produce the skills required. The juggling of objectives, characteristic of the AOTA period, does not seem to be part of the spirit underlying the National Training Program. In its present form, at least, the emphasis is undoubtedly on the elimination of shortages.

Central to such an approach, of course, is the ability to anticipate future imbalances. As noted above, such ability has generally been lacking until now. Accordingly, the development of an accurate occupational information and projection system represents the cornerstone of the federal proposal. It is envisioned that conventional employment forecasting models and qualitative information from a number of sources — including the private sector, educational institutions, and provincial governments — will be reconciled in some fashion in order to identify future shortages and surpluses. These estimates, then, would be used as the basis for allocating federal training funds.

Provincial Initiatives

It should be noted that some provincial governments have already established priority on improved information. Alberta, Ontario, and British Columbia, in particular, have made significant efforts in this area in recent years. In fact, the federal government's vision of a system for identifying the training needs through forecasting models and extensive data collection corresponds broadly to the approaches already in place in these provinces.

Provincial initiatives aimed at encouraging market-oriented training are not limited to information gathering. For example, in Ontario, we have seen the development of a network of community training councils, composed of representatives from industry, labour, and the education sector. The more successful of these councils appear to have been very effective in identifying local manpower needs and marshalling available resources to provide the required training. This type of arrangement is particularly advantageous with respect to the delivery of training. Educational institutes and employers are able to co-ordinate classroom and on-the-job periods; in some cases, groups of employers sponsor trainees, thus reducing the risks and costs for any single firm.

Labour demand pressures in Western Canada have stimulated provincial governments in that region to intensify their vocational education efforts. Alberta has witnessed an impressive escalation in its apprenticeship programs: in the past five years, enrolment has nearly doubled, and that province now accounts for over one-quarter of the country's apprentices. In both Alberta and Saskatchewan, training opportunities for trades and technology have increased through the opening of new facilities and through the expansion of "outreach" initiatives, designed to spread training programs beyond the urban centres.

Special Considerations

Although responsiveness to anticipated labour demand must be central to a future training system in this country, there are equity-related considerations that should also be addressed by policy makers. Canadians do not share equally in the benefits associated with the labour market. An analysis of unemployment in this country (see Chapter 6) reveals a surprisingly high incidence of long-term joblessness. Moreover, among those with jobs, there are significant discrepancies in wages, benefits, opportunities for advancement, and conditions of work. While such variations are unavoidable, at least to some extent, it is disturbing that these poor labour market outcomes, with attendant hardships, seem to be concentrated among certain segments of the population.

It is our view that governments must take the lead in improving the work-related prospects of all Canadians. As we argued in Chapter 6, for example, a strong and precisely targeted employment creation program is needed to address the considerable long-term component of the country's joblessness. Indeed, a persuasive case could be made for transferring to job creation some of the public monies previously used for low-level training. Rather than developing people with productive and desirable skills, much of the activity under AOTA has seemingly served merely as a temporary palliative for unemployment. In many situations, creating employment would seem preferable to carrying out training courses that do not lead to stable and rewarding work.

While the best training for a job may just simply be a job, there is still a place for education and training as a policy mechanism by which to pursue equity considerations. A case in point is the problem of functional illiteracy, which is surprisingly extensive in Canada. While there are definitional difficulties associated with this phenomenon, if one considers as functionally illiterate people who are at least 15 years of age, who are not attending school full-time, and who have only completed Grade 8 or less, there were over 4 million Canadians in that category in 1976,

according to that year's Census. As might be expected, employment-related problems figure prominently among the myriad of difficulties experienced by these people. In comparison with the national average, their rate of joblessness is high, and their employment is largely restricted to low-paying jobs. Certainly, such hardship could be reduced if education credentials were eliminated from jobs or training positions where they bear no relationship to performance. On the other hand, literacy and mathematical skills, at least at the basic level, are undoubtedly necessary for most types of employment.

In addition to providing for basic adult education, governments must also continue to recognize skill training as a vehicle for overcoming the traditional barriers that have restricted labour market opportunities for certain groups of Canadians. These barriers, often based on stereotypes, are particularly evident in the case of women and the native people. Admittedly, the development of vocational skills cannot be viewed as a panacea for these groups. Yet, at a time when particular kinds of shortages are so prominent, there is reason to believe that workers, regardless of their demographic characteristics, have better access to stable and well-paying employment if they have the needed skills. Training programs, focused on occupations in demand, could thus lead to an opportune wedding of both equity and efficiency objectives.

Women

The experience of women in the labour market has generally not been good. Their story has become quite familiar: located, for the most part, in "job ghettos" — the clerical, sales, and service occupations — women have tended to be concentrated in low-income positions with relatively little opportunity for advancement. While some movement of female workers into managerial and professional skills has been witnessed in recent years, the persistent overall wage differential between the sexes testifies to the real lack of progress. Moreover, if today's trainees are tomorrow's workers, there is little reason to believe that change is imminent. Of all the women who started CMTP Skill Training in 1979/80, some 54 per cent were enrolled in clerical-related courses, and 14 per cent were training for service occupations.[10] Over two-thirds, then, were receiving vocational preparation for traditional female jobs that are not in high demand.

Demand continues to be great, however, for many high-level, blue-collar skills. With the expectations that women will account for a major share of labour force growth in upcoming years, it would seem advantageous for them to enter these critical short-age positions. Yet the data show that trainees in such occupations remain almost exclusively male. In fact, in 1979/80, men accounted for 95.2 per cent of the CMTP machining trainees and for 81.4 per cent of those in product fabricating and repair. Provincial apprenticeship programs represent another means of entry into high-demand trades; but, here as well, women are not participating. In Ontario, for example, when hairdressing and cooking trainees are excluded, only 0.4 per cent of the apprentices in 1979 were female.

The failure of women to escape the job ghettos and move into better-paying, high-skill work is undoubtedly a complex phenomenon. Although many of these occupations are characterized by critical shortages, they have been historically dominated by men; and, as we know well, attitudes die hard. Socialization patterns exert a strong influence on individual expectations, and the traditional sex roles persist. While counselling within education and at employment centres may offer opportunities for altering the status quo, there is little evidence that this is happening. According to testimony received by the Parliamentary Task Force on Employment Opportunities for the '80s, some "outreach" counselling projects, designed to broaden employment horizons for women, have been successful. The overall impact of such initiatives, however, has been limited by their small numbers, as well as by tenuous and short-term public funding practices.

Even if women choose to enter traditionally male-dominated occupations, they often face another rigidity in the form of employer attitudes. A federal government program was recently instituted to address problems of this nature. This program, Non Traditional Training for Women, will fund 75 per cent of the wages of women being trained in generally male-dominated occupations. Unfortunately, at the present time only $2 million has been allocated for this initiative.

Looking ahead, the segregation of women in the labour market poses another concern, in that many of the traditional areas of female employment may be jeopardized by the anticipated trends stemming from technological innovations. More specifically, the diffusion of the microchip is likely to have a major effect on the clerical occupations, which account for about one-third of all female jobs. While the eventual impact of this technological development is uncertain, it appears likely that the demand for clerical skills will diminish. A recent study concluded that, depending on its diffusion rate and its productivity effect, the chip could result in an unemployment rate of up to 35 per cent for female clerical workers by 1990.[11] Much of this job loss could well be offset by the increased demand for technical and professional workers; however, according to the study, few of the displaced workers have access to the training opportunities required to fill the new positions. The sober conclusion of the study is that, unless women move away from traditional jobs into demand-oriented occupations, they will likely face severe structural unemployment in the 1990s.

The Indigenous Peoples

The work-related problems of the native people — the Indians, the Metis, and the Inuit — is another major issue of concern in this country. While the lack of data precludes a precise empirical description, it is obvious that the situation is lamentable. As noted in Chapter 2, unemployment among the native people is higher than for any other segment of Canadian society. Those who are employed are largely confined to unskilled jobs, characterized by low wages and poor prospects for advancement.

All indications suggest that in the 1980s native people will become an increasingly important component of the labour supply. Because they experienced a later baby boom and their participation rates are rising, the working-age native population is expected to grow at an annual rate of 2.9 per cent during the 1980s — well over double that projected for the rest of the country.[12] Much of this growth will occur in Western Canada, where the strongest labour demand pressures are anticipated. Accordingly, opportunities should exist for improved labour market experiences for native people. Indeed, serious imbalances would seem inevitable without their increased employment in high-demand occupations.

Unfortunately, the obstacles to be overcome are great. The current problems of natives in the labour market derive from the historical experiences that have followed the arrival of the first Europeans to the New World. Cultural, political, and economic factors have, together, shaped the developments that have taken place since that time. The universal nature of the situation facing the native people in this country was emphasized in many of the presentations made to the Parliamentary Task Force. Repeatedly it was stressed that employment problems must not be viewed in isolation and that they are inseparable from the rest of the native's reality. Accordingly, the National Indian Brotherhood and others have rejected "band-aid" government involvement as the preferred course of action. Rather, they argue, an enhanced level of unconditional development funding, administered by the native communities, would constitute a more appropriate economic strategy.

While it is not the purview of this report to examine the ramifications of this overall problem, it is clear that, whatever the arrangements, greater opportunities for education and training will be necessary. Admittedly, the development of skills cannot be viewed as the only solution to the labour market problems of native people. Nevertheless, basic deficiencies in education and an overall lack of skill training are major barriers at present. And, while market segmentation and discrimination are undoubtedly significant obstacles, it is important to note that a study on natives in the Winnipeg area found that the level of education did have a positive impact on employment experiences.[13]

Earlier, the problems associated with a lack of basic educational skills were briefly discussed. This issue is certainly applicable to the native population, which is characterized by very high dropout rates. This lack of general education bars many natives from access to training courses and to employment. Yet, surprisingly enough, in recent years the federal government has discontinued adult education programs on Indian reserves. Without these basic capabilities, the natives are unable to receive training in many of the skills that are currently in such short supply in the western and northern regions of the country.

To conclude, it must be emphasized that the attitude underlying any training or education efforts involving natives is of critical importance. Cultural differences and a history of discrimination would seem to make self-determination an attractive feature of any program. Indeed, it is in this spirit that developmental funding has been recommended. Government money is necessary if the native people are to experience improved labour market outcomes. On the basis of past experiences, however, the benefits of such funding appear greatest when decision making is carried out within the native population.

Other Avenues for Skill Development

In addition to public occupational training programs, there are other avenues for the development of vocational skills. Most prominent among these are apprenticeship training and postsecondary education. Provisions for continuing education are also relevant to our concerns in this chapter.

Apprenticeship Training

Apprenticeships are essentially an institutionalized form of training that mixes classroom and on-the-job instruction. A discussion of apprenticeships in Canada is complicated somewhat by two features of the prevailing arrangements. First of all, there is the distinction between registered and nonregistered programs; because only the former explicitly involves governments, our focus here will be on this type. Second, the registered or public apprenticeships are provincially controlled, and there is considerable variation in the operation of the different systems. Thus, while the federal government does not play a central role in apprenticeship training, it is involved nevertheless, through funding for the institutional component and through the Red Seal program, which is concerned with the national standardization of provincial certificates.

A primary virtue of apprenticeship training is its incorporation of both institutional and industrial components. From a pedagogical point of view, the best method of transmitting skills is, in many cases, through such a mixed approach. Industrial training, because it takes place "on the job," ensures that the skills transmitted are relevant and up-to-date. Moreover, familiarity with other aspects of work, such as health and safety, will inevitably accompany the actual vocational development. Institutional instruction, for its part, provides a theoretical background that not only facilitates on-the-job learning but is essential for future adaptability to new techniques. In addition to the mixed format, regulation of the curriculum and standards of most apprenticeship programs ensures that they will produce workers with an accepted competency over a comprehensive package of skills.

In recent years, the effectiveness of Canada's apprenticeship systems has been called into question. More than anything, this criticism has been associated with the shortages in high-skill, blue-collar occupations, many of which are apprenticeable trades. While an apprenticeship-style approach has much to offer, then, there are clearly problems with the existing arrangements in this country. It has therefore become appropriate to ask whether it is desirable to maintain this form of training and, if it is, how the programs could be improved.

The most prominent signal of the difficulties of the apprenticeship system has been the overall inability of the programs to produce the numbers of skilled workers needed by the economy. While there has been impressive growth in some provinces, notably Alberta, apprenticeship training on a national basis has not experienced the expansion that one would expect, given the excess demand for many trades (see Chart 8-4). This is particularly true of the industrial trades, where the annual output of less than 3,000 new journeymen seems very inadequate.

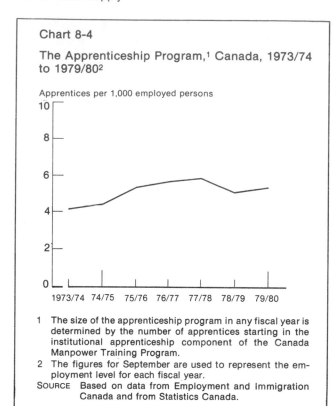

Chart 8-4

The Apprenticeship Program,[1] Canada, 1973/74 to 1979/80[2]

Apprentices per 1,000 employed persons

1 The size of the apprenticeship program in any fiscal year is determined by the number of apprentices starting in the institutional apprenticeship component of the Canada Manpower Training Program.
2 The figures for September are used to represent the employment level for each fiscal year.
SOURCE   Based on data from Employment and Immigration Canada and from Statistics Canada.

In a critical look at the present systems, entry, the training process, and certification all merit close attention. Facilitating entry, of course, is essential to the expansion of the trades "pipeline." The relatively low social status associated with blue-collar occupations unfortunately remains a significant barrier that is understandably difficult to disassemble. Furthermore, with the high degree of subsidization of schooling and the lifelong patterns of income returns to postsecondary education, an apprenticeship in the trades has simply not been a rational career choice for many young people. The need for the potential apprentices to find an employer willing to hire and train them represents another disadvantage. The duration of apprenticeships is generally three or four years, and employers tend to be reluctant to undertake lengthy and costly training of this nature, particularly during downturns in the business cycle. It has to be said, however, that the apprentices who are brought in during these periods will be fully trained and productive when output picks up a few years later.

Some barriers to entry are institutional in nature; educational requirements, in particular, have been cited as unnecessarily high. In some trades, for example, high school completion is demanded. As a result, many who are not academically oriented but who may have vocational talents are excluded. Indeed, the considerable variation, internationally,

with respect to educational requirements certainly casts doubt about whether Canadian standards are too high.

The content of training programs varies considerably between provinces. It is agreed, however, that the quality of the on-the-job component is generally a problem. While the apprentice/journeyman ratios are intended to avoid such problems, they are not always sufficient. As a result, a number of provinces are using additional mechanisms to improve the employer-based component. Saskatchewan, Manitoba, and Nova Scotia, for example, have attempted to provide improved information and counselling to industry. British Columbia, on the other hand, has enforced stricter quality regulations. Other provinces, such as Alberta, Newfoundland, and Ontario, are employing a combination of these two approaches. A strengthened institutional component, better linked to the on-the-job portion, can also upgrade the overall training quality. A lengthy introductory segment in the classroom, for example, is one modification of this type, whereby a strong foundation can be established, enabling the trainee to benefit more from subsequent on-the-job instruction.

In light of Canada's regional imbalances, it is vitally important for skilled people to be able to work in different parts of the country. With our 12 different apprenticeship systems, however, it is not surprising that certification problems exist. Many occupations, for example, are apprenticeable trades in some provinces and not in others. As of the end of 1980, apprenticeship programs were provided for 153 occupations; of these, only 11 were designated as apprenticeable trades in every jurisdiction.

Where certification does exist, the standards required may well vary considerably. Accordingly, a national Red Seal program has been set up to establish interprovincial assessments and certification. While this program included only 23 trades in 1981, they covered 80 per cent of the country's apprentices. Thus, in most cases, certification at the provincial level is not, in itself, an obstacle; however, more serious problems stem from differences between jurisdictions in terms of the quality of training.

Postsecondary Education

While the arrangements for training constitute the primary focus of this chapter, our analysis would not be complete without some mention of the education system, particularly at the postsecondary level. The colleges and universities of Canada have a number of functions, among which is the provision of a highly qualified population, well endowed with intellectual, scientific, and technical resources. In making observations and drawing conclusions about postsecondary education, we limit ourselves to this vocational development aspect – a focus dictated only by the theme of our report.

From this limited perspective, the central issue facing the postsecondary system concerns its ability to respond to the demand for skills. Some interesting data, relevant to this question, can be found in the results of a recent Statistics Canada survey, which questioned 1976 graduates about their career development two years after having completed their studies.[14] The findings of this project must be interpreted with some caution, primarily because of the limitations associated with any solitary, "one-shot" effort. Nevertheless, the data do tell us something about the responsiveness of postsecondary education.

Overall, a surprisingly small proportion of the university graduates seemed to be making optimal use of their educational investment once they were in the labour market. Their unemployment rate was 8.2 per cent – a level very close to the national figure at the time of the survey (Table 8-4).[15] Moreover, the incidence of respondents either underemployed or doing work unrelated to past studies suggests that, in many instances, the transition from school to work for many university graduates does not occur in the manner that one might expect.

The apparent absence of "fit" between field of study and subsequent employment, however, need not necessarily occasion surprise or alarm. From the standpoint of neither the worker nor even the employer should such a fit be necessary. From the individual's point of view, considerations other than career may determine fields of study. For employers, educational qualification is frequently a screening device that aids in the selection of candidates for training on the job.

The absence of such correspondence seems particularly evident in general fields – such as the social sciences and the humanities, which together accounted for about 40 per cent of all university graduates – that do not have strong labour market orientations. On the other hand, professional and technical disciplines, which enjoyed favourable employment outcomes, had relatively small enrolments.

The survey results show that, in comparison with the universities, college programs are more responsive to the needs of the labour market (Table 8-5). Given the stronger training mandate of the colleges, this could be expected.

Table 8-4

Labour Force Experience of 1976 University Graduates, by Field of Study, Canada,[1] June 1978

		Labour force experience[2]		
	Number of graduates	Unemployment rate	Employed in work unrelated to studies	Employed who are "underemployed"
		(Per cent)		
Business, management, and commerce	5,030	4.4	8.9	27.6
Education	12,769	4.6	11.7	26.8
Fine and applied arts	2,115	14.3	20.0	38.5
Humanities	10,888	10.8	28.2	45.9
Social sciences	17,479	10.0	26.3	42.7
Agriculture and biology	5,443	11.0	25.3	37.5
Engineering and applied sciences	3,573	4.4	7.4	13.8
Health	3,266	4.4	2.7	18.8
Mathematics and physical sciences	4,274	9.7	18.1	29.8
General	759	8.5	24.3	46.8
All graduates	66,481	8.2	18.8	34.3

1 Excluding Quebec.
2 Based on three separate tabulations.
SOURCE W. Clark and Z. Zsigmond, *Job Market Reality for Postsecondary Graduates* (Ottawa: Statistics Canada, 1981).

Table 8-5

Labour Force Experience of 1976 College Graduates, by Field of Study, Canada,[1] June 1978

| | Number of graduates | Unemployment rate | Labour force experience[2] | |
			Employed doing work unrelated to studies	Employed who are "underemployed"
		(Per cent)		
Business, management, and commerce	3,103	6.4	17.4	39.9
Community service and social welfare	2,400	10.0	12.8	28.7
Data processing and computer science	556	--	7.5	19.8
Fine, applied, and performing arts	1,309	11.9	26.7	36.1
General arts, science, education, and law	1,861	8.3	18.4	28.6
Mass communications	827	6.8	16.3	37.2
Medical and dental services	7,624	6.1	3.3	6.2
Primary industries	1,183	7.2	15.2	28.4
Secretarial arts and science	2,188	5.6	8.0	40.9
Technological	4,273	5.2	11.7	28.9
Transportation	290	--	19.5	52.7
All graduates	26,250	6.7	11.1	25.3

1 Excluding Quebec.
2 Based on three separate tabulations.
SOURCE Clark and Zsigmond, *Job Market Reality*.

It should be noted that in recent years there appears to have been some response in postsecondary enrolments to labour demands. Evidence of this is provided in Table 8-6, which documents the growth in business and engineering faculties over the past eight years. Nevertheless, data such as those collected in Statistics Canada's survey on graduates suggest that stresses related to the labour market do result from the existing orientation of postsecondary education in this country. A complex industrial economy does have impressive requirements for highly educated scientific and technical personnel; in the light of the shortages in many highly qualified skills, it appears that these needs are not being adequately met in Canada.

Opportunities for Continuing Development

Another area that should be addressed in a critical review of existing public policy is that of adult education and training. Thus far, government intervention in the development of human resources has been directed, for the most part, towards young people entering the labour force. Evidence of this focus on youth comes from an examination of the demographic characteristics of government-sponsored trainees. In 1979/80, for example, over half of those who started training under CMTP and CMITP were single, and close to three-quarters had no dependants. One of every two participants was under 25 years of age.

Table 8-6

University Enrolments[1] in Engineering and Applied Sciences, Commerce and Business Administration, and All Disciplines, Canada, 1972-73 and 1980-81

| | 1972/73 | | 1980/81 (preliminary) | | Annual growth rate, 1972/73 to 1980/81 |
	Number	Proportion	Number	Proportion	
		(Per cent)		(Per cent)	(Per cent)
Engineering and applied sciences	27,111	6.5	41,696	7.5	6.7
Commerce and business administration	33,712	8.1	72,823	13.2	14.5
All disciplines	417,397	100.0	552,738	100.0	4.1

1 Enrolments include full-time and part-time students at the undergraduate level.
SOURCE Statistics Canada, *Education in Canada*, Cat. 81-229, 1975 and 1981

Generally, then, existing initiatives are primarily concerned with the transition from the school system to the world of work. There is little, if any, provision for a "life-cycle" view of education and training sharing the stage with employment. For a number of reasons, it would now appear more important than ever that public policies incorporate such a perspective. In the first place, the traditional notion of the one-career work cycle is becoming less relevant. Economic shifts and technological innovations are occurring with increasing rapidity; as a consequence, there is a diminished guarantee that there will always be a demand for the occupation in which one was initially trained. Also, demographic developments, such as the aging of the population, will inevitably lead to shifts in participation patterns; and these, in turn, will dictate changing education and training requisites. The emergence of new sociocultural values, too, must be considered. The growing emphasis on personal development can be expected to lead to an increased demand for lifelong education and training opportunities.

In light of factors such as these, there has been a growing interest in concepts related to the educational development of working adults. In Canada, this issue was recently investigated by a special commission of inquiry under the auspices of the federal Department of Labour. Its findings were not particularly encouraging, as the Commission concluded that "the opportunities available to working Canadians to prepare for occupational careers, to advance upward in organizational hierarchies, and to upgrade and maintain their skills are inadequate."[16] The commission also pointed out that opportunities for general educational development and trade union education were quite insufficient.

Compared with Canada, the European experience is superior. The federal group found that, at least with respect to vocational training and trade union education, possibilities do exist in Western Europe for the continued development of adult workers. These have been ensured, in all cases, by government intervention; in order for such opportunities to exist in Canada, public policies will need to address the issue of lifelong education and training.

Future Directions

Our examination of training and vocational education has led us to emphasize its importance in the pursuit of a wide range of economic and social goals. Although public expenditures in this area have been relatively high, there are strong indications that the present arrangements need to be reconsidered.

Obviously, the critical shortages in several occupations attest to the fact that the demands of the labour market are not being adequately met. Moreover, there is little evidence to suggest that the existing initiatives have been very successful in improving the opportunities for Canadians with poor employment prospects.

These observations lead us to conclude that Canada needs fresh approaches to the development of vocational skills. The challenge for the policy maker in this area is essentially twofold: first, to reduce employment and income disparities; and, second, to strengthen the contribution of vocational education and training to economic performance and development. While these two concerns are somewhat interrelated, we believe that they are sufficiently distinct to warrant separate policy attention. Indeed, we believe that it was the failure to do so that undermined the effectiveness of the AOTA programs.

With respect to equity considerations, we are convinced that there is an important role to be played by government. We do not believe, however, that short-term, low-skill training programs, such as those offered under CMTP, constitute the best method for improving employment prospects when work is generally unavailable. Rather, a more promising approach might well rest with greater emphasis on job creation, particularly through the targeted use of wage subsidies.

Naturally, we do not rule out the usefulness of education and training as mechanisms for pursuing equity-related objectives. Functional illiteracy, for example, impedes the labour market participation of a surprisingly high number of Canadians; in these cases, educational upgrading is obviously necessary. In addition, there is a need for considerably greater training activity within certain segments of society such as women and the native people. Until now, these and other groups have faced a variety of social, cultural, and political barriers in the labour market. The result has been high rates of joblessness and/or relegation into low-skill, low-wage occupations. During the 1980s, natives and women, in particular, will swell Canada's labour supply to a degree heretofore unparalleled; as a consequence, it will be necessary to provide for them employment possibilities that were previously denied. The realization of these opportunities will depend on a number of factors, including access to training.

Future growth in this country will depend on an improved domestic capacity to develop the skills needed by the economy. We have found many faults with the existing arrangements. In fact, with these problems in mind, we have come to question the present allocation of responsibilities for training between the private and public sectors. Many observers, including the Commission on Educational Leave and Productivity and the Parliamentary Task Force on Employment Opportunities for the '80s, have determined that there should be a significant shift in these responsibilities.

Those two task forces are joined by a number of other voices in recommending some form of levy-grant or levy-credit scheme. While there are some attractive features to this option, they should not obscure its undeniable problems.[17] In Britain, for example, the levy-grant initially changed the training behaviour of employers in the desired fashion, but it is not clear whether this trend continued. Moreover, this experience has provided first-rate evidence that bureaucracy is not only a government phenomenon. By all accounts, the system has been an administrative nightmare. In addition, the levy-grant poses particular difficulties for small firms, which for a variety of reasons tend to be the net losers overall. In fact, in recognition of this, the British government has excluded small establishments from the system for the past nine years.

While the shortcomings of a national industrial levy-grant scheme cannot be ignored, this approach does question the role of government, and it also reminds us of the responsibilities of the private sector in the development of vocational skills. This is not to say that government has no part to play in training for the needs of the economy. For a variety of reasons, the labour market does not work in true "textbook fashion." Accordingly, we recognize the need for selective public policies facilitating the kind of training that would not likely occur without intervention.

It is apparent that the success of future programs will depend greatly on an improved process for identifying training needs. To understand the Canadian labour market, its diversity must be recognized. Impressive documentation of this need has been collected by the Parliamentary Task Force; from the reams of evidence heard by this body, diversity alone seems to have emerged as a constant.

The implications of this variation for labour market policies are obvious. No monolithic system can reasonably be expected to accommodate the wide range of needs in this country, although this is essentially what past arrangements have tried to do. Uniform programs can conceivably respond to regional and local requirements if these concerns are incorporated into the planning process. While the existing Manpower Needs Committees were perhaps established with this in mind, on balance they do not seem to have decentralized decision making to any

great extent. The effectiveness of these committees does vary, to some extent, from one to the other; yet all face limitations stemming from the considerable authority that emanates from national headquarters.

In light of this imperative for diversity, we feel that serious consideration should be given to a new training approach that would allow more scope for decision making and delivery at the local labour market level. We do not deny the importance of some degree of centralized policy setting and co-ordination. There are, however, advantages to a more disaggregated approach. First, there is perhaps no better way at present to overcome the current lack of labour market information. Given the problems associated with forecasting and large-scale surveys, the collection of necessary data on training needs at the local level is perhaps the best alternative. Familiarity with likely issues, a workable size frame, and co-operation are all plausible reasons for this belief. Moreover, a local setting is likely to be a relatively acceptable setting for multipartite decision making. In a single community, all those involved who have a stake in vocational training may be more successful than their representatives at the national or even provincial levels. A decentralized approach has already been undertaken in Ontario through the Local Industrial Training Advisory Councils; this experiment deserves the close attention of policy makers.

Leaving aside the local council plan and turning now to apprenticeships, we recognize the role of these programs in developing highly trained workers with comprehensive skill packages. An expansion of apprenticeship training in the future is particularly critical in light of the anticipated demand in the trades during the 1980s. Consequently, it is important that the regulations facilitate an increase in the volume of the system. In this vein, it would seem imperative that flexibility be pursued with respect to program organization. Our research suggests that there are a number of barriers to the expansion of apprenticeship training, particularly with respect to entry and placement. Some mechanisms to facilitate placement should therefore be considered by the provinces. The training process itself may, in some cases, be unnecessarily long. Pre-training institutional preparation, recognition of past experiences, and competency-based accreditation are all promising solutions to this problem. We have also looked with interest at recent efforts in some provinces to improve the co-ordination of the institutional and on-the-job components of apprenticeship training.

While we have not carried out original research on postsecondary education, we recognize its importance in developing the intellectual, scientific, and technical resources of this country. Jurisdictionally, postsecondary education is a contentious issue in Canada. Nevertheless, this Council asserted its belief, in a recent report, that strong financial support from the federal government should be maintained in this area.[18] From the federal government's point of view, we understand the problems associated with its largely unconditional contributions under the Established Programs Financing arrangements. There are national interests in postsecondary education such as the development of highly skilled personnel, however,

and Ottawa should continue its financial support while negotiating with the provinces regarding ways to improve the co-ordination of policy formulation.

A final issue that we would like to mention is that of continuing education. The old cycle of schooling, training, and work is likely to be replaced by a sequence punctuated by frequent periods of retraining and re-education. In recognition of this, arrangements for lifelong skill development must be investigated carefully.

9 Conclusions and Recommendations

In this report, we have dealt with the way the labour market works and with measures that might be taken when it does not. Thus we have focused upon labour demand and supply in the past and in the future, and on the problems that are posed when these forces do not balance. We have looked at shortages of skills in particular occupations, industries, locations, and time periods. We have examined the unemployment of particular groups of workers, their patterns of job search, its duration, and its degree of success. We have also been concerned with some of the processes and mechanisms by which the labour market adjusts to economic growth and development, the stresses of societal change, and the shocks of external forces. Our examination of the performance of the market has suggested that in certain areas, at certain times, this allocative adjustment mechanism does not function optimally and that some intervention is required to improve its efficiency.

For the discussion of policy issues and recommendations, the principal conclusions of our analysis may be summarized as follows:

• The continuing high levels of inflation and unemployment in Canada are reflected in the deterioration of labour market performance since the mid-1970s.

• This shortcoming is manifested not only in record rates of unemployment generally but also in even more severe hardship for specific groups and, at the same time, in shortages of certain categories of skilled workers.

• These imbalances have worsened in recent years and could, in view of the considerable adjustments that anticipated developments in the labour market will require, remain severe in the future.

• It is apparent that in the present economic climate the ability of traditional monetary and fiscal policy instruments to combat unemployment and skill shortages is severely constrained. Thus finer, more specific remedies must be found.

• Manpower training has the potential to fill current and projected manpower requirements and to alleviate the joblessness that derives from skill deficiency, but the system must be redirected to fit more closely the changing employment requirements of various sectors.

• Information is crucial to the design, implementation, and maintenance of a national training system, as well as to the job search of unemployed workers, the acquisition of skilled manpower by employers, and determination of the need for future action by decision makers in all sectors. Our present capacity to produce and project detailed occupational information is, however, limited.

• While part of the joint problem of joblessness and skill shortages may be alleviated by improvement in the quality of information and by skill training, another part requires policy initiatives on the demand side of the market.

• A comprehensive manpower policy package requires job creation programs serving individual and social needs, not just as a short-term palliative but as part of a long-run strategic framework, to maximize access to work and skill formation.

• Both efficiency and equity must continue to be viewed as central objectives of labour market policy. Whenever possible, measures should be designed to pursue these goals in a mutually reinforcing way.

On the basis of these broad conclusions, we discuss issues and recommendations in three main policy areas: vocational skill development, labour market information, and job creation.

Vocational Skill Development

Throughout this document, and particularly in the preceding chapter, we have emphasized the critical importance of skill development for the future of this country, recognizing the contribution of training and vocational education to a wide array of economic and social objectives. Indeed, a highly skilled and efficiently allocated labour force is viewed as essential if Canada is to realize its potential for growth in the upcoming decade. This imperative is likely to be complicated by a host of factors, including the planned massive resource developments, the shifting industrial structure, and anticipated technological innovations. Growing out of these events will be demands for labour that are unprecedented, not only in terms of numbers but also with respect to the types of skills needed. The task of adjustment in the 1980s will be considerable.

New demands, though, hold the promise of new opportunities, particularly for those Canadians who, until now, have not shared in the benefits that derive from labour market participation. The possession of needed skills has the potential for overcoming traditional barriers and other forces that have excluded certain groups from favourable employment outcomes. In this view, training constitutes an important, even powerful, mechanism for the realization of equity-oriented social goals.

That Canadians recognize the significance of vocational training is evidenced by past government expenditures in this area. In terms of dollars spent, public training programs have represented the single largest component in the labour market policy package. Despite this, our research suggests that past efforts have not been effective in achieving the objectives outlined above. Most prominently, the critical shortages of skills, identified by the Human Resources Survey and other inquiries, indicate the failure of the system to meet all of the demands of the labour market. Moreover, we do not easily arrive at the conclusion that existing initiatives have been very successful in improving the opportunities for those Canadians who are experiencing long-term joblessness and other employment-related problems.

This questionable past performance, coupled with the imposing demands of the future, led the Council to seriously reconsider the arrangements for the development of vocational skills in this country. In doing this, we looked, first, at the question of the appropriate roles of the public and private sectors in training. Certainly, we agree with the sentiment, popular in many quarters, that Canadian employers must heighten their emphasis on human resources. Indeed, our nationwide establishment survey indicated clearly that the training and development effort within industry is inadequate. While stressing the importance of a greater role for the private sector, the Council believes nonetheless that governments must retain a central role in vocational training. Much of the comprehensive and transferable skill development, so crucial to long-term labour market well-being, is unlikely to be identified and carried out by the private sector alone.

While it is apparent to us that a co-operative partnership between government, labour, and industry is necessary, the need for co-ordination between the federal and provincial governments also deserves attention. Both levels have legitimate concerns associated with the development of vocational skills, but neither has fully respected the presence of the other. Unfortunately, Canadians have been ill-served by this confrontation, and the Council emphasizes the importance of a constructive partnership in any future arrangements.

Turning to more particular objectives, we have concluded that the desired system must incorporate 1/ a capacity to identify training needs, and 2/ flexibility to accommodate the diversity of labour market conditions that characterizes this country.

With respect to the former, it is obvious that improved information is necessary – a consistent theme throughout this report. Within the context of training, the projection of future imbalances is of critical importance, but such forecasting is, at present, severely hampered by data limitations. While urging that high priority be assigned to solving this problem, we appreciate the difficulties associated with improving information, and we understand that the forecasting capabilities required remain at a developmental stage.

Thus the training needs for the entire country cannot be completely identified, for the time being anyway, in any centralized fashion. This observation leads us to the other imperative mentioned above, that of accommodating the diverse labour market conditions in Canada. One of the major criticisms about the existing program that we encountered during our work was related to its inflexible, monolithic structure. The administrative neatness of uniform standards entails a system that is tailored to the requirements of no particular locale. In practice, however, the needs of rural and urban areas, of mining sites and manufacturing cities, of fishing villages and boom towns, vary substantially.

This diversity leads us to look, with a great deal of interest, towards a training approach that would allow for greater input in the decision-making process at the local level. As mentioned in the preceding chapter, a more disaggregated system would have a number of attractive features. By determining needs and initiating programs locally, such an approach, by its very nature, would be sensitive to the diversity of the conditions facing different areas of the country. Moreover, given the existing problems associated with large-scale information efforts, decentralized data collection might be a better alternative. With these and other advantages in mind,

1   **We recommend that the federal and provincial governments enter into discussions with representatives of industry and labour to consider arrangements for the creation of local training**

councils. **The mandate of these councils would be to identify the training needs within their markets and to initiate and co-ordinate programs to meet these needs.**

While advocating the usefulness of such an approach, we do not necessarily believe that a uniform network of similar councils is desirable. Indeed, some regions of the country — for example, those sparsely industrialized or those dominated by one employer — might not be appropriate locales for such an arrangement. In other areas, particularly major urban centres, a number of councils organized along industry lines might be a better approach.

In our view, another advantage to a localized approach is the potential that it offers for the participation of all those involved in vocational training. In particular, the local councils, as we envisage them, would place major emphasis on industry and labour as initiators of training. Co-operation among all parties, though, would be essential; and, although multipartite decision making might face many obstacles at the national level, the familiarity and shared concerns within a community would facilitate consensus. Therefore,

2 **We recommend that the local training councils include representatives from labour, business, and the federal and provincial governments, along with education officials.**

The Local Industrial Training Advisory Councils, in Ontario, are promising examples of the kind of institutional arrangement that we have in mind. We believe that a policy based on such principles, administratively supported by public funds, would represent a significant contribution to the planning of human-resource development. Naturally, we recognize the need for provincewide and national planning and co-ordination. On the basis of our analysis of the existing training system, however, we have concluded that greater local input in the decision-making process is needed.

We applaud the recent federal proposals to direct government funding more towards the demands of the labour market, as our research suggests that this is necessary. We do, however, advise caution in this reorientation. While certain specific vocational skills may be needed immediately, public policies must nevertheless give priority to the development of workers endowed with a set of comprehensive skills. Only in this way can this country adjust continually to the rapidly changing labour market. Institutional preparation is essential to such a process, and continuing support in this area would seem desirable. Institutional instruction should, however, be oriented more towards anticipated employment opportunities than was the case under CMTP.

Turning to industrial training, it is clear that greater effort at all skill levels is needed in this country. Particular attention should be paid to the promotion of training in small firms where relatively little activity of this kind seems to occur. In our view, the appropriate role for government is to fill the gaps left by the private sector. Our work indicates that this has not been the case in the past. Thus our suggestion would result in a significant shift in the types of industrial training funded. In particular,

3 **We recommend that government support for training in industry focus on high-level, long-duration programs for technical and trades occupations.**

Within the present context, it is clear, for example, that on a national basis, more training in industry for machinery mechanics, industrial electricians, machinists, computer specialists, and engineering technicians and technologists is required. It should be noted, however, that in some parts of the country, other needs may be more pressing.

We believe that specific funding should be made available to facilitate access to training for all Canadians who are underrepresented and/or absent from many skilled occupations. Here, we refer particularly to women. Problems also exist for indigenous people and others who have found themselves largely excluded from the labour market. Therefore, we welcome any positive attempts to improve the employment opportunities for all workers in this country.

While we recognize that training, by itself, cannot be a panacea, it is nevertheless essential. For a variety of social and cultural reasons, many groups have been unable to flourish in traditional programs. As a result, control of the design and delivery of training would seem to be a reasonable consideration. Indeed, the "outreach" counselling and training programs are founded on this strategy and we have been favourably impressed by many of these efforts. With more certain and long-term funding practices, initiatives of this nature could have a significant impact.

Particularly with respect to women, the major policy thrust must address the historical patterns of job segregation. Not only have many of the jobs most threatened by anticipated changes in labour demand traditionally been held by women, but the latter also account for a very small share of the employment in many occupations where emerging opportunities are the greatest. The federal government has recently instituted a training initiative — a program called Non Traditional Training for Women — aimed at improving access for women to traditionally male vocations. While endorsing this program, we believe that at present the scale of this effort is inadequate. There-fore,

4   We recommend that the federal government increase considerably its funding for Non Traditional Training for Women. Moreover, in order to increase the breadth of this program, we urge that the occupations covered be broadened.

Indigenous people, too, tend to be located in segments of the labour market that are characterized by low wages and poor long-term prospects. We acknowledge that these problems cannot be easily separated from the host of social and economic conditions that describe the native reality in this country. While this situation, and its possible solu-tions, go beyond the scope of our report, it is evident that initiatives designed to enhance vocational skill development, both on and off reserves, are badly needed. We have noted, for example, that a lack of basic educational foundations constitutes a major barrier for native people. Unfortunately, programs addressing this problem have been dropped by the federal government.

We would be remiss if we did not once again draw attention to the particular need for increasing the potential for older people to participate in the labour market, not as a substitute for a better retirement income system but rather on the basis of the strong social and medical arguments that have been advanced in this respect and as a way of easing the present shortcomings of the labour market. This Council has already recommended measures to this effect in its report on the Canadian retirement income system.[1]

Apprenticeship training is another avenue of skill development that has received considerable attention in our work. In our view, apprenticeships constitute an effective method for producing workers highly trained in a comprehensive package of skills and capable of adapting to rapidly changing labour markets. With this in mind, we believe that the expansion of this form of training is desirable. Our research suggests, however, that reforms are neces-sary in order to achieve this objective. For example, educational prerequisites may not always be neces-sary; where this is the case, they should be removed. The difficulty in finding employers willing to take on apprentices may be an even more significant barrier to entry. This problem is exacerbated during cyclical downturns, when, in principle, the volume of appren-ticeships should be greatest. Therefore,

5   We recommend that the provincial governments consider incorporating within their apprentice-ship offices an agency designed to facilitate the placement of aspiring apprentices within industry.

Flexibility in program organization would also be essential. Without jeopardizing the integrity of the institution, the training process itself might be short-ened in some cases. Thus,

6   We recommend that, wherever possible, the qualifications required for the certification of apprentices be competency-based rather than time-based, that past experience be accredited, and that pre-training institutional preparation be employed in order to shorten the training period.

While it has many functions, postsecondary education, of course, plays a critical role in develop-ing highly qualified personnel for the labour market. Although this Council has not carried out a compre-hensive study of these matters in recent years, it touched on certain aspects in its recent report on fiscal federalism.[2] The Council recognized, with one dissenting voice, the continuation of the interests of both national and provincial governments in post-secondary education. It supported the continued sharing by the federal government in the financing of such education, but through arrangements that ensure more effective accountability to Parliament and to the Canadian public than under the 1977-82 Established Programs Financing arrangements. The Council urged the federal and provincial governments to work out more explicitly, in the next year or two, their respective interests and roles in postsecondary education and the means of discharging their respon-sibilities in this area.

To conclude this section, we would like to point out that for a variety of reasons, among which technolog-ical change is particularly important, the traditional view of the lifelong career is unlikely to survive in the labour market of the future. Forward-looking policies should provide for such "re-tooling" by ensuring reasonable access for working Canadians to educa-tional institutions and programs. Not only would this enhance the career opportunities of individuals, but it would also guard against skill obsolescence and contribute to the country's productivity.

While there may be many types of arrangements appropriate to such objectives, one that has received some attention is that of paid educational leave. In 1974, the International Labour Organization adopted a general convention (number 140) recommending that each member country formulate and apply a policy for the promotion of paid educational leave.[3] Although such policies have been implemented in several European countries, Canada has not yet moved in this direction. In fact, the ILO convention has never been ratified in this country. Accordingly, in light of the importance the Council attaches to lifelong vocational development,

7   We recommend that Canada ratify the ILO convention on paid educational leave (number 140) and that the federal and provincial governments, along with industry and labour, consider the means for its implementation.

Ratification of this convention would be an indication of Canada's concern for the concept of access for workers to education and training. Naturally, in formulating a policy for paid educational leave, the parties involved would have to examine closely a number of critical issues, including eligibility and safeguards from abuse, and, particularly, the appropriate funding arrangements.

The Role of Information

Labour markets do not, of their own accord, automatically generate the best allocation of human resources. This also holds for labour market information: Canadian labour markets have not always produced the quantity and quality of information considered ideal by participants in those markets. Since information is an essential element in the process of labour market adjustment, its shortcomings have contributed to the observed imbalances and, hence, to losses in gross national product.

It would be an understatement to say that the process of allocating human resources is very complex, depending, as it does, on the individual decisions of millions of labour market participants — workers and employers — whose interaction affects the forces of supply and demand. These forces are, at the same time, also influenced by the interventions of governments and other organized economic institutions. The resulting network of relationships requires for its smooth functioning an equally complex set of information networks. Although there are obvious overlaps, it is useful to think of information needs that are specific to employees, to employers, to labour market analysts, and to policy makers. Each of these classes of information users requires not only information that may be classified as current intelligence but also prospective data that can be used for long-term planning. Another dimension of information that should be borne in mind is the level of data aggregation — ranging from the national, on the one hand, to the most disaggregated local levels, on the other.

Consider the information needs of workers. Current and prospective labour market participants need to consider alternative jobs that feature differing skill requirements, remuneration, fringe benefits, and career prospects, and to evaluate them in the context of their own skill endowments and aspirations. The need for prospective information arises, of course, because many education and training decisions must be taken years in advance. Employers, too, are faced with exacting requirements with respect to labour market information. They must determine their human resource needs in the face of shifting demand for their products and of changes in the technology they employ. They must then attempt to meet these requirements, without interruptions and bottlenecks, from a potential work force whose size cannot be known with precision. This they must do by offering terms and conditions of employment that must not only be competitive but also be consistent with the profitability of the enterprise and that offer a harmonious working environment.

While the need for labour market information may thus be apparent, the economic costs that can arise because of information deficiencies may not be widely appreciated. This has led, in our view, to a discounting of the importance attached to the gathering, dissemination, and use of information. And yet it is not difficult to imagine the exorbitant costs that faulty information could impose on an economic system.

In view of the vast information requirements described above, it is small wonder that the demand and supply of labour do not always adjust; a degree of imbalance is therefore to be expected. With the multitude of decision makers acting and reacting, however, the information generated by the labour market is itself subject to constant flux and a high rate of obsolescence. Of course, decisions based on obsolete information can only make the adjustment process more difficult. The problem, as we have shown, arises when these imbalances loom large, and it can be traced in no small measure to inadequacies in the information system. Where decisions have to be taken years in advance, any planning error caused by faulty prospective information is magnified manifold. The periodic under- and oversupply of certain skills that our economy has experienced from time to time are classic illustrations of the tyranny of inappropriate information. It not only misallocates labour and reduces output of the economy, but it also generates the very real human problems that emerge when the work force is not appropriately matched with the jobs that are available.

The adjustment problems become even further complicated when their diagnosis and the subsequent policy responses are made on the basis of faulty information. Under such circumstances, correct policy prescriptions can only be expected through sheer accident. It is in this perspective that the labour market information needs of analysts and policy framers can be properly appreciated and become a critical concern.

Deficiencies in the Information System

Our studies suggest that the requirements of the four major groups of data users identified above are not being met adequately by the present information system. Consider the case of the work force. In recent months, more than one million labour force participants are reported monthly by Statistics Canada to be looking for jobs; of these, one-quarter are employed persons looking for alternative opportunities. The methods of search employed by these people suffer from major inefficiencies caused by inadequate data, in the sense that the utilization rates of various methods seem quite unrelated to their relative success. Public employment services provided by the Canada Employment Centres (CEC) and the Quebec Manpower Centres are beset with many weaknesses. It is widely believed that the share of job vacancies available to these centres is very small, concentrated mainly in the low-level skill categories. No adequate service exists for medium- and high-level skills. Nor can employed job seekers expect to be served by the Centres.

Job information over the medium and long term fares even worse. Workers often quit their jobs without being properly aware of the employment opportunities awaiting them. Although they are eligible for unemployment insurance benefits and register for this purpose, the vacancies they generate in the process often do not get reported to the CECs. Other examples include the periodic oversupply of such highly qualified manpower as engineers, chemists, physicists, and so on; and a recent survey of young people, in which it was found that most respondents had not heard about apprenticeship opportunities in their province. In brief, information about job prospects is very inadequate, both quantitatively and qualitatively; it is concentrated on the low-skill categories, and it does not receive wide dissemination.

Employer groups fare no better. The major deficiency here relates to prospective information – a vital element in human-resource planning. While there are notable examples of Canadian expertise in this area, our studies tend to support the view that Canadian industry exerts much less energy and ingenuity in the acquisition, maintenance, and improvement of human capital than it does in the case of physical capital. The shortage of high-level, blue-collar skills and the aging of the work force in such occupations, without any steps being taken over the years to ensure a continuous flow of skills through new recruitment, illustrate our general point. The fact is that, at this time, little is known about the volume and nature of training and manpower planning activities in Canada's private sector.

The plight of labour market analysts has been underlined again in this report: the forecasting of occupational imbalances in Canada is severely handicapped by data shortcomings (Chapters 3 and 4), and the gross flow data utilized in Chapter 6 point out the importance of longitudinal data in evaluating long-term labour market experiences, as well as the serious deficiency that their absence represents at present. Whether the high unemployment rates experienced by certain youth groups leave a permanent mark on their long-term prospects can be appropriately evaluated only by using a longitudinal design. The demise of the Job Vacancy Survey leaves an alarming gap in labour market statistics. A major problem facing analysts is that some of the data they require are jealously guarded by the various government departments that generate them. In brief, not only are there major gaps in the information available, but the system also suffers from a lack of co-ordination, especially with respect to dissemination.

To the extent that labour market policy makers rely on analysts, they are also hampered by these weaknesses. They may also not be making use of such labour market information and analysis as do exist. For example, prospective analysis of the demographic structure and of fertility behaviour was apparently not a major element of the considerations that led to a massive infusion of capital into universities and colleges during the 1960s. There is, therefore, the need for co-ordinated planning between the various sectors of the economy that have an impact on the labour market. The need to bring education and labour market planners closer together is especially underscored.

Directions for Change

Why, then, does the market mechanism itself fail to generate, in adequate quantity, the types of information that are required by different groups of users? The answer, in the first instance, lies in the fact that information has some of the attributes of a public good. While its benefits to society as a whole are large, the cost of developing and maintaining such a system is very high. But the benefits to society arise only if such information is widely disseminated. Obviously, there are selective circumstances in which either these general conditions do not hold or they apply with limited effect, so that specialized agencies dealing with selected labour market information can be run on a profit basis. Such agencies not only generate and disseminate information, but they also serve as intermediaries between employers and job seekers. One promising approach, therefore, would be to explore the possibilities whereby markets of this type could be encouraged to take root.

It is apparent, however, that certain labour markets are well served by a highly developed information system. Some professional organizations, such as those in the engineering field, have a sophisticated data base with highly specific information on the characteristics of jobs. For markets of this type, our concern is not with the quality or availability of information for employers and employees but rather with the regular, continuous, and systematic extraction of that information for the broader planning and policy needs of a national manpower strategy.

In devising an overall strategy, therefore, it must be recognized that the information needs of the Canadian labour market are many and varied; as a consequence, the current deficiencies in the system do not lend themselves to global solutions. Some of these deficiencies would require only marginal adjustments in existing structures; others could not so easily be handled and would require fresh approaches. A revamping of the current system must proceed with the recognition that there are diverse categories of information users. Also, each class of users requires not only information that can be categorized as current intelligence but also prospective information that can serve long-term planning needs. The level of data aggregation is another dimension that must be taken into consideration. Accordingly, in formulating our recommendations we consider, first, a major step that will ensure that the various needs are met and, second, the additional steps that are necessary in order to provide information that will be specific to labour force participants, employers, labour market analysts, and policy makers.

As outlined above and described more fully in Chapter 7, the three major deficiencies in the current system are: 1/ a lack of co-ordination in data development, dissemination, and analysis; 2/ weaknesses in human-resource planning at the firm level; and 3/ inadequate linkages between the educational system and the world of work. In our judgment, there is at present no institutional structure that can address these problems adequately. Therefore,

8   We recommend the establishment of an independent research institute charged specifically with developing and co-ordinating a human-resource information network to meet the needs of each of the major groups of information consumers — workers, employers, analysts, and policy makers.

In particular, the institute should put special effort into diagnosing the difficulties currently being encountered in planning at the firm level and should develop approaches for their alleviation. It should also undertake steps to bridge the gaps that currently exist between educational planners and labour market policy makers. The institute should monitor the labour market information system with a view to identifying gaps and suggesting improvements in light of developments in information technology, but it should also have as a major priority the more efficient exploitation of existing data sets and sources. As part of its co-ordinating and disseminating activities, the institute should be empowered with sufficient legal authority to extract from government agencies and departments, for disseminating to the public, data that are not of a confidential nature and whose development has been paid for by the taxpayers. In order to carry out these functions effectively, it is essential that the institute, though funded by governments, be run independently, with an advisory board consisting of representatives from labour, management, the federal and provincial governments, and the education sector. In addition to the continuing research and current analysis of labour market issues, the institute would act as a clearinghouse and would maintain an information network for Canadian research.

Rather than establish a costly organization, we propose that the existing research manpower and funds of federal and provincial departments be reallocated, with industry, labour, and academic and government agencies supplying manpower and funds to support short-term (up to one year) internships. As an additional safeguard against the establishment of another institutional overlay, it might be useful to include a "sunset clause" in the legislation creating such an institute. In this way, its success and future usefulness would have to be demonstrated to justify an extension of its life.

Since Canada is rather ill-served as far as labour journals are concerned, it is suggested that the responsibility for current analysis should entail the publication of a quarterly bulletin similar in format to the *Monthly Labor Review* of the U.S. Bureau of Labor Statistics.[4] More detailed accounts of research findings could be published in a more formal, semi-annual journal of applied labour economics.

For labour force participants, the two basic information shortcomings relate to current job vacancies and to the linkages between the educational system and the world of work. While the latter would be addressed by the recommendation made above, steps to improve the performance of the public employment service (PES) may be of only limited use to meet the first problem. A number of studies over the years have commented on the limited share of job vacancies that are reported through the PES. Efforts to increase this share have not borne fruit; in fact, some deterioration has been noted in recent years. It is time that these limitations were recognized and, given the segmentation of Canadian labour markets, that attempts were made to improve its effectiveness within the particular skill categories in which service dominates. These efforts could take the form of an extension of the "metropolitan order processing system" (MOPS) to all main cities in Canada and their direct linkages with each other. Alternative approaches must also be sought, however, since the vast majority of vacancies do not go through the public employment service and a large number of job seekers, especially those who are employed, receive no assistance from this service. Specialized private-sector employment agencies, for example, could serve as intermediaries in some of the higher-skill areas. In our opinion, there is room for considerable expansion of this kind of service in the private sector, since ingredients necessary for the emergence of such intermediation already exist: as both the employers and the employees could cut their search costs significantly through organized exchanges, they should be willing to pay for these services.

Finally, there are several gaps in the labour market information system that can be filled by agencies currently involved in the provision of similar data. The forecasting of occupational imbalances is one example that we have noted. While broad national projections of occupational demands and supplies consistent with macroeconomic models and forecasts are indispensable, the evidence reported earlier (Chapter 5) strongly suggests the practical value of surveys, such as our own Human Resources Survey, that provide greater geographical and industry detail. We are aware that some surveys can entail costs to industry, but we are encouraged by our own experience, which shows that relatively simple instruments can yield data that are useful to analysts and, more importantly, to the respondents themselves.

Our research on the gross flows and duration of joblessness strongly suggested the need for longitudinal labour market data. A variety of important policy questions could be addressed advantageously with such data: the life-cycle patterns of labour force participation, skill acquisition, geographical and occupational mobility, and the stability of employment, for example. We believe that attempts to create a longitudinal data base by linking various data sources would be complex and costly. A survey along the lines of that undertaken in the United States would be more appropriate. Other obvious gaps relate to estimates of the significance of discouraged workers, of the underutilization of labour by

firms (popularly known as labour hoarding), and of hiring and separations data. In light of these considerations,

9 **We recommend that the federal and provincial governments assign high priority to the regular production of information concerning the labour force, employment, vacancies and labour compensation,** *by occupation,* **and that a regular skill shortage survey be conducted as a complement.**

Further,

10 **We recommend that Statistics Canada attempt to institute a longitudinal survey of the behaviour of labour market participants and plan to make available hiring and separations data on a regular and continuing basis. The agency should continue to provide annual estimates of discouraged workers and conduct a survey that would address the issue of labour hoarding directly.**

Job Creation

The general economic rationale for direct employment programs was spelled out in some detail in Chapter 7. The more specific case for such programs in the Canadian context involves a number of considerations that should be seen in the light of the framework discussed at the beginning of the present chapter.

The first consideration flows directly from our analysis of Canadian joblessness, in which we established the importance of long-term unemployment. This, in turn, strongly suggests that job availability, rather than the difficulty in matching people and jobs, is the overriding concern for some groups of workers. The scope for aggregate monetary or fiscal stimulus to create the required employment is, however, constrained by the possible inflationary consequences. While training programs may give people new skills and mobility programs may move them, these measures will be useless if jobs do not exist. In a macroeconomic perspective, therefore, the payoff is the potential to create jobs in a way that is cheaper than by conventional aggregate measures and, because of the targeted nature of direct job creation, less inflationary.

The second consideration concerns the case for job creation at the firm level. This rests on the observation that in today's complex labour market, there are a number of important programs that safeguard the rights and well-being of workers but nevertheless constrain purely economic forces and may lead to disincentives and allocative distortions. Some employers feel that with respect to lower-skilled workers, there is a considerable gap between expected productivity and the gross wage that must be paid. Direct job creation, by lowering the wage cost, could therefore correct distortions and remove allocative failure.

Equity, however, is an important third consideration. Our analysis of joblessness demonstrated that the burden of long-term unemployment is shouldered by a relatively small group of workers. Thus unemployment is *not* borne more or less equally: there is a clear distributional problem. The ability of job creation programs to be targeted at particular groups is therefore an attractive feature. In the context of equity, we must also look at the interrelationship of job creation and other policy measures. In Canada recently, there have been suggestions (with which we are in broad agreement) that federal training programs should be geared more closely to market needs. Such a move could well prove to be a more *efficient* way to operate programs of this type, but it could also have undesirable implications with respect to their former equity components. Certain disadvantaged groups with low skills and poor labour market experience could, in some cases, be left behind by a training system oriented primarily to market demand. The creation of jobs for those specific groups might afford them the work experience that would enable them to form a more permanent attachment to the labour force.

While emphasizing the importance of the equity objective, we are persuaded that job creation programs should not — and need not — project the unfortunate "make work" image cast by inferior stop-gap palliatives. Such unemployment "sponges," which have no clearly useful end product or service, do not produce useful skills; they are demeaning to the participants and, ultimately, costly to taxpayers. We favour programs with clearly identifiable objectives that are beneficial to individual workers and to society.

To the extent that they were successful, such measures would have important longer-run consequences in addition to the alleviation of a short-run problem. For participants, the work provided would have value in itself as an alternative to idleness, and it would offer them a chance to gain work experience and obtain income from earnings rather than from government handouts. From the longer-term, strategic point of view, these (albeit nonquantifiable) socio-psychological benefits could well be of overwhelming importance to those for whom the welfare-dependency cycle was broken.

We do not wish to suggest, however, that job creation programs are in any sense a panacea for the ills of the labour market. It is clear, for example, that they should complement, rather than replace, policy measures that affect the process of labour market adjustment and allocation. Of these, training is the most obvious example. Our analysis suggests, very simply, that some problems could best be addressed by training, and others by job creation. In some cases, a combination of the two might be the best way to help certain groups. A recent Swedish initiative to stimulate employment requires that employers offer at least two months' training, with any additional costs to be covered by a subsidy. Such mutually supporting measures might also be appropriate in Canada. Similarly, direct job creation programs must not compete or conflict with regional incentive and subsidy programs such as those administered by the Department of Regional Economic Expansion (DREE) and its successor, the Department of Regional Industrial Expansion.

Next, quite apart from the general problems of displacement and fiscal substitution, which detract from their net job creation effects, we are aware that these measures pose a number of specific design problems. In attempting to ensure that new jobs are created, for example, there is the problem of defining the "normal" work force, with respect to which new positions are considered to be incremental. In the case of private-sector programs, it is probably impossible to be certain that the new jobs would not have been forthcoming in the absence of the subsidy. Experience with the Canadian Employment Tax Credit Program (ETCP) suggests that employers are leery of signing certificates of incrementality. There is obviously a trade-off between the need to emphasize *net* employment creation and the potential danger of discouraging employers from participating.

Nevertheless, we view direct job creation programs as a legitimate component of overall public labour market policy. Moreover, we believe that, since the bulk of the present federal effort is in the public sector, attention needs to be focused on some policy issues concerning employment creation in the private sector as well. Our analysis of private-sector programs suggests that they may have certain advantages over public-employment programs in terms of cost effectiveness and employment stability. Furthermore, in urban, industrialized areas, they may simply afford more relevant, saleable work experience to the participants. This country's major program of wage subsidy in the private sector is the ETCP, which was phased out at the end of fiscal year 1980/81. Thus, while we endorse job creation programs for the private sector, we recognize that there are alternative means of delivering the wage subsidy.

In restrospect, the ETCP appears to have enjoyed some degree of success, and some of its design features are instructive. Compared with a straightforward cash subsidy, the tax credit approach has some advantages. Program officials estimate that tax credits may yield a faster payoff to employers because they can apply them periodically against their interim tax assessments, while cash payments may require long processing delays. The tax credit system uses the existing tax framework and its administrative machinery, taking advantage of the auditing safeguards that it affords. Cash transfers, by contrast, may require a much more elaborate system of field visits to employers for inspection and verification purposes, as well as a larger complement of head office staff to process claims. On the other hand, under the tax credit system just phased out, the credits themselves were taxable so that some employers found the benefits realized to be less than anticipated. And, of course, the firms that pay no taxes – a significant proportion of the total – would be potentially excluded from any tax credit scheme unless the tax credit was refundable.

Some very important trade-offs are involved here. From the standpoint of the agency administering it (CEIC), the tax credit system is appealing because of its simplicity. Although this is an important aspect of a short-run, stop-gap, policy measure, it fails to help all potential employers because the nonprofit sector and the non-tax-paying firms are excluded. Furthermore, the utilization of the tax system itself is not without costs. The system depends, in the first instance, on the voluntary compliance of taxpayers. In addition, the form-filling and auditing procedures required by a scheme like ETCP impose an additional burden upon such a system. Furthermore, it is understood that officials of both the Department of Finance and Revenue Canada might oppose the refundability concept on the grounds that it would set a precedent for *all* tax credit programs, none of which, at the moment, involves refundability.

It is our contention that a major dimension of these issues has to do with the short-run/long-run distinction that we emphasized earlier. That is, a job creation program of limited duration to meet a short-term problem might well be based on the administratively simplest delivery machinery. For a longer-run program, however – one that is viewed as an enduring and integral part of overall labour market policy strategy, though varying in size as conditions change – a major concern might be simplicity from the user's point of view and avoidance of a burden on the tax system. This would involve a heavier investment in head office staff by the administering agency, the streamlining of claim-processing procedures, and the hiring of field staff for monitoring and inspection purposes. The advantage would be that such a program would avoid a burden on the tax system, would cast its net over more potential employers, and

would, by paying direct cash subsidies, be intuitively simpler.

In view of the urgency of the present unemployment problem in this country and in the light of the need to consider direct job creation in the private sector as an integral part of a long-run labour market policy framework, we suggest a role for both approaches. First, we recognize the need to use a familiar system that can be easily geared up; therefore,

11 We recommend that the federal government institute a short-run direct employment creation program in the private sector, based on the employment tax credit system and targeted at those groups who bear a disproportionate burden of unemployment.

Furthermore, in recognition of the longer-run strategic role of private-sector direct employment programs,

12 We recommend that the federal government take steps to put in place the administrative machinery necessary to establish a system involving a direct cash wage subsidy to private employers for the purpose of job creation.

We recognize that even a simple cash subsidy scheme, with streamlined claim procedures, is not without possible blemishes. From the employer's standpoint the monitoring that is required to establish the principle of incrementality might be considered an unnecessary intrusion, but it may be no worse than the auditing requirements of a tax credit system. The government and the taxpayers, by contrast, may be anxious to ensure that job creation is truly incremental – i.e., over and above "normal" manning levels. Suffice it to say that there is obviously a trade-off between take-up and control and that, if equity is an important consideration, what administrators refer to as "additionality" (rather than incrementality) is a useful criterion. (By "additionality" is meant the idea that the persons hired would not, in the absence of the program, have found jobs.) Thus the targeting feature of such programs is highlighted.

A further interesting question has to do with whether the subsidy for job creation should be paid to the employer or given (by means of a voucher) to the individual. The evidence in Canada is rather unclear on this point. The one program that has used the voucher system is rather small; it involves a portable wage subsidy for essentially older, well-established workers who have been laid off in certain economically depressed areas. Such people are perhaps unwilling to break away from established homes and neighbourhoods; hence it is difficult to know whether the relatively low acceptance of the scheme is due to reluctance to move or to the frequently cited objection that the voucher system stigmatizes the workers by labeling them as a target group.

The targeting of the subsidy at the long-term unemployed is also a concern, since the instinctive lack of enthusiasm on the part of employers concerning the productive potential of such workers has to be overcome. In this respect, the fact that a large majority of the people hired under ETCP were either young or female is encouraging, but the fact that it was necessary to substantially relax the minimum period of unemployment (eight weeks) is not. To overcome this latter problem, the program might benefit from better local identification of the long-term jobless; furthermore, employers might be more attracted to a scheme that would enhance longer-run productivity through a built-in training requirement, the costs of which would be offset by a correspondingly richer subsidy.

As for the scale of the program, we note simply that in its last year the ETCP provided roughly 50,000 jobs at a cost of about $100 million. In the light of the recent worsening of the overall unemployment problem and in view of the equity considerations outlined earlier, we suggest that the overall job creation target be increased. Because of this and because of the need to increase the absolute value of the hourly wage subsidy in order to maintain proportionality with the going wage rates, the dollar commitment would also need to be considerably enlarged. It should be emphasized, however, that a large part of the job creation effort that we are proposing is no more than a replacement for the ETCP, which was terminated in March 1981.

It is clear to us that wage subsidies to the private sector alone are insufficient to achieve the government's overall direct job creation task. We are convinced that both private- and public-sector programs have their roles to play, but in different areas. Private-sector programs are generally more advantageous, we believe, in urban areas with a substantial industrial base. The experience of a job in such an environment is often more saleable than the experience of a specialized public-sector project. The probability of continued employment after the duration of the subsidy is, we believe, greater in the case of private-sector programs. Public-sector programs have a vital role to play in areas where private-sector employment is absent; they are particularly well-suited to areas where the major employment opportunities are seasonal. In short, a mix of private- and public-sector direct employment programs seems warranted. While supporting the continuation of existing public-sector programs, however, we wish to register our concern about the designation of the output of such programs. A clearly specified, easily visible public good that has wide support should be the key objective of such programs. Their acceptance by both taxpayers and participants is likely to be enhanced in this way, and the stigma of "make work" programs could be avoided.

Conclusion

The policy questions that we have addressed refer to only a few aspects of the broad range of issues that come under the umbrella of "labour market policy." In keeping with the main thrust of our analysis, we have concentrated upon a few measures that relate directly to the adjustment of labour demand and supply and to the elimination of imbalances.

The general tenor of our discussion has been that, on the basis of our analysis of the labour market and of some projections of possible future developments, significant shifts are in train — shifts that will require a modification of policy responses. In this respect our suggestions concerning manpower training are not unlike those of the Employment and Immigration Canada Task Force in a number of areas, although we tend to place more emphasis on the local labour market as the focus of planning and on the equity objective.

We see information as a crucial ingredient in the labour allocation process and, more specifically, in the decisions of workers, employers, and policy makers. We have emphasized this crucial role of information so that our recommendations on this subject will escape from the "benign neglect" that the standard pleas for more and better data typically receive.

As far as job creation is concerned, we have tried to draw attention to the need for a balanced approach that would focus upon both the private and the public sectors. In recommending wage subsidies as an ingredient of private-sector programs, our conclusions reflect a different emphasis from that of the Employment and Immigration Canada Task Force report, which tends to concentrate more heavily on the community development model of public-sector job creation. Furthermore, we raise the possibility of viewing job creation measures not only as short-term, cyclical responses to high unemployment but also as a continuing, long-run component of a strategic policy package designed to lower the equilibrium unemployment rate.

Finally, we emphasize that we view these policy options and recommendations as the mutually supporting elements of a policy framework. They are designed to address, simultaneously, certain aspects of both the demand and the supply side of the labour market, as well as the information requirements to reconcile the two effectively.

Appendixes

Appendix A

Table A-1

Selected Labour Market Indicators,[1] Canada, 1960-80

	Unemployment rate	Employment ratio[2]	Job vacancy rate[3]	Change in real GNE[4] per person-hour	Change in real hourly earnings[4]	Change in unit labour costs
			(Per cent)			
1960	7.0	50.4	0.39	2.1	3.1	2.2
1961	7.1	50.2	0.39	2.4	2.9	1.4
1962	5.9	50.7	0.52	4.3	3.2	0.1
1963	5.5	50.9	0.53	3.5	3.1	1.3
1964	4.7	51.6	0.63	3.9	4.0	1.9
1965	3.9	52.3	0.76	3.2	4.8	4.0
1966	3.4	55.4	0.79	4.0	5.9	5.7
1967	3.8	55.4	0.67	1.1	4.7	7.2
1968	4.5	55.0	0.58	6.5	5.1	2.7
1969	4.4	55.3	0.68	2.7	4.2	6.1
Average	5.0	52.7	0.59	3.4	4.1	3.3
1970	5.7	54.5	0.55	2.4	4.7	5.7
1971	6.2	54.5	0.46	5.3	5.5	3.0
1972	6.2	54.9	0.79	3.3	3.7	5.2
1973	5.5	56.4	0.98	2.9	3.0	7.8
1974	5.3	57.3	1.11	0.1	4.4	15.7
1975	6.9	56.9	0.68	-0.4	4.3	15.0
1976	7.1	56.7	0.54	4.1	6.1	9.5
1977	8.1	56.6	0.46	1.2	1.2	7.9
1978	8.4	57.4	0.45	0.4	-3.9	5.1
1979	7.5	58.6	..	-0.3	-1.0	8.3
Average	6.7	56.4	0.75	1.8	2.8	8.3
1980	7.5	59.2	..	-2.1	-0.6	11.8

1 Prior to 1966, figures for the unemployment rate, the employment ratio, and the job vacancy rate include 14-year olds.
2 Total employment as a proportion of the working-age population.
3 Total number of vacancies as a proportion of total employment; strictly speaking, these two series are not comparable, as the latter includes employment in agriculture, fishing and trapping, and domestic service, while the former does not.
4 In 1971 dollars.
SOURCE   Statistics Canada, CANSIM data bank; Economic Council of Canada, CANDIDE data bank; vacancy series up to 1970 from Frank Denton et al., "Patterns of Unemployment Behaviour in Canada," Economic Council of Canada Discussion Paper 36, 1975, p. 62.

Appendix B

Table B-1

Occupations Included in Projections

Code	Description
113/114	Managers and administrators, other than government
117	Occupations related to management and administration
211	Occupations in physical sciences
213	Occupations in life sciences
214/215	Architects and engineers
216	Other occupations in architecture and engineering
218	Occupations in mathematics, statistics, systems analysis, and related fields
231	Occupations in social sciences
233	Occupations in social work and related fields
234	Occupations in law and jurisprudence
235	Occupations in library, museum, and archival sciences
239	Other occupations in social sciences and related fields
25	Occupations in religion
271	University teaching and related occupations
273	Elementary and secondary school teaching and related occupations
279	Other teaching and related occupations
311	Health diagnosing and treating occupations
313	Nursing, therapy, and related assisting occupations
315	Other occupations in medicine and health
331	Occupations in fine and commercial art, photography, and related fields
333	Occupations in performing and audio-visual arts
335	Occupations in writing
337	Occupations in sport and recreation
411	Stenographic and typing occupations
413	Bookkeeping, account recording, and related occupations
414	Office machine and electronic data-processing equipment operators
415	Material recording, scheduling, and distributing occupations
416	Library, file and correspondence clerks, and related occupations
417	Reception, information, and mail and message distribution occupations
419	Other clerical and related occupations
513/514	Sales occupations – commodities
517	Sales occupations – services
519	Other sales occupations
611	Protective service occupations
612	Food and beverage preparation and related service occupations
613	Occupations in lodging and other accommodation
614	Personal service occupations
616	Apparel and furnishing service occupations
619	Other service occupations
71	Farming, horticultural, and animal husbandry occupations
73	Fishing, hunting, trapping, and related occupations

Table B-1 (Concl'd)

Code	Description
75	Forestry and logging occupations
77	Mining and quarrying, including oil and gas field occupations
811	Mineral ore treating occupations
813/814	Metal processing and related occupations
815	Clay, glass and stone processing, forming, and related occupations
816/817	Chemicals, petroleum, rubber, plastics, and related materials processing occupations
821/822	Food, beverage, and related processing occupations
823	Wood processing occupations, except pulp and papermaking
825	Pulp and papermaking, and related occupations
826/827	Textile processing occupations
829	Other processing occupations
831	Metal machining occupations
833	Metal shaping and forming occupations, except machining
835	Wood machining occupations
837	Clay, glass and stone, and related materials machining occupations
839	Other machining and related occupations
851/852	Fabricating and assembling occupations, metal products, n.e.c.
853	Fabricating, assembling, installing, and repairing occupations – electrical, electronic, and related equipment
854	Fabricating, assembling, and repairing occupations – wood products
855/856	Fabricating, assembling, and repairing occupations – textile, fur, and leather products
857	Fabricating, assembling, and repairing occupations – rubber, plastic, and related products
858	Mechanics and repairmen, except electrical
859	Other product fabricating, assembling, and repairing occupations
871	Excavating, grading, paving, and related occupations
873	Electrical power, lighting and wire communications equipment erecting, installing, and repairing occupations
878	Other construction trades occupations
911	Air transport operating occupations
913	Railway transport operating occupations
915	Water transport operating occupations
917	Motor transport operating occupations
919	Other transport equipment operating occupations
93	Materials handling and related occupation, n.e.c.
951	Printing and related occupations
953	Stationary engine and utilities equipment operating and related occupations
955	Electronic and related communications equipment operating occupations, n.e.c.
959	Other crafts and equipment operating occupations, n.e.c.

n.e.c. = not elsewhere classified.

SOURCE Dominion Bureau of Statistics, *Occupational Classification Manual*, Volume II (Ottawa: Information Canada, 1971).

Appendix C

Table C-1

Source Population,[1] by Age-Sex Group, Canada, 1975-85

	15-24		25-44		45-64		65 and over		Total		
	Men	Women	Men	Women	Men	Women	Men	Women	Men	Women	Both sexes
	(Thousands)										
1975	2,157.0	2,141.0	2,973.0	2,970.0	2,089.0	2,185.0	807.0	1,001.0	8,026.0	8,297.0	16,323.0
1976	2,206.0	2,188.0	3,055.0	3,054.0	2,120.0	2,220.0	828.0	1,034.0	8,209.0	8,496.0	16,706.0
1977	2,248.0	2,222.0	3,130.0	3,135.0	2,146.0	2,248.0	853.0	1,074.0	8,378.0	8,679.0	17,057.0
1978	2,283.0	2,247.0	3,202.0	3,214.0	2,168.0	2,274.0	878.0	1,116.0	8,531.0	8,851.0	17,381.0
1979	2,305.0	2,262.0	3,282.0	3,302.0	2,182.0	2,292.0	905.0	1,161.0	8,676.0	9,017.0	17,691.0
1980	2,316.0	2,262.0	3,380.0	3,401.0	2,198.0	2,310.0	933.0	1,206.0	8,826.0	9,179.0	18,004.0
1981	2,309.0	2,247.0	3,484.0	3,505.0	2,217.0	2,330.0	955.0	1,247.0	8,966.0	9,329.0	18,295.0
1982	2,257.5	2,201.0	3,600.6	3,610.3	2,226.7	2,327.6	984.2	1,290.6	9,069.0	9,429.5	18,498.5
1983	2,213.7	2,161.4	3,722.9	3,717.1	2,246.3	2,341.7	1,010.4	1,333.7	9,193.3	9,553.9	18,747.2
1984	2,165.6	2,117.8	3,838.9	3,819.1	2,271.5	2,363.1	1,036.6	1,376.8	9,312.6	9,676.8	18,989.4
1985	2,119.4	2,072.8	3,929.9	3,917.6	2,283.0	2,381.8	1,062.8	1,419.9	9,395.1	9,792.0	19,187.1

1   The source population, as defined by the Labour Force Survey, includes all persons aged 15 and over residing in Canada, with the exception of the following: residents of the Yukon and Northwest Territories, persons living on Indian reserves, inmates of institutions, and full-time members of the armed forces.
SOURCE   Data from Statistics Canada; and calculations from Economic Council of Canada, "base case" solution of CANDIDE 2.0 model, September 1981.

Table C-2

Labour Force,[1] by Age-Sex Group, Canada, 1975-85

	15-24		25-44		45-64		65 and over		Total		
	Men	Women	Men	Women	Men	Women	Men	Women	Men	Women	Both sexes
	(Thousands)										
1975	1,485.0	1,217.0	2,843.0	1,553.0	1,817.0	861.0	149.0	50.0	6,294.0	3,680.0	9,974.0
1976	1,498.0	1,244.0	2,922.0	1,638.0	1,816.0	912.0	133.0	44.0	6,369.0	3,837.0	10,206.0
1977	1,548.0	1,277.0	2,991.0	1,736.0	1,834.0	934.0	133.0	47.0	6,505.0	3,994.0	10,498.0
1978	1,591.0	1,324.0	3,068.0	1,887.0	1,857.0	970.0	133.0	51.0	6,650.0	4,232.0	10,882.0
1979	1,646.0	1,379.0	3,150.0	1,980.0	1,865.0	1,000.0	138.0	49.0	6,799.0	4,408.0	11,207.0
1980	1,667.0	1,416.0	3,232.0	2,117.0	1,873.0	1,027.0	137.0	52.0	6,909.0	4,613.0	11,522.0
1981	1,673.0	1,421.0	3,331.0	2,282.0	1,880.0	1,053.0	134.0	55.0	7,019.0	4,811.0	11,830.0
1982	1,678.0	1,419.2	3,438.9	2,351.5	1,892.8	1,097.2	139.8	55.8	7,149.4	4,923.7	12,073.0
1983	1,662.0	1,399.4	3,554.2	2,487.5	1,907.3	1,129.7	140.4	57.6	7,263.9	5,074.2	12,338.1
1984	1,644.7	1,386.6	3,662.7	2,637.0	1,924.3	1,162.6	141.0	59.1	7,372.6	5,245.3	12,618.0
1985	1,624.0	1,370.3	3,746.4	2,785.9	1,936.9	1,195.4	141.3	61.3	7,448.6	5,413.0	12,861.6

1   The labour force is composed of that portion of the civilian noninstitutional population aged 15 and over who were employed or unemployed.
SOURCE   Data from Statistics Canada; and calculations from the Economic Council of Canada, "base case" solution of CANDIDE 2.0 model, September 1981.

Appendix D

Table D-1

Distribution of Persons with Some Unemployment, by Number of Unemployment Spells, Canada, 1973-78 and 1979

	LFTS[1] 1973-78	AWPS[2] 1979
	(Per cent)	
Number of spells		
1	65.1	83.6
2	21.1	13.2
3	7.3	2.3
4 or more	6.5	0.9
Total	100.0	100.0

1 Labour Force Tracking Survey, Department of Industry, Trade and Commerce.
2 Annual Work Pattern Survey, Statistics Canada.
SOURCE Estimates by the Economic Council of Canada based on special tabulation from the AWPS (1980) and from the LFTS (1978).

Table D-2

Distribution of Persons with Some Unemployment and of Total Unemployment, by Duration of Unemployment, Canada, 1979

	Duration in weeks				
	1-4	5-13	14-26	27 or more	Total
	(Per cent)				
Persons with some unemployment	32.2	31.4	20.2	16.2	100.0
Total unemployment	5.8	20.2	28.9	45.1	100.0

SOURCE Estimates by the Economic Council of Canada based on Statistics Canada's Annual Work Pattern Survey, 1980.

Table D-3

Proportion of Unemployment Spells Ending in Withdrawal from the Labour Force, and Average Duration of Unemployment for "Indomitable Job Seekers," Canada, 1976-80

	1976	1977	1978	1979	1980
	(Per cent)				
Unemployment spells ending in withdrawal	44.1	44.9	45.0	44.3	44.2
	(Months)				
Average duration of unemployment for "indomitable job seekers"	4.2	4.6	4.6	4.4	4.5

SOURCE Estimates by the Economic Council of Canada based on gross flow data provided by Statistics Canada.

Table D-4

Discouraged Job Seekers and Their Impact on the Unemployment Rate,[1] by Region and by Sex, Average Monthly Estimates, Canada, 1980

	Atlantic region	Quebec	Ontario	Prairie region	British Columbia	Canada
	(Thousands)					
Discouraged job seekers						
Men	8 – 17	29 – 55	17 – 32	2 – 6	3 – 6	57 – 112
Women	8 – 14	24 – 51	15 – 37	3 – 6	4 – 9	48 – 113
Both sexes	16 – 31	52 – 106	32 – 69	5 – 12	7 – 15	106 – 225
	(Percentage points)					
Addition to the unemployment rate						
Men	1.4 – 2.9	1.6 – 2.9	0.7 – 1.2	0.2 – 0.5	0.4 – 0.8	0.8 – 1.6
Women	2.2 – 3.8	2.1 – 4.3	0.8 – 2.0	0.4 – 0.8	0.8 – 1.7	1.0 – 2.4
Both sexes	1.7 – 3.4	1.7 – 3.5	0.7 – 1.6	0.2 – 0.6	0.5 – 1.2	0.9 – 1.9

1   In each pair of figures, the first represents the stock of those persons who, at any point in 1980, were no longer in the labour force, having left it after five months or more of job search; the second figure applies to those who left the labour force after three months or more of search. The estimates for men and women may not add up to the total for both sexes, and regional estimates may not add up to the total for Canada, because each estimate is calculated independently and is rounded.
SOURCE   Estimates by the Economic Council of Canada based on gross flow data provided by Statistics Canada.

Table D-5

Discouraged Job Seekers and Their Impact on the Unemployment Rate,[1] by Age Group and by Sex, Average Monthly Estimates, Canada, 1980

	Age group				
	15-19	20-24	25-44	45-64	All age groups
	(Thousands)				
Discouraged job seekers					
Men	8 – 20	14 – 25	22 – 38	13 – 26	57 – 112
Women	5 – 17	11 – 24	20 – 46	12 – 25	48 – 113
Both sexes	13 – 37	26 – 49	43 – 87	24 – 49	106 – 225
	(Percentage points)				
Addition to the unemployment rate					
Men	1.2 – 2.9	1.4 – 2.5	0.7 – 1.2	0.7 – 1.4	0.8 – 1.6
Women	0.8 – 2.8	1.3 – 2.8	0.9 – 2.1	1.2 – 2.4	1.0 – 2.4
Both sexes	1.0 – 2.8	1.4 – 2.6	0.8 – 1.5	0.8 – 1.7	0.9 – 1.9

1   In each pair of figures, the first represents the stock of those persons who, at any point in 1980, were no longer in the labour force, having left it after five months or more of job search; the second figure applies to those who left the labour force after three months or more of search. The estimates for men and women may not add up to the total for both sexes, and estimates for each group may not add up to the total for all age groups, because each estimate is calculated independently and is rounded.
SOURCE   Estimates by the Economic Council of Canada based on gross flow data provided by Statistics Canada.

Table D-6

Logit Coefficients[1] of the Probability of Being
Unemployed More than Six Months, Canada, 1973-78

	Logit coefficients
Characteristics of participants:	
Demographic	
15-19 – Men	1.273*
– Women	1.970*
20-24 – Men	0.357***
– Women	2.743*
25-44 – Men	--
– Women	3.053*
45-64 – Men	0.660*
– Women	3.859*
Married	-0.320**
Single	--
Human capital	
Education (years)	-0.037*
Training	-0.033***
No training	--
Experience (weeks)	0.001*
Occupation	
White-collar	-0.104
Blue-collar	--
Industry	
Manufacturing	-0.873*
Construction	--
Transportation	0.212
Trade, finance, and public administration	0.387
Region	
Newfoundland	0.597**
New Brunswick	1.238*
Quebec	0.359**
Ontario	--
Manitoba	-3.958*
British Columbia	-1.018*
Union status	
Belonging to union	-0.404*
Not belonging to union	--
Motivational	
Wage expectations	-1.827*
Financial	
Unemployment insurance benefits	3.043*
No benefits	--
Working part-time	2.584
Not working part-time	--
Constant	-4.269*
R^2	0.0391
F-statistic	25.34*
Number of observations	15,588

1 Confidence levels: * = 0.99; ** = 0.95; *** = 0.90; the double dash (--)
designates the reference group for the set of variables under
consideration.
SOURCE Estimates by the Economic Council of Canada based on data
from the LFTS, 1978.

Table D-7

Proportion of Long-Term Unemployment[1] in Multiple
Spells, by Duration of the First Spell, Canada,
1973-78

Duration of first spell	Proportion of persons experiencing long-duration unemployment in:			
	Second spell	Third spell	Fourth spell	Fifth spell
	(Per cent)			
Number of spells experienced:				
2 Long	41.5			
Short	29.8			
3 Long	40.6	43.3		
Short	24.5	29.2		
4 Long	65.2	68.1	56.0	
Short	20.9	30.0	38.1	
5 Long	51.1	57.4	48.9	44.7
Short	13.0	28.2	35.1	32.1

1 By definition, long-term unemployment is that lasting more than six
months. The percentages shown have been calculated independently;
in other words, among those people who experienced three unemployment spells, for example, 43.3 per cent of those whose first spell
lasted more than six months ("long-duration") experienced a third
spell that also lasted more than six months, whereas only 29.2 per
cent of those whose first spell lasted less than six months ("short-
duration") experienced a third spell lasting more than six months.
SOURCE Based on data from the LFTS, 1978.

ble E-1

umber of Jobs Created and Program Expenditure, by Program, Canada, 1971/72 to 1981/82

	1971/72	1972/73	1973/74	1974/75	1975/76	1976/77	1977/78	1978/79	1979/80	1980/81	1981/82
cal Initiatives Program (LIP)											
Number of jobs created	92,300	85,876	30,157	31,610	40,650	43,083	. . .	. . .	. . .	. . .	. . .
Program expenditure ($ millions)	182.8	192.5	67.6	79.9	128.3	177.2	. . .	. . .	. . .	. . .	. . .
nada Works (CW)											
Number of jobs created	. . .	. . .	. . .	. . .	. . .	. . .	69,739	75,631	45,456	17,648	. . .
Program expenditure ($ millions)	. . .	. . .	. . .	. . .	. . .	. . .	320.8	168.1	96.3	96.5	. . .
onomic Growth Component											
Number of jobs created[1]	. . .	. . .	. . .	. . .	. . .	. . .	. . .	15,076	4,714	. . .	. . .
Program expenditure ($ millions)	. . .	. . .	. . .	. . .	. . .	. . .	. . .	28.4	16.5	. . .	. . .
cal Employment Assistance ogram (LEAP)											
Number of jobs created	. . .	. . .	1,534	1,856	1,639	1,504	2,219	3,006	6,892	8,807	. . .
Program expenditure ($ millions)	. . .	. . .	5.4	11.8	13.3	14.0	19.0	24.1	48.2	. .	. . .
portunities for Youth (OFY)											
Number of summer jobs created	27,832	29,954	37,392	27,525	29,312	. . .	. . .	. . .	. . .	. . .	. . .
Program expenditure ($ millions)	23.1	31.0	35.9	26.3	32.3	. . .	. . .	. . .	. . .	. . .	. . .
ung Canadian Works (YCW) ogram											
Number of summer jobs created	. . .	. . .	. . .	. . .	. . .	. . .	30,157	27,635	33,037	. . .	. . .
Program expenditure ($ millions)	. . .	. . .	. . .	. . .	. . .	. . .	43.6	42.5	52.4	. . .	. . .
mmer Job Corps (SJC) ogram											
Number of summer jobs created	. . .	. . .	. . .	. . .	. . .	. . .	5,348	6,413	. . .	. . .	. . .
Program expenditure ($ millions)	. . .	. . .	. . .	. . .	. . .	. . .	8.5	11.5	. . .	. . .	. . .
uth Job Corps (YJC) Program											
Student summer projects											
Number of summer jobs created	. . .	. . .	. . .	. . .	. . .	. . .	. . .	. . .	7,954	. . .	. . .
Program expenditure ($ millions)	. . .	. . .	. . .	. . .	. . .	. . .	. . .	. . .	17.1	. . .	
Year-round nonstudent projects											
Number of summer jobs created	. . .	. . .	. . .	. . .	. . .	. . .	. . .	. . .	8,419	. . .	. . .
Program expenditure ($ millions)	. . .	. . .	. . .	. . .	. . .	. . .	. . .	. . .	29.8	. . .	. . .
mployment Tax Credit (ETC) rogram											
Number of jobs created	. . .	. . .	. . .	. . .	. . .	. . .	. . .	19,811	50,786	. .	. . .
Program expenditure ($ millions)	. . .	. . .	. . .	. . .	. . .	. . .	. . .	. .	90.0	. .	. . .
ummer Youth Employment (SYE) rogram											
Number of summer jobs created	. . .	. . .	. . .	. . .	. . .	. . .	. . .	. . .	. . .	45,335	. . .
Program expenditure ($ millions)	. . .	. . .	. . .	. . .	. . .	. . .	. . .	. . .	. . .	53.4	. . .
ummer Canada (SC)											
Number of summer jobs created[2]	. . .	. . .	. . .	. . .	. . .	. . .	. . .	. . .	. . .	. . .	18,623
Program expenditure ($ millions)	. . .	. . .	. . .	. . .	. . .	. . .	. . .	. . .	. . .	. . .	34.5
anada Community Development rogram (CCDP)											
Number of jobs created	. . .	. . .	. . .	. . .	. . .	. . .	. . .	. . .	. . .	19,780	. . .
Program expenditure ($ millions)	. . .	. . .	. . .	. . .	. . .	. . .	. . .	. . .	. . .	109.5	. . .
anada Community Services roject (CCSP)											
Number of jobs created[3]	. . .	. . .	. . .	. . .	. . .	. . .	. . .	. . .	. . .	1,635	. . .
Program expenditure ($ millions)	. . .	. . .	. . .	. . .	. . .	. . .	. . .	. . .	. . .	11.6	. . .

Includes short-term jobs, numbering 3,174 and 1,974 for 1978/79 and 1979/80, respectively.
The program started in May 1981. The figures reported are tentative.
The figures reported are tentative.
SOURCE   Data from Employment and Immigration Canada.

CHAPTER 2

Other labour market indicators manifested a similar deterioration in the 1970s, compared with the 1960s, as the figures for output per person-hour, real hourly earnings, and unit labour costs in Appendix Table A-1 show.

See Pierre Fortin and Keith Newton, "Labour Market Tightness and Wage Inflation in Canada," in *Workers, Jobs, and Inflation* (Washington, D.C.: The Brookings Institution, forthcoming).

Edwin G. West and Michael McKee, *Minimum Wages: The New Issues in Theory, Evidence, Policy, and Politics*, Economic Council of Canada and the Institute for Research on Public Policy (Ottawa: Supply and Services Canada, 1980).

It should be emphasized, in all fairness, that while the evidence suggests that the labour market policies we have described have added to the official unemployment count, each of these programs has its own very valid rationale. Our own work shows, for example, that in addition to helping workers to avert the sheer privation of joblessness, the much-maligned institution of unemployment insurance may very well, by permitting more-intensive job search, augment labour productivity.

See Economic Council of Canada, *People and Jobs: A Study of the Canadian Labour Market* (Ottawa: Information Canada, 1976), pp. 34-38; and Economic Council, *A Time for Reason: Fifteenth Annual Review* (Ottawa: Supply and Services Canada, 1978), pp. 83-90.

Economic Council of Canada, *Two Cheers for the Eighties: Sixteenth Annual Review* (Ottawa: Supply and Services Canada, 1979), p. 14.

It should be noted that if such a tightening takes place in an environment of worsening employment prospects, other levels of government may be called upon to extend the "social safety net."

See Tom Siedule and Keith Newton, "The Unemployment Gap in Canada, 1961-1978"; and Siedule and Newton, "Tentative Measure of Labour Hoarding, 1961-1977"; Economic Council of Canada Discussion Papers 145 and 128, Ottawa, December and March 1979, respectively.

Stewart J. Clatworthy, "Patterns of Native Employment in the Winnipeg Labour Market," Employment and Immigration Canada Task Force on Labour Market Development, Technical Study No. 6, Ottawa, July 1981.

10 See, for example, the briefs of the Federation of Saskatchewan Indians and the Indian Association of Alberta to the Parliamentary Special Committee on Employment Opportunities for the '80s (the Allmand Committee). This Committee was also known as the Parliamentary Task Force on Employment Opportunities for the '80s, and its final report was published under that name; see *Work for Tomorrow: Employment Opportunities for the '80s* (Ottawa: Supply and Services Canada, 1981).

11 National Indian Brotherhood, "Employment Opportunities for the 1980's: A Development Strategy for Indian Society," in *Minutes of Proceedings and Evidence of the Special Committee on Employment Opportunities for the '80s*, Issue No. 22, February 13, 1981 (Ottawa: Supply and Services Canada, 1981), pp. 22A:1 to 22A:22.

CHAPTER 3

1 The depressing cycle of shortage and surplus that is more reminiscent of the markets for hogs and corn than for college graduates is vividly described in Richard Freeman, *The Overeducated American* (New York: Academic Press, 1976), pp. 60-62.

2 See J. F. Helliwell et al., *The Structure of RDX2*, Bank of Canada Staff Research Study No. 7 (Ottawa: Bank of Canada, 1971); Institute for Policy Analysis, *The Focus Model*, and *The Trace Model* (Toronto, 1978); Michael C. McCracken, *An Overview of CANDIDE 1.0* (Ottawa: Economic Council of Canada, 1973); and the Conference Board in Canada, *The Aeric Short-Term Quarterly Forecasting Model of the Canadian Economy* (Ottawa, 1977).

3 A more detailed discussion of this issue can be found in David K. Foot, *Labour Market Analysis with Canadian Macroeconomic Models: A Review* (Toronto: Ontario Manpower Commission, 1980); and in Norman Leckie and Tom Siedule, "Labour Demand by Occupation: Estimation and Projection," a paper prepared for the Economic Council of Canada (in progress).

4 The JVS, a sample survey of establishments, was subject to certain deficiencies relating to size and reporting, but it nevertheless provides useful indications of quantitative change.

5   Economic Council, *People and Jobs*, Chapter 10.

6   This is the classic form of the unemployment/vacancies relationship, known as the "*UV* map." Strictly speaking, a given *UV* curve is defined for a given magnitude of "structural maladjustment" — what we refer to as "mismatching."

7   If the basic ability of the labour market to match unemployed workers and vacant jobs in a given time period remains constant, then any cyclical changes in the relative availability of jobs will trace out a *UV* curve as described above. If this basic matching ability were to improve or deteriorate, the *UV* curve would depict more or less acceptable combinations of the unemployment and vacancy rates. Generally speaking, the further to the "northeast" are the *UV* observations on the map, the greater is the amount of labour market mismatching.

8   This system is described in Department of Manpower and Immigration, *Canadian Classification and Dictionary of Occupations*, Volume I (Ottawa: Information Canada, 1971).

9   Gordon Betcherman, *Meeting Skill Requirements: Report of the Human Resources Survey*, Economic Council of Canada (Ottawa: Supply and Services Canada, 1982).

10 For example, it should be noted that vacancies recorded for other sales occupations (519); textile processing occupations (826); clay, glass, and stone and related materials machining occupations (837); and material handling and related occupations, n.e.c. (93) are statistical artifacts rather than occupations with a real shortage problem. When the historical data for these occupations are examined in conjunction with the projected levels of vacancies, it can be seen that these levels became relatively high very early in the 1970s. They declined sharply until the mid-1970s and then started to rise again gradually. Therefore, if the average levels of vacancies of the 1970s are used as bench marks, these occupations may be said to have no meaningful growth for the 1981-85 period.

Chapter 4

1   A "census family" consists of the husband, wife, and any unmarried children resident with them, or of one parent and any unmarried children. This concept is used throughout this section.

2   Dan Ciuriak and Harvey Sims, "Participation Rate and Labour Force Growth in Canada," Department of Finance, Ottawa, April 1980.

3   Frank T. Denton, Christine H. Feaver, and Byron G. Spencer, *The Future Population and Labour Force of Canada: Projections to the Year 2051*, Economic Council of Canada (Ottawa: Supply and Services Canada, 1980).

4   David K. Foot, "A Challenge of the 1980s: Unemployment and Labour Force Growth in Canada and the Provinces," Institute for Policy Analysis, University of Toronto, March 1981.

5   Employment and Immigration Canada, Task Force Labour Market Development, *Labour Market Development in the 1980s*, a report prepared for the Minister Employment and Immigration (the "Dodge Report July 1981 (Ottawa: Supply and Services Canada 1981).

6   Comprehensive occupational data are in limited supply in Canada. Detailed occupational data, at the four-digit CCDO level, are available from the 1971 census. F subsequent years, however, data are available only the two-digit CCDO level. Even at the latter level, the are breaks in the time series, introduced by a change in the occupational classification in 1973 and by t revision of the Labour Force Survey in 1975.

7   The particular groupings used in these tables a maintained throughout our report; they differ some what from the groupings generally used for the ma population, for reasons related to the occupation dimension discussed later in this chapter.

8   See the Ciurak and Sims paper, which presents resu for both Canada and the United States; this pap constitutes a particularly good analysis and summa of participation rate changes.

9   The "base case" solution was prepared in Septemb 1981. Adjustments were made to the CANDIDE outp to establish this report on a revised Labour For Survey basis.

10 See Alfred J. Kahn and Sheila B. Kamerman, "Incor Maintenance Policies and Programs from a Fam Policy Perspective," a preliminary report, Washingto D.C., April 28-30, 1981; the final report is currently preparation.

11 While the examination of such a tax credit is beyo the scope of this document, some features that wou be required are readily apparent. To be of use, such tax credit would have to be of meaningful size, relation to potential working expenses, and refundab As with the Child Tax Credit, it should not affect t operation of provincial social assistance programs, b it should be prorated to labour market participati and be taxed-back at higher levels of income, w above the range at which social assistance paymer are a consideration. At these higher income levels, t existing deductions for child care expenses have positive impact.

Chapter 5

1   See, for example, William Dodge, *Skilled Labour Supp Imbalances: The Canadian Experience* (Montre British North American Committee, 1977); and Fra T. Denton and Byron G. Spencer, "On the Prospect a Labour Shortage," *Canadian Public Policy* IV, no. (Winter 1978):101-18.

2   This problem, in the context of shortages, is address in Keith Newton, Gordon Betcherman, and Noah Mel "Diagnosing Labour Market Imbalances in Canada *Canadian Public Policy* VII, no. 1 (Winter 1981):94-10

3 A detailed discussion of the methodology and findings of the Human Resources Survey is presented in Betcherman, *Meeting Skill Requirements*.

4 Note that there are difficulties inherent in the measurement of shortages. The phenomenon itself is easily understood: vacant jobs cannot be filled because there are not enough workers with the required skills. More precisely, there is agreement among most labour market observers that a shortage exists when employers, for a prolonged period of time, are unable to hire people at the going rate of compensation. Operationalizing concepts such as "a prolonged period of time" and "the going rate of compensation" poses significant problems, however. As a result, a subjective approach was used in the Human Resources Survey, whereby the responding organization identified shortages as it perceived them. Admittedly, this may result in some overstatement of the imbalances.

5 Mining Association of Canada, "Preliminary Report on Human Resource Planning in the Canadian Mining Industry: Co-operative Approaches for the Eighties," Toronto, November 1980.

6 Ontario Manpower Commission, "Manpower Requirements and Hiring Plans of Ontario Employers in Manufacturing Industries," Toronto, October 1979.

7 Machinery and Equipment Manufacturers' Association of Canada, "Results of a Survey of Skilled Tradesman Requirement and Training in the Industrial Machinery and Equipment Manufacturing Sector from 1979 to 1982," Ottawa, 1979.

8 British Columbia Ministry of Labour, "Critical Skills," a study prepared for the Occupational Training Council of British Columbia, Victoria, March 1980.

9 For example, *A Report by the Sector Task Force on Mobility in the Construction Industry* (Ottawa: Canadian Employment and Immigration Commission, 1980); Department of Regional Economic Expansion (Western Region), "Gap Analysis of Western Canada Labour Market, 1980-1990," Saskatoon, February 1980; and B. A. Keys and D. M. Caskie, "The Medium-Term Employment Outlook: Construction Industry," Employment and Immigration Canada Task Force on Labour Market Development, Technical Study No. 19, Ottawa, July 1981.

10 Noah M. Meltz, *Economic Analysis of Labour Shortages: The Case of Tool and Die Makers in Ontario*, Ontario Economic Council, Occasional Paper No. 15 (Toronto: Ontario Economic Council, 1982), p. 7.

11 Robertson, Nickerson, Group Associates Limited, "Case Studies on Aspects of Training Upper Skilled Blue Collar Industrial Workers: The Analysis," a study prepared for the Department of Manpower and Immigration, Ottawa, 1978.

12 Conestoga College of Applied Arts and Technology, "Survey of Metal Machining Industry: Phase 1 – Identification of Human and Physical Resources," Kitchener, January 1979; R. G. Thompson, "Summary of Survey of Metals Machining Industry," conducted by Seneca College of Applied Arts and Technology, the North York Board of Education, and the York County Board of Education for the North York and York Regional Community Industrial Training Committee, Toronto, January 1980.

13 This "white-collar ethos" has been documented through sociological research on prestige rankings accorded to different occupations. For the best-known work of this type in Canada, see Peter C. Pineo and John Porter, "Occupational Prestige in Canada," *Canadian Review of Sociology and Anthropology* IV, no. 1 (1967):24-40.

14 Economic Council of Canada, *Reforming Regulation* (Ottawa: Supply and Services Canada, 1981), p. 118.

CHAPTER 6

1 See, also, Frank T. Denton, Christine H. Feaver, and Leslie A. Robb, *The Short-Run Dynamics of the Canadian Labour Market*, Economic Council of Canada (Ottawa: Supply and Services Canada, 1976); and Economic Council, *A Time for Reason*, Chapter 6.

2 Statistics Canada defines the unemployed as "those persons who during the reference week were without work, had actively looked for work in the past four weeks [...] and were available for work." People not in the labour force are defined as those "15 years of age and over who during the reference week were neither employed nor unemployed" (as defined above). Statistics Canada, *The Labour Force*, Cat. 71-001 (monthly), ' Notes."

3 Martin S. Feldstein, *Lowering the Permanent Rate of Unemployment*, a study prepared for the use of the Joint Economic Committee, Congress of the United States (Washington: U.S. Government Printing Office, 1973), p. 11.

4 Strictly speaking, it is completed spells of unemployment that concern us here. As explained later, the official statistics on unemployment duration estimate how long individuals have been unemployed up to the time of the survey; they do not take into account the unemployment that people may continue to experience *after* that point. (Paradoxically, as we shall see, the official measure nevertheless overestimates duration!)

5 The calculated unemployment rate is somewhat lower than the actual rate for some groups (especially youths), because the equation is based on the "steady state" assumption, which implies that the labour market is in a state of equilibrium during the period concerned – i.e., that the flows into and out of a labour force state are equal. Roughly speaking, this amounts to saying: "If, over a period of time, the numbers of people entering, and leaving, the unemployment pool each month are about equal, then the number of unemployed in any given month will depend on a/ the number joining the unemployment pool, and b/ how long they stay in it." Obviously, this assumption is a simplification of the real world, which is constantly changing. Thus a gap may occur between the unemployment rate calculated on the basis of the "steady state" assumption and the actual rate. When unemployment is rising – when the flows into the pool are larger than the flows out of it – the calculated rate

tends to underestimate the actual rate; and the reverse is true when unemployment is declining. Since these consequences are inherent in the application of the "steady state" assumption, one must use it cautiously and apply it to a period in which it provides a good approximation of actual conditions.

6   Here, as in the rest of the chapter, data pertaining to 1980 have been used to illustrate our findings, which also apply to the other years examined (1976 to 1979).

7   The differences in average duration between some regions – between Ontario and the Atlantic provinces, for example – are not large. If proper adjustments were made for withdrawal spells, however, a larger difference would be observed. See the section on withdrawals later in this chapter.

8   Female teenagers and young adults among men stand out as the categories for which the incidence of unemployment plays a much greater role.

9   See Abrar Hasan and Patrice de Broucker, "The Dynamics of the Canadian Labour Market," a study prepared for the Economic Council of Canada (in progress).

10   The LFTS concentrated on selected local labour markets. A description of the LFTS can be found in Abrar Hasan and Surendra Gera, *Job Search Behaviour, Unemployment, and Wage Gains in Canadian Labour Markets*, Economic Council of Canada (forthcoming).

11   Economic Council of Canada, *Newfoundland: From Dependency to Self-Reliance* (Ottawa: Supply and Services Canada, 1980). For details, see Harry H. Postner, *A New Approach to Frictional Unemployment: An Application to Newfoundland and Canada*, Economic Council of Canada (Ottawa: Supply and Services Canada, 1980).

12   For various reasons detailed elsewhere, this estimate should be regarded as conservative. See Hasan and de Broucker, "The Dynamics of the Canadian Labour Market"; and Charles M. Beach and Stephan F. Kaliski, "Unemployment Frequency and Duration: Preliminary Estimates for Canada for 1978 from the AWPS," Queen's University, Kingston, May 1981.

13   Tom Siedule and Keith Newton, "Discouraged and Additional Workers Revisited," Economic Council of Canada Discussion Paper 141, December 1979.

14   Statistics Canada, *The Labour Force*, January 1981, pp. 75-105.

15   According to the convention adopted in the survey, in husband-and-wife families the husband is tabulated as the "head of the family."

16   The Employment and Immigration Canada Task Force on Labour Market Development also found that individuals with extended unemployment are not concentrated in the lowest wage categories; see *Labour Market Development in the 1980s*, p. 41.

17   The general character of these results is supported by longitudinal data applying to Canada as a whole. See S. D. Magun, "Unemployment Experience in Canada: A Five-Year Longitudinal Analysis," a paper prepared

for the Canadian Economics Association meetings, Ottawa, June 1982.

CHAPTER 7

1   Economic Council of Canada, *Design for Decision-Making: Eighth Annual Review* (Ottawa: Information Canada, 1971), Chapter 8; and Dennis R. Maki, *Search Behaviour in Canadian Job Markets*, Economic Council of Canada Special Study 15 (Ottawa: Information Canada, 1972).

2   Hasan and Gera, *Job Search Behaviour*.

3   See Norman Leckie and Keith Newton, "Occupational Choice in Canada: Theory and Evidence," a paper prepared for the Economic Council of Canada (in progress).

4   In this context, it is worth noting that the pay increase provisions of the Anti-Inflation Board, which specified maximum absolute dollar increases for higher-level occupations, exerted a narrowing effect on the wage structure.

5   The major exception to the pattern described is the occupation of millwright, for which an increasing differential was observed over the last decade.

6   Employment and Immigration Canada, *Labour Market Development in the 1980s*, p. 29.

7   Economic Council, *Newfoundland: From Dependency to Self-Reliance*, Chapter 4.

8   Employment and Immigration Canada, *Unemployment Insurance in the 1980s*, (Ottawa: Supply and Services Canada, 1981).

9   Many such obstacles are spelled out in *A report of the Sector Task Force on Mobility in the Construction Industry*.

10   See Newton, Betcherman, and Meltz, "Diagnosing Labour Market Imbalances"; and Noah Meltz, "Labour Market Information in Canada: The Current Situation and A Proposal," *Relations Industrielles* (forthcoming) for a fuller discussion of these issues.

11   See Organisation for Economic Co-operation and Development, Working Party on Employment, "Inventory of Employment and Manpower Measures," MAS/WP5(80)1/04, Paris, November 5, 1981, p. 55.

12   S. D. Magun, *The Impact of the Canadian Placement Service on the Labour Market* (Ottawa: Employment and Immigration Canada, 1981).

13   For an overview of quality-of-working-life concepts, see Keith Newton, Norman Leckie, and Barrie O. Pettman, *The Quality of Working Life* (Bradford, U.K.: MCB Publications, 1979).

14   See Keith Newton, "The Theory and Practice of Industrial Democracy: A Canadian Perspective," Economic Council of Canada Discussion Paper 94, Ottawa, August 1977.

15   This section is based on Surendra Gera, "Job Creation in Canada: Issues, Evidence, and Implications," a paper prepared for the Economic Council of Canada (in progress).

CHAPTER 8

1 The Economic Council's recent report on regulatory reform is an example of this.

2 A. C. Pigou, *The Economics of Welfare* (London: Macmillan, 1932), pp. 24-30.

3 There seems to have been two major problems with the shared-cost approach. First, federal contributions were tied to provincial expenditures; as a result, most of the federal grants went to the rich provinces (notably Ontario), which had some of their own money to spend. In this way, regional disparities were exacerbated, as assistance bore an inverse relationship to need. The other major problem was, in fact, purely a federal problem. Under TVTA, the federal government spent a lot of money but had neither visibility nor control.

4 The political story of the transition from TVTA to AOTA is well documented in J. Stefan Dupré, David M. Cameron, Graeme H. McKechnie, and Theodore B. Rotenberg, *Federalism and Policy Development* (Toronto: University of Toronto Press, 1973); and A.G.S. Careless, *Initiative and Response: The Adaptation of Canadian Federalism to Regional Economic Development* (Montreal: McGill-Queen's University Press, 1977).

5 In Alberta, the Manpower Needs Committee has been replaced by two separate processes – one for institutional training and one for industrial training. Each of these is governed by bilateral agreements between the federal government and the province. Responsibility for the planning and purchase of institutional training lies with officials at both levels. Industrial training is steered by an advisory committee consisting of representatives from both levels of government as well as from industry and labour.

6 Economic Council, *Design for Decision-Making*, p. 123.

7 Information shortcomings are greatest for the training where there is no government involvement. There have been periodical investigations of employer training, but these tend to be intermittent and incomplete. For results on two of the more comprehensive undertakings, see Statistics Canada, *Training in Industry, 1969-70*, Cat. 81-555, Ottawa, 1973; and Commission of Inquiry on Educational Leave and Productivity, *Education and Working Canadians* (Ottawa: Labour Canada, 1979).

8 See Betcherman, *Meeting Skill Requirements*, p. 50.

9 Recognizing the methodological difficulties involved, evidence from follow-up surveys of former trainees suggests that the employability benefits of participants in the AOTA programs (particularly CMTP) are directly linked to the availability of jobs after training. See Employment and Immigration Canada, "Interdepartmental Evaluation Study of the Canada Manpower Training Program: Technical Report," Ottawa, 1977.

10 See Employment and Immigration Canada, *Canada Manpower Training Program: Annual Statistical Bulletin, 1979-80* (Ottawa, December 1980).

11 Heather Menzies, *Women and the Chip: Case Studies of the Effects of Informatics on Employment in Canada* (Montreal: Institute for Research on Public Policy, 1981).

12 Employment and Immigration Canada, *Labour Market Development in the 1980s*, p. 58.

13 See Clatworthy, "Patterns of Native Employment."

14 W. Clark and Z. Zsigmond, *Job Market Reality for Postsecondary Graduates*, Statistics Canada (Ottawa: Supply and Services Canada, 1981).

15 In contrast, a 1979 survey in Ontario found that the unemployment rate for 1978 university graduates was only 4.9 per cent. The difference between this figure and that of the Statistics Canada survey underlines the risks inherent in "snapshot" efforts. It should be noted, though, that in many respects similar results did emerge from the two studies. For details of the Ontario survey, see Ontario Ministry of Colleges and Universities, "Employment Survey of 1979 Graduates of Ontario Universities," University Affairs Division, Toronto, 1980.

16 Commission of Inquiry on Educational Leave and Productivity, *Education and Working Canadians*, p. 219.

17 See, for example, Manpower Services Commission, *Outlook on Training: Review of the Employment and Training Act, 1973* (London, 1980); and Employment and Immigration Canada, *Labour Market Development in the 1980s*, Appendix B.

18 Economic Council of Canada, *Financing Confederation: Today and Tomorrow* (Ottawa: Supply and Services Canada, 1982).

CHAPTER 9

1 Economic Council of Canada, *One in Three: Pensions for Canadians to 2030* (Ottawa: Supply and Services Canada, 1979), p. 108.

2 Economic Council, *Financing Confederation*, pp. 127-28.

3 The ILO convention states that "each Member [country] shall formulate and apply a policy designed to promote, by methods appropriate to national conditions and practice and by stages as necessary, the granting of paid educational leave." In using the term, "paid educational leave," the convention refers to "leave granted to a worker for educational purposes for a specified period during working hours, with adequate financial entitlements."

4 This journal serves practitioners and analysts in the labour field, with short, nontechnical articles and notes about current developments in labour and industrial relations, brief analyses of particular data sets, and reviews of books and articles.

List of Tables and Charts